But The Crackling Is Superb

When in 1982 at a televised dinner I served a roast loin of pork, half of which was tenderized with fresh pineapple juice, Michel Roux, the famous chef, remarked that the tenderizing worked well, almost too well, then that he preferred the untenderized firm half and added 'BUT THE CRACKLING IS SUPERB'.

BBC TV *QED*, 20 April 1982

But The Crackling Is Superb

An Anthology on Food and Drink
by Fellows and Foreign Members

of

The Royal Society

Edited by
Nicholas and Giana Kurti

with a Foreword by
Sir George Porter,
President of the Royal Society

Adam Hilger, Bristol and Philadelphia

British Library Cataloguing in Publication Data

But the crackling is superb
  1. Food & drinks
  I. Kurti, Nicholas   II. Kurti, Giana
  III. Royal Society
  641

ISBN 0-85274-301-7

Library of Congress Cataloging-in-Publication Data available

ISBN 0-85274-301-7

First published 1988
Reprinted 1989

Published under the Adam Hilger imprint by IOP Publishing Ltd
Techno House, Redcliffe Way, Bristol BS1 6NX, England
242 Cherry Street, Philadelphia, PA 19106, USA

Typeset by Mathematical Composition Setters Ltd, Salisbury, UK
Printed in Great Britain by J W Arrowsmith Ltd

We dedicate this book
to the memory of our dear friend
SIR FRANCIS SIMON, CBE, FRS,
Dr Lee's Professor of Experimental Philosophy
in the University of Oxford
who, in addition to being a great scientist,
was also a discriminating lover
of food and drink

Nicholas and Giana Kurti

The use of science is so to explain the operations which take place in the practice of the arts, and to discover the means of improving them; and there is no process, however simple it may appear to be, that does not afford an ample field for curious and interesting investigations.

Opening paragraph of the essay: OF THE EXCELLENT QUALITIES OF COFFEE by Sir Benjamin Thompson, Count Rumford, FRS, 1812.

Contents

IX Recipes

Editors' notes appear in an italic typeface enclosed by square brackets.

Foreword

It may not have been previously known that so many Fellows of the Royal Society enjoy food and take its preparation seriously enough to transfer their scientific skills from the laboratory bench to the kitchen table. They have not generally rushed into the publication of their recipes in the *Philosophical Transactions* nor, with the notable exception of the senior Editor of this book, have they lectured on them widely in scientific establishments.

But the latent *cordon bleu*, which is within us all, needed only the catalyst of the Kurtis to burst forth from 80 Fellows. Nearly another 400 of them responded, but modestly disclaimed their own results in this field as unoriginal or not yet ready for publication.

This response may be slightly less surprising when one remembers that the Royal Society began as several dining clubs, at least one of which continues today as a subset of feasting Fellows. The early records show little evidence of Epicurean niceties. A typical repast of the eighteenth century was reported in 1784, by a guest from France, as follows:

> We sat down to table about five o'clock. Sir Joseph Banks presided and filled the place of honour. No napkins were laid before us; indeed there were none used; the dinner was truly in English style. The dishes were of the solid kind, such as roast beef, boiled beef and mutton prepared in various ways with abundance of potatoes and other vegetables which each person seasoned as he pleased with the different sauces which were placed on the table in bottles of different shapes.
>
> The beef-steaks and the roast beef were at first drenched with

copious bumpers of strong beer, called porter, drunk out of cylindrical pewter pots, which are much prefered to glasses because one can swallow a whole pint at a draft. This prelude being finished, the cloth was removed, and a handsome and well polished table was covered, as if it were by magic, with a number of fine crystal decanters, filled with the best port, madeira and claret... and the libations began on a grand scale, in the midst of different kinds of cheese, which, rolling in mahogany boxes from one end of the table to the other, provoke the thirst of the drinkers.... A few bottles of champagne completed the enlivement of every one. Tea came next with bread and butter and all the usual accompaniments: coffee followed.... Brandy, rum and some other strong liqueurs closed this philosophic banquet which terminated at half past seven as we had to be at a meeting of the Royal Society summoned for eight o'clock.

Today, even with less copious food and drink, it is generally accepted that the Society's meetings are more safely conducted before dinner. Although more modest in size, the dinners have not decreased in number, especially for the President. Lord Florey once remarked, in the middle of his term of office, 'The President is the corporate stomach of the Society!'

But it was not all prodigality and indulgence. Fellows who made serious studies of food and its preparation were principally concerned with feeding the poor, and their efforts were towards improving the cooking and the nutritional value of food at the lowest cost. Count Rumford, who is mentioned frequently in this anthology, was as interested in how to keep things hot or cold in the kitchen as in the nature of heat itself. He asked himself, for example, how it was that his apple sauce remained too hot to eat, long after his soup had cooled, in spite of the fact that both articles are largely made of water. He made careful measurements in a 'passage thermometer', on the relative rates of cooling of apple sauce and water which led him eventually to the discovery of the importance of convection in heat transfer. This early example of the scientific method, of seeking first an understanding, however mundane the practical problem may appear to be, has successors today which are to be found within these pages.

I am not sure what refereeing procedure was used on these papers and certainly the Royal Society can accept no responsibility for even the mildest indigestion resulting from repeating any of the experiments published by its Fellows. Some should quite clearly be taken with a pinch of salt. The referees would also have to look carefully at the units used and at the place of fluid ounces and pounds in the recommended SI system. Perhaps we should be lenient on the grounds that some effort has been made towards standardisation, as evidenced by the use of pounds in the recipe for Rumford Soups on page 130 in place of Rumford's original which was expressed in Viertls, albeit with the explanation that the Viertl is one twelfth of a Schäfl and that the Bavarial Schäfl is equal to 6 31/300 Winchester bushels. And today's cook worries about metrication!

Nicholas Kurti gave his famous Friday Evening Discourse 'The Physicist in the Kitchen' in 1969, when I was Director of the Royal Institution. It broke with tradition in several ways: it was televised, the lecturer refused to be locked up beforehand in the customary way because he had to get on with his cooking, and his enthusiasm made the audience so hungry that immediately the lecture was over they descended like starving wolves on the famous lecture table and demolished, to the last morsel, a four pound leg of lamb, a two pound fillet of pork, an eight-egg soufflé and a large baked Alaska. It was all quite memorable; my own favourite recollection is of the lecturer with, before him, a large soufflé riddled with thermocouples recording the temperature at all depths, asking with much feeling 'Is it not quite amazing that today we know more about the temperature distribution in the atmosphere of the planet Venus than that in the centre of our soufflé?'

The preparation of food and drink is a science where the amateur may still sometimes prevail over the professional, and the artist over the scientist. The ingredient common to all the contributors of this volume, the FRSs and For. Mem. RSs, can only serve as a top dressing. But only one of Hungarian birth could put them all together in such an original goulash.

Sir George Porter, PRS,
June 1988

Introduction

THIS IS NOT A COOKERY BOOK. Nor is it a collection of articles about the use of scientific techniques for the preparation of food. The motivation for this anthology is explained by its origin.

In 1969 I gave a Friday Evening Discourse at the Royal Institution under the title 'The Physicist in the Kitchen'. I showed, with the help of demonstrations, how novel or hitherto little-used techniques, or even new concepts, could be transferred from the laboratory into the domestic kitchen and could lead to the improvement of existing, or the creation of new dishes. I finished the lecture by voicing my conviction that the great culinary creations would continue to be the result of artistic imagination seasoned with a blend of tradition and empiricism but with only a soupçon of science. I nevertheless felt that scientists should not regard the established practices of the art of cookery as sacrosanct but should use their ingenuity and expertise to adapt new or unfamiliar techniques to culinary use and even to create new dishes by hitherto little-used processes. However, it seemed to me that, while scientists on the whole enjoy good food and are often expert cooks, they shy away from a serious application of their profession in the kitchen. Could it be that they do not regard cooking as sufficiently dignified to deserve research effort using scientific techniques and methods?

It was not until 1986 that I decided to put these speculations to a test. I chose a group of scientists which, while not a representative sample, was well defined, and wrote to the Fellows and Foreign Members of the Royal Society asking them whether they would be willing to contribute to an anthology of recipes, views on cooking, new ideas etc. I explained that the contributions could be anything from remarks of a few words to elaborate recipes or learned essays.

Anything concerning food and drink and their enjoyment would be acceptable, from the profound to the frivolous, from the ridiculous to the sublime.

I sent out about 1000 questionnaires and the response was most gratifying—450 replied and of those 85 agreed to contribute. Nearly a quarter of those who felt that their lack of culinary skills or of interest in food prevented them from contributing were nevertheless encouraging, wished the venture well and looked forward to reading the book. Only one Fellow felt that the publication of a "Cook-Book" by FRSs would damage the reputation of the Society and lay it open to ridicule.

I also include excerpts from the writings of FRSs no longer among the living: Michael Faraday, Benjamin Franklin, Stephen Hales, F A Lindemann (Lord Cherwell), Samuel Pepys and Sir Benjamin Thompson, Count Rumford, as well as from two Fellows elected under Statute 12, i.e. otherwise than by virtue of their scientific achievements, Sir Winston Churchill and Sir Stafford Cripps. Living Statute 12 Fellows were not, however, approached. Apart from a couple of exceptions all other contributions were specially written or arranged for this anthology.

As was to be expected the contributions varied enormously both in length and in nature. The shortest contribution consists of 6 words, the longest runs to nearly 3000. The articles cover a great variety of subjects. There are comments on the nastiness of whale's milk and the excellence of skylark and house sparrow. Recipes are given for tournedo of seal and other antarctic delicacies and the palatability of human flesh, of Patagonian Petises and of barbecued elephant receive due attention. Technical advice, mathematical treatments, computerized recipes abound and there are also descriptions of meals consumed in fashionable restaurants and more modest places.

With so many topics and authors it would have been neither possible nor desirable to aim at editorial uniformity. I only hope that professional food writers will not object to differing formats of recipes, to inconsistent and occasionally tongue-in-cheek mixing of units of measurements and to the rediscovery of old recipes and accepted techniques by some of the contributors.

The grouping of the articles into nine chapters is also somewhat arbitrary. The last chapter contains straightforward recipes, but recipes may also be found in many of the other contributions.

The Editors' notes which we have added appear in an italic type-face enclosed by square brackets.

Many aspects of culinary science are represented in the anthology but, to my great disappointment, deep freezing and microwaves are not, although they are, in my view, the most important twentieth century science-based techniques in food production. There are Fellows who could have enlightened the public why it is that bull's sperm or nematodes can be deep frozen with impunity whereas strawberries turn mushy and lose their flavour on being warmed up. Is there no research on cryoprotective agents for culinary use? Similarly other Fellows might have given a lead on how microwaves could revolutionize culinary art by adding to traditional cookery, which relies on heat conduction (rare steaks, pink roast beef, crisp rolls etc), microwave cookery which, in principle, permits the introduction of heat into any chosen region of the food. We know how to make an inverted Baked Alaska, or, as it is now called, Frozen Florida, but there must be other microwave-based dishes waiting to be invented.

I have tried to persuade some Fellows to write about these topics but they declined. I am nevertheless not without hope that, even now, they are perhaps preparing papers on the enhancement by science of the pleasures of eating, for publication in the *Proceedings of the Royal Society*. They would thus prove that they shared the sentiments of Rumford who, writing in 1800 about the application of natural philosophy to the art of cookery, asked: 'IN WHAT ART OR SCIENCE COULD IMPROVEMENTS BE MADE THAT WOULD MORE POWERFULLY CONTRIBUTE TO INCREASE THE COMFORTS AND THE ENJOYMENTS OF MANKIND?'

Acknowledgments. My grateful thanks are due to Dr Tom Kuhn, Fellow of Brasenose College, for enlightenment on some obscure quotations and to Mrs Audrey Ellison, nutritionist and food writer, for expert advice on outlandish ingredients and culinary practices.

I am much indebted to the members of the Physics Photographic Unit of the University of Oxford (C W Band, S Bebb, J Burrage and P Flint) for their help and advice so generously given.

I thank the contributors for tolerating with good humour my chivvying and my occasional criticisms.

I am particularly grateful to Professor George Pickett of the

Physics Department, University of Lancaster, who entered into the spirit of this venture and, by combining scientific insight with artistic sense, produced amusing and telling illustrations.

And finally, my affectionate thanks to my wife Giana for the many months of hard work as co-editor, secretary, typist, literary adviser and proof-reader.

Nicholas Kurti
June 1988

4

Section I Aphorisms, Observations and Quotations

Hannes Alfvén

'DER MENSCH IST WAS ER ISST'
(ONE IS WHAT ONE EATS)

[*The author of this German punning aphorism is the German philosopher Ludwig Feuerbach (1804–1872) who in his prospectus for J Moleschott's* Treatise on Food for the People *(1850) wrote 'Do you want to improve the people? Then, instead of preaching against sin give them better food. Man is (ist) what he eats (isst).'*† *One recognizes two forerunners of this view:*

(1) A. Brillat-Savarin (1755–1826) with the following aphorism in the preface to his 'La Physiologie du Goût',

> *'Dis moi ce que tu manges, je te dirai ce que tu es' (Tell me what you eat and I will tell you what you are)*

(2) Sir Benjamin Thompson, Count Rumford, FRS (1753–1814) with the rationale for the establishment of soup kitchens to feed the numerous beggars of Munich‡

---

† Büchmann's *Geflügelte Worte* (Frankfurt am Main: Ulstein) p. 163 (1986).
‡ S C Brown (ed) (1970) *Collected Works of Count Rumford* (Cambridge, MA: Harvard University Press) Vol. V p. 29.

They ... had been so long familiarized with every crime that they had become perfectly callous to all sense of shame and remorse.

With persons of this description, it is easy to be conceived that precepts, admonitions, and punishments would be of little or no avail. But, where precepts fail, habits may sometimes be successful.

To make vicious and abandoned people happy, it has generally been supposed necessary, first to make them virtuous. But why not reverse this order! Why not make them first happy, and then virtuous! If happiness and virtue are inseparable, the end will be as certainly obtained by the one method as by the other; and it is undoubtedly much easier to contribute to the happiness and comfort of persons in a state of poverty and misery than by admonitions and punishments to reform their morals.

The same view was expressed 100 years later by Brecht in his Threepenny Opera (music by Kurt Weill), 'Erst kommt das Fressen, dann kommt die Moral' ('Food is the first thing—morals follow on', as given in the English version by Hugh MacDiarmid).]

Kenneth Blaxter

Man does not ingest nutrients, he eats food
Attributed to R L M Synge

Hugh Ford

THE ECONOMICS OF THE FOOD CHAIN

It is a sad reflection that the calorific value of the packaging (including the energy consumed in making it) which brings the cereal to the breakfast table is about the same as that of all the cereal it contains.

Harry Pitt

THOUGHTS ON FOOD AND EDUCATION

(1) It is quite astonishing that an activity that has taken up so much time and effort over thousands of years should not have been studied and recorded properly.

(2) It is only recently that cooking on a *large* scale has been treated scientifically as Food Science (or whatever). This is now, but only recently, academically respectable and there are large departments at Reading and elsewhere.

(3) But cooking on a small domestic scale is still a much bigger and more widespread activity and virtually no genuine study has been done. In some parts of the world it is *the* dominant activity.

(4) Why not ask the Education Committee of the Royal Society to think about the place of Home Economics in the school science curriculum?

(5) How, in fact, *do* people in Britain learn—or fail to learn—to cook? The main sources, I suppose, are parents, schools, cookery books and TV programmes, and it would be interesting to know why the outcome is so abysmal and whether there is enough objective evidence to confirm the common view that it is worse here than in most other countries.

(6) On cookery books my own experience is that most are comprehensible only to those who know the subject already but there are exceptions like Delia Smith, for example, who accepts that a teaspoon is an imperfect measure of volume. Incidentally, has the metrication programme got completely stuck? And how many generations will have to deal with two systems of measurement?

(7) Fellows of the Royal Society who think cooking insufficiently 'dignified' should try living without it for a first experiment.

Uli Arndt

A MIXED BAG OF QUOTATIONS

So much water, so much fruit, unrelieved by any alcohol, turned his blood gangrenous by lowering the vital spirits, and weakened his digestion by nightly sweating.

Saint-Simon on Louis XIV

Can that which is unsavoury be eaten without salt? Or is there any taste in the white of an egg?

Job VI:6

It would certainly be far better policy to substitute for tea, which must be brought from China, the coffee which grows in the English colonies: such a change might, perhaps, tend to diminish that alarming consumption of wine which occasions in this country so many diseases and especially so many excesses caused by drunkeness.

B Faujas de Saint-Fond *A Journey through England and Scotland to the Hebrides in 1784*

The end of a work, like the end of a children's dinner party, must be made up of sweetmeats and sugar-plums.

Trollope *Barchester Towers*

Give me a little ham and egg
And let me be alone, I beg.
Give me my tea, hot, sweet and weak
Bring me The Times *and do not speak.*

A P Herbert

Ah, what an excellent thing is an English pudding!

Misson de Valbourg (1690)

Gentlemen do not take soup at luncheon.

G N Curzon's comment on a proposed menu

Whoever is interested in furnishing is not interested in food. The important thing is to eat well.

O V Bismarck

Sweets [are] strange, [such as] the stewed stems of the rhubarb plant whose medicinal properties are well known; yet these prudish people (the English) openly advertise the defects of their most private

8

internal economy by their shameless partiality for this amazing fare!
Francis Wey *A Frenchman sees the English in the 'Fifties*

[*The writer of the last quotation is wrong. The roots, not the stems, of the rhubarb plant have purgative properties.*]

David Finney

CULINARY CHAUVINISM

[*Date: 1805. Place: the Sussex coast. Squire Carne, who is in league with the French, courts Dolly, Admiral Darling's daughter. He describes to her how happy and peaceful the country will be once the French have landed and France and England are united.*]

One of the cows best loved by Dolly had come up to ask who this man was who had been sitting with her. She was gifted with a white face and large soft eyes, short little horns and a delicate fringe around her pleasant nostrils and above her clovey lips. She hoped that Dolly had obtained a lover as good as could be found upon a single pair of legs. Carne was attired with some bravery of the French manner and swung round his cane of heavy snakewood at the cow, and struck her poor horns so sharply that her head went round.

'Is that universal peace, and gentleness, and justice' cried Dolly, springing up and hastening to console her cow. 'Is this the way the lofty French redress the wrongs of England? What had poor Dewlips done, I should like to know? Kiss me, my pretty, and tell me how you would like the French army to land, as a matter of form! The form you would take would be beef, I'm afraid; not even good roast beef, but bouillon, potage, fricandeau, friture—anything one cannot taste any meat in; and that is how your wrongs could be redressed, after having had both your horns knocked off ...'

R D Blackmore (1887) *Springhaven* (Sampson, Low, Marston and
Company)
Vol. 3 Ch. III p. 36

R A McCance

THE NURSERY RHYMES

Prior to the 15th century few of the population could read or write. Wishful thinking of hungry men and women, cradle songs, popular tastes and feelings and lampoons, often political, have come down to us as the nursery rhymes. Similar rhymes with different motifs occur in many countries:

Pease porridge hot, Pease porridge cold,
Pease porridge in the pot, nine days old.

The necessity for making one cooking last for several days was commonly caused by a shortage of fuel due to the local deforestation so common in the rural surroundings of any English village. Boiling dried peas with water, moreover, was not only a very primitive form of cooking but the only way to make dried peas palatable, or oatmeal too for that matter, for which the only alternative was flat unleavened cakes.

Little Miss Muffet sat on a tuffet
Eating her curds and whey   [a well known food for children].

Unfortunately we are not told whether rennet was used to prepare it, or the natural acidification due to the lactic acid bacteria.

Little Tommy Tucker who sang for his supper was rewarded by white bread and butter. This taste for white bread originated certainly as early as Roman times and has persisted throughout history for the simple reason that white flour baked a larger, softer loaf, or cake, than flour of any higher extraction, i.e. wholemeal or any of the intermediates. So:

Pat-a-cake, pat-a-cake, baker's man,
Bake me a cake as fast as you can

or

Ride a cock-horse to Banbury Cross,
To see what Tommy can buy;
A penny white loaf, a penny white cake,
and a two-penny apple-pie.

10

The penny white loaf was always listed in the 'Assize of Bread' which fixed the price of bread according to the price of grain. In the 18th century chalk was often added to the flour used for bread making to improve the whiteness, if not the baking quality! This alteration was forbidden by Statute in 1758. Nowadays, however, the law demands that chalk be added to flour to increase our intake of calcium, which most people think is already high enough!

In a country virtually without sugar honey was naturally a food of great value:

> The King was in his counting-house,
> Counting out his money;
> The Queen was in the parlour,
> Eating bread and honey.

Of the cereals eaten oats have already been mentioned though they were not much eaten except in the North of England and Scotland. There is abundant evidence that wheat flour was preferred above all the others, but two more cereals were in common use. Rye was easier to grow in poor soil than wheat but it was not much sought after in England for baking, although rye bread was eaten all over North Germany. It was, however, used in England for pies.

> Sing a song of sixpence,
> A pocket full of rye,
> Four-and-twenty blackbirds
> Baked in a pie.

There were, moreover, several kinds of pie. One was the kind in which the blackbirds were baked and an allied type made for little King Pippin with apples in it and 'pie crust, and pastry building up the wall'. The other kind of pie was enclosed by a hard pastry and contained possibly fruit but more often meat of some kind similar to the familiar pork pie or the Glasgow mutton pie of more modern times. These were the kind bought by Simple Simon on his way to the fair and that the old woman had to sell cold or hot that could be followed by the smell.

Barley was less highly regarded than rye. It was all right for pigs, but the only way to make it palatable for man was to follow the advice of good King Arthur.

11

When good King Arthur ruled this land,
  He was a clever King
He stole three packs of barley meal
  To make a bag pudding.
A bag pudding the King did make
  And stuffed it well with plums
And in it put great lumps of fat,
  As big as my two thumbs.
The King and Queen did eat thereof,
  and noblemen beside;
And what they could not eat that night
  The Queen next morning fried.

The problem is what were the plums? Were they dried English plums, or French sugar plums, or were they raisins and currants, i.e. dried large and small grapes. Cold plum porridge was what burned the mouth of the man in the moon!

The context is sometimes a help, for example

Little Jack Horner sat in the corner,
  Eating his Christmas pie,
He put in his thumb and pulled out a plum,
  And said, what a good boy am I!

Tasty animal products of many kinds were looked forward to by all classes, for when the tailor accidentally shot his pig:

Zooks quoth the tailor, I care not a louse!
For we shall eat black puddings, chitterlings and souse.

The foods eaten were really not so very different then from now: sausages, stews, sheep's head, haggis, giblet pie, roast beef, gammon and spinach and pancakes all feature in nursery rhymes and they are just as tasty now as then.

Mrs Bond she flew down to the pond in a rage
With plenty of onions and plenty of sage
She cried Dilly Dilly Dilly Dilly come to be killed
For you must be stuffed and my customers filled.

The cooks of the 17th century may have been able to get parsley, sage, rosemary and thyme from their own gardens, but certainly not 'nutmeg and ginger, cinnamon and cloves', which gave the writer his jolly red nose!

These smack of the East Indies, but the Portuguese, the Dutch and the British were opening up the East Indies about this time and the 'oranges and lemons' associated with 'the Bells of St Clement's' probably came direct from Portugal.

BIBLIOGRAPHY

Opie I and Opie P 1951 *Oxford Dictionary of Nursery Rhymes* (Oxford: Oxford University Press)
McCance R A and Widdowson E M 1956 *Breads White and Brown—Their place in thought and social history* (London: Pitmans Medical Publishing)
Thomas K E 1930 *The Real Personages of Mother Goose* (Lothrop, Lee and Sheperd)

James Dyson

A smiling woman bringing food is the
beginning of happiness.

Desmond King-Hele

FRUITS OF NATURE

Green miracle

The sunshine strong-eyed
and carbon dioxide,
    with chlorophyll
        and H_2O,
make trees and all things green
    on plain or hill
        serenely grow
to beautify the scene;
    make fruit and wheat
    for us to eat,
    and new-born oxygen
    to let us breathe again.

13

The magic hand this is
of photosynthesis,
our life's botanic basis,
the origin of species.

Fruits of Earth

When you cut a slice
Through the polar ice,
    The Earth is like a pear.
But sliced along the equato
She looks like a potato,
    A giant *pomme de terre*.

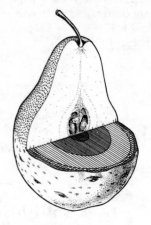

Orange peal

An orange needs a peeling,
but what we find appealing
is the supersonic spray—
a juicy rind is made that way.
        What we find
            incredible
                is
            that the rind
                is
            inedible,
        and has to be made
        into marmalade.

PLAY-MEATS

Wait for it

The diners start the long ordeal
of waiting for their evening meal.
    They call out, 'Waiter'.
    He calls back, 'Later'.

He thought they needed a lengthy wait
to make them relish the food they ate,
'You'll eat anything, tender or tough,
if I keep you waiting long enough'.

    'That's logical', they said;
    and, since they wished to be fed,
    they deprived him of life
    with his carving knife.

So you see
    not the diners
    waiting for the waiter,
    nor the waiter
    waiting on the diners,
    but the diners
    dining on the waiter.

And you see
    how restaurantal crimes
    give rise to ruthless rhymes.

Petrified menu

    Don't try to bite
    a trilobite:
    it isn't possible
    to eat a fossible.

    We dine no more
    on the dinosaur:
    its every bone
    has turned to stone.

Though oil is fossil fuel,
it takes a greedy fool
    to drink a tin
    of paraffin.

Fresh seeds of wheat
we knead and eat,
but stony fossil seeds
    would B A CD FEG
    of poor digestibility,
unfit to meet our needs.

Nut-case

The Colonel ate
a burning plate
    of nuts, too fast;
and his guts revolted
at the nuts he bolted
    in this repast.

As the surgeon sadly said
on giving him up for dead,
    'Inside nuts
        are kernels;
    inside Colonels
        are nuts'.

Debate a bull

Beef-
    eaters eating eatable
beef
    will in due course eat a bull.
Bull-
    fighters fighting defeatable
bulls
    will in the end defeat a bull.
But when debaters bait a bull
the end is more debatable.

Peter and Paul
decline and fall

A compulsive eater
was portly Peter:
what ails this doughty eater-out?
His heart's about to peter out.

His skinny brother Paul
who scarcely eats at all
has reached the grave-side all-in
through carrying Peter's pall in.

In due course

The first course
is the work of a horse,
the next course
is a platter of fish,
the third course
is the principal dish,
the fourth course
is just dessert,
with coffee of course
to keep alert.

From *Animal Spirits* (Farnham: The X Press) (1983)

Section II Scientific Insight and Culinary Art

E Lester Smith

THE BAKERY GRAPH

Any recipe for bread, scones, biscuits, sponges, pastry, pancakes and cakes contains some or all of five basic ingredients: these are flour, fat, egg, liquid (milk or water) and sugar. The proportions of the first three can be represented as a single point on triangular graph paper (see figures 1 and 2). This is based on the fact that if we consider any point within an equilateral triangle the sum of the perpendicular distances of this point measured from the three sides is constant. The three apices of the graph represent respectively pure flour, pure egg and pure fat. As we travel away from an apex to the opposite side the fractional quantity is reduced as shown by the scale. A point lying on a side represents a mixture of only two ingredients, for example point X (figure 1) represents 20% egg and 80% fat, a reasonable recipe for sauce hollandaise. To represent a mixture of fl grams (or oz etc.) of flour, f of fat and e of egg we first convert these quantities into percentages by dividing each quantity by the sum of all three and multiplying by 100. Thus $100e/(fl + f + e)$ is the percentage of egg, e%, which is represented on the graph by the line A. Similarly B corresponds to fl% and the intersection of A and B at Y represents the composition, the line C corresponding to f%. The recipe defined by Y is in fact Mrs

18

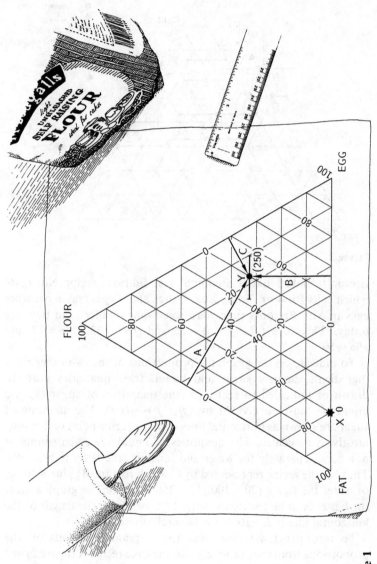

Figure 1

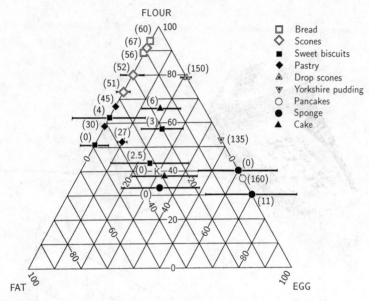

Figure 2

Beeton's 'Baked Batter Pudding' (1st Edition, recipe No. 1246) which calls for 4 oz. flour, 2 oz. butter and 4 eggs, say 6 oz. since eggs in Mrs Beeton's time were somewhat smaller than they are today. Therefore $(fl + f + e) = 12$ and $fl\% = 33$, $f\% = 17$ and $e\% = 50$.

To indicate on the graph the proportions of the two other main ingredients, namely sugar and liquid, their quantities must be drawn or indicated to scale, i.e. the quantities of sugar (s) and liquid (l) must be divided by $(fl + f + e)/100$. The amounts of sugar are shown as horizontal lines with the recipe point on the line, mostly in its centre. The quantities of liquid are given simply as numbers, separately for water and for milk, the latter in brackets. Thus for the recipe represented by C which requires $1\frac{1}{2}$ pint = 30 oz. of water the figure $(30 \times 100)/12 = 250$ is put on the graph and, if the batter is to be sweetened with 2 oz. of sugar, the length of the horizontal line is $2 \times 100/12 = 17$ small divisions.

To reconstruct a recipe from the diagram one reads off the proportions from the graph, e.g. for the cake recipe K (figure 2) one finds 38 parts flour, 29 parts fat, 33 parts egg and 29 parts sugar.

Different recipes for each product will bunch into regions on the

20

diagram. Conversely, to reconstruct the recipe from the diagram, the five coordinates are read off as grams and multiplied by 5 or 10 for a family-size bake. Minor ingredients must be added back to the recipe. Flour signifies plain white flour for pastry, batters and breads using yeast; otherwise self-raising flour. In many recipes brown flour can be substituted wholly or in part. Fat signifies butter or margarine; for pastry it is traditional, but not essential, to include lard or suet.

Obviously it is easier to use the original recipe than the graphical diagram. Its value is to *compare* recipes within a group, and between groups, and hopefully to devise improved ones. In addition, study of the whole diagram will show what compositional features differentiate one group of recipes from another. One may thus come to a better understanding of the whole art of bakery. It can become more of a science instead of 'just cookery'. It may be noted, for example, that all the points cluster towards the flour corner, as might be expected. No recipe contains *less* than 30% flour, nor *more* than 50% of fat or 70% of egg (as percentages of the total of these three ingredients). These three components, represented by the plotted points, exert major control over the *texture* and *character* of the product. However, it is also important to get the liquid content 'right' (numbers in brackets) as also the baking conditions, to avoid a product that is too doughy or dry. Sugar (horizontal lines) influences mainly the flavour, as do the omitted minor ingredients. Study of the diagram may also suggest formulations for new and interesting bakery products outside the conventional range. An experienced cook should be able to gauge their likely characteristics before trying out such newly-devised recipes.

The various groups of recipes may now be considered in more detail. For example, the exact centre of the diagram represents a Victoria sponge mix, with equal parts of flour, fat, egg, and also of sugar, with no extra liquid. So this is roughly midway between bread and a sweet omelette! Replacing the fat by more egg, (i.e. moving to the right-hand side of the triangle) gives a sponge with 70% of egg, even closer to a sweet omelette, and to a Swiss roll mix. So the sponges are the most variable in composition; any recipe with more than 30% of egg can yield a sponge. This is not surprising when one reflects that egg alone can yield a fluffy omelette of spongy texture.

21

Returning to the centre (Victoria sponge) and omitting egg (i.e. moving left-hand to the edge) gives a shortcake biscuit recipe. Starting again from the flour apex, along the left-hand edge, leads to the bread recipes and then to the scones. Judging from some scones I have eaten, there is scope for improvement in their formulation. But improvement in the gastronomic sense, towards 'richer' products, implies substituting milk for water, and additional fat and/or egg. A little egg may indeed be added to some scone formulations with advantage. All these changes increase the cost, especially extra egg. This is common knowledge, of course, but the diagram permits quick comparison of recipes in this respect. Usually a compromise is needed; the more expensive mixes may be too 'rich' for some palates.

Adding a little egg and sugar (and some cake-fruit) to suitable scone recipes leads to a rock-cake formulation, as might be expected. The only other cake formulation included, near the centre of the diagram, is for a general-purpose rich cake mix. It can serve, with suitable additions, for fruit cake, cherry cake, Madeira cake, chocolate cake and Dundee cake. Other cake recipes would fall near a line joining these points, and continuing a little further for a rich Christmas cake. This line passes through a point representing a soft cakey biscuit. Other biscuit recipes are all along the left-hand edge, to the left of this cake line, namely eggless mixes with very little water. Two pastry formulations are in the same position, and another just to the right, with 10% of egg; but pastry recipes are without sugar and use much more water than for biscuits. Also the mixing technique is different, especially for flaky pastry.

Returning to the flour corner and moving down the right-hand edge of the triangle leads to fat-free recipes for batters, again with no sugar but a lot of water. Increasing proportions of egg lead to formulations for drop scones, Yorkshire pudding and pancakes. Also to the sponge formulations already mentioned.

Regretfully, there does not seem much scope for devising new types of bakery products. For example, it can be seen that somewhere between the Yorkshire pudding and rich cake formulations must lie a recipe for a soft, moist dough-cake—but that has already been invented.

O V S Heath

THE BINOMIAL DISTRIBUTION AND DOMESTIC HARMONY

Occasionally the results of an experiment in the kitchen may be something so delicious that the only question is 'can you do it again?' (and adequate notes should help there) or so horrible that you don't want to. More often, assessment poses a major problem and can be as much a matter of psychology as of physiology. Preferences for food and drink can change with mood or state of health and with time of day—the same coffee tastes different first thing in the morning or at night after a good dinner. One should aim at improvements that are consistently appreciated as such, at least under specified circumstances. In *The Design of Experiments* R A Fisher discussed a test of a lady's claim that she could distinguish by the taste whether tea had been poured out before the milk or after it. A wife might not appreciate being subjected by a sceptical husband to such a test of her beliefs, but if she could be persuaded to act in a husband–wife team, with mutual testing, domestic harmony might be preserved (or not!).

There are probably even more ways of making coffee than of brewing tea and most coffee drinkers have views on the subject. If the couple breakfast and sup together and are willing to share each other's coffee, two methods or blends A and B can be compared in pairs of cups or jugs—prepared one day by the husband for the wife to judge (without knowing which is which) and vice versa another day. In each pair of days the order husband–wife or wife–husband should preferably be randomised, e.g. by tossing a coin; which of the two cups is tasted first should certainly be similarly randomised. Different methods or blends can if desired be used for the breakfast and after dinner coffee, if the 'time of day effect' is not of interest. Husband and wife should record the other's preferences with a + or − sign according to whether A or B is preferred and not reveal them until the end of the experiment— say after 20 days. There will then be four columns with ten plus or minus signs in each: his and her preferences at breakfast; his and her preferences after dinner. To avoid being misled it is desirable to

test the statistical significance of the results by means of the 'sign test' based on the binomial distribution and explained in several text-books, e.g. *Statistics for Biologists* by R C Campbell (Cambridge University Press), page 53.

If we want to have an assurance that the preference found in N tests ($N = 10$ in the above example) is probably real with a not more than 5% chance of its being due to random or uncontrolled causes we check whether the *smaller* of the number of pluses or minuses equals or is less than the value of S given in the table below.

N	10	12	14	16	18	20	24
S	1	2	2	3	4	5	6

Thus with $N = 10$ and a 'minority vote' of 0 or 1 the preference is 'real' while with $N = 20$ the minority must be 5 or less.

The limitation of comparing only two methods or blends at a time means that arriving at the 'best' one can take a long while, but it involves relatively little disturbance of domestic routine. If foods or drinks not consumed every day are compared in pairs, the delay is of course much greater. A comparison of more than two foods or drinks at a time is much more difficult to judge accurately and involves much more organization in preparation. Few people, for instance, would wish to prepare five different sorts of Christmas

24

pudding or to compare them at one meal, let alone repeat the whole process a number of times. Finally, it should be pointed out that if no consistent difference has been detected between two foods or drinks the experiment has not failed—the easier method or the cheaper ingredients can be adopted!

Joseph Keller

SPILLING

Sometimes when a liquid is poured from one container into another, some of the liquid flows along the outside of the pouring container. Then it spills onto the tablecloth, floor or clothing of the person pouring. This phenomenon has been called 'the teapot effect' because it is especially common and particularly troublesome when it occurs with hot tea.

In 1956, a famous Israeli rheologist, Marcus Reiner, published an article about the physical explanation of this phenomenon (M Reiner 1956 *Physics Today* **9** 16–20). He wrote that he had asked many physicists what was responsible for it, and almost everyone said 'surface tension'. This is the force that acts on the surface between a liquid and air, which tends to make the surface contract like a rubber membrane. Reiner did a simple experiment to test that explanation. He filled a teapot with salt water coloured blue with ink, and held it in a glass-walled aquarium tank filled with fresh water. Then he poured out the blue salt water, which was heavier than the surrounding clear fresh water, and he found that the teapot effect still occurred. Since there was no sharp surface between the salt water and the fresh water, there was practically no surface tension acting on the salt water. Thus he ruled out surface tension as the explanation, but he didn't propose any other explanation.

The author of the present article proposed a new explanation in 1957 (J B Keller 1957 The teapot effect *J. Appl. Phys.* **28** 859–64; 1958 *Math. Rev.* **19** 348). It is simply that at the pouring lip the pressure in the liquid is lower than the pressure in the surrounding air, so the air pushes the liquid against the lip and against the outside of the pouring container. This happens because the liquid at the lip flows faster than the liquid away from the lip, and Bernoulli showed 200 years ago that the pressure is lowest where a liquid moves fastest. The author supported his proposal with a mathematical analysis which showed that this explanation was plausible.

The explanation was accepted and it has been incorporated into texts on fluid flow. Recently, Jerl Wilson in *Scientific American* described the teapot effect together with the explanation, and presented photographs and drawings of his own experiments on it (J Wilson 1984 The amateur scientist *Scientific American* (October)). In 1986 Jean-Marc Vanden-Broeck and the author used this explanation to calculate the velocity of the liquid and the shape of its surface for a variety of pouring flows (J M Vanden-Broeck and J B Keller 1986 Pouring flows *Phys. Fluids* **29** 3958).

In some cases the teapot effect is desirable. For example when a chemist pours an acid from one beaker to another, he may pour it along a glass stirring rod which rests against the pouring lip and has its lower end in the receiving beaker. In this case the flow is held against the rod, rather than against the outside of the pouring beaker.

To avoid the teapot effect there are a number of precautions which can be taken. The best one is to use a teapot which has the end of its spout pointing straight down, or nearly so. Then the flow would have to turn through $180°$ and go straight up if it were to flow along the outside of the spout. It's also good to have a thin or sharp lip so that the liquid is forced to leave the surface at its edge, rather than a thick rounded lip which the liquid starts flowing around and tends to continue doing.

When pouring from a glass (or other wide-mouthed container) it is best to have the glass only partly full. Then the glass must be tipped a good deal before the flow begins. This has two advantages. First the liquid would have to turn through a large angle to flow along the outside of the glass, which it is unlikely to do. Second the liquid is flowing faster when it comes out, and this also makes it less likely to turn back onto the outside of the glass.

Once this major type of spilling is avoided, which occurs when pouring begins, one can consider how to avoid spilling the last drop.

H B G Casimir

WINE AND WATER

And Noah he often said to his wife when
he sat down to dine,
'I don't care where the water goes if it
doesn't get into the wine.'

G K Chesterton

Water, as a drink, can be somewhat improved by adding wine. Even that fanatically convinced water drinker Doctor Sangrado—immortal character in Lesage's *Gil Blas*—indulged in later life in drinking such a mixture. But wine is certainly ruined by adding water and we can concur wholeheartedly with Noah in Chesterton's poem. Why then should I be interested all the same in some details of mixing wine and water? Because I was intrigued by the following well-known problem.

A glass of water and a glass of wine are standing side by side. Take a spoonful of wine out of the wineglass, add it to the water, stir well and then put a spoonful of the mixture back into the wine. Question: as a final result have you put more wine into the water than water into the wine, or is it the other way round? At first sight the answer seems ridiculously simple. Since you removed a spoonful and put a spoonful back, the total content of each glass after the operation is the same as before, therefore the total volume of wine removed from the wineglass must be equal to the volume of water put into the wine.

Now I once attended a lecture on the teaching of physics where this problem and its elementary solution were discussed and while the speaker enlarged on the didactical value of such problems I began to wonder what the real answer would be. I arrived at the conclusion that the answer probably depended on non-linear terms in the relation between the density of a mixture and its percentage of alcohol, but that was as far as I could get there and then. And I never got around to work out the solution until the invitation to contribute to the present volume made me overcome my usual laziness.

27

I simplify the problem by considering instead of wine a mixture of water and ethyl alcohol with 10% alcohol by weight. A table of densities of water–alcohol mixtures in the *Handwörterbuch der Naturwissenschaften*—an impressive handbook in ten volumes published in 1912—was the only one I could find in my own library. It gives the relative density, that is the density divided by that of pure water, at a temperature of 15°C. This density can be represented by the formula (p is the percentage of alcohol by weight)

$$s_p = 1 - \alpha p + \beta p^2$$

with $\alpha = 1910.83 \times 10^{-6}$ and $\beta = 30.417 \times 10^{-6}$. I shall write G and l for the volumes of liquid in each glass and in the spoon corrected by a factor d_{15} which is the density of pure water at 15°C, so that Gs and ls are weights in grams.

Let us take a spoonful of wine. It will weigh ls_{10} grams and contain $0.1 ls_{10}$ grams of alcohol. If this is put into the water the total weight will become $G + ls_{10}$ and the percentage by weight is

$$p^* = \frac{10 ls_{10}}{G + ls_{10}}.$$

From this we can derive the density of the mixture, s^*, and its total volume

$$G^* = \frac{G + ls_{10}}{s^*}.$$

A simple calculation gives

$$G^* = G + l + 100\beta l$$

the remaining terms being less than $20\beta l$, as long as $G > 10l$. So we have $G^* = G + l + \delta$ with δ roughly given by $0.003l$. Of course, precise values of δ can easily be calculated.

We are now ready to take the next step: we take a volume l, and that is a fraction $l/(G + l + \delta)$ of the total mixture, back to the wineglass. Since the waterglass contained ls_{10} grams of wine after the first operation, the total weight of wine removed is

$$ls_{10} - \frac{l}{G + l + \delta} ls_{10}$$

28

corresponding to a volume

$$V_{\text{wine}} = \frac{G + \delta}{G + l + \delta} \, l.$$

On the other hand we find for the volume of water that is moved

$$V_{\text{water}} = \frac{G}{G + l + \delta} \, l.$$

So, if we start putting wine into water then the final result will be that there is more wine in the water than water in the wine. If we begin putting water in the wine it is just the other way round as can be shown by a similar analysis.

The effect is extremely small and of no importance—and certainly of no culinary importance—whatever. But I am glad that I finally know the answer and can add it to my cherished store of useless knowledge. And it is really the non-linear term that does the trick!

Peter Richardson

LORD RAYLEIGH AND THICK PANCAKES

Lord Rayleigh was noted for his energetic pursuit of science, sometimes in unexpected places. He was a passionate observer; I recall that he studied creep in marble as a consequence of an opportunity presented by a fire-mantle during some refurbishing in his quarters. When I was an undergraduate at Imperial College an elderly employee there told me of his recollections of milk carts of Lord Rayleigh's Dairy passing in Exhibition Road, the sounds of the wheels and the horses' hooves muffled by straw spread regularly in the road by the occupants of the houses there. In the science of fluid mechanics, the development of self-stirring motions in a flat, horizontal layer of fluid heated from below is assessed using the Rayleigh number. A pancake batter is a flat, horizontal layer of fluid heated from below and so it seems entirely appropriate to dedicate this slightly scientific description of pancakes to Lord Rayleigh.

Before I give my recipe for thick, eggless pancakes I should give a brief explanation. Many years ago, when I said I'd like eggless pancakes I was told this was not done—pancakes had to have eggs. Not only is this not true, but one can make many different dishes based on eggless pancakes, including a type of pizza.

A fluid dynamic problem of pancakes arises in turning them over. If the batter has too low a viscosity, the uncooked part of the batter runs off the cooked part as one is in the process of turning it over. Raising the speed of turning—flipping fast—does not solve this problem; it tends to spread the uncooked batter over the environment. Egg in the batter overcomes this problem because of the polymerization process in the cooking egg. But the problem can be overcome as well by making a batter of high viscosity without any egg. The half-cooked pancake can be turned over without any spillage then.

A batter of high viscosity requires precise measuring of the ingredients. High viscosity is achieved by having a fine filler (mainly flour) of true volume fraction between 52 and 56 per cent. The mixing has to be carried out carefully to avoid the formation of lumps. My recipe provides for this.

Mixing of the ingredients (and refrigerated storage of unused mix) can be carried out easily in a glass jar with a screw top. Mixing goes well if the height of jar is about twice the diameter. For the amounts given in this recipe (for four pancakes) a jar with a capacity of about 1000 ml (or 1 quart) works well. The jar should have a wide mouth, around 2 inches in diameter.

Put 175 ml milk (whole or semi-skimmed) in the bottom of the glass jar; gently add 8 oz plain flour (not self-raising), a level teaspoon of baking soda, a level teaspoon of baking powder, and $1\frac{1}{2}$ oz dried milk. Do not stir, shake or mix yet. Add, by gentle pouring on top of these solids, 225 ml cold water. Screw the top firmly onto the glass jar. Pick up the jar, holding it vertically, and swirl for about 5 seconds to mix the dried milk somewhat with the cold water. Now grasp the jar firmly with both hands and shake vigorously up and down, keeping the jar vertical. The amplitude of shaking can be about 4–6 inches at 2–4 cycles per second. You should be able to feel the mixing taking place with progressive thickening. Ten seconds of shaking should be ample. Put the jar down and open the top; the mix should look free of dry solids, and when the jar is tilted sideways the viscosity of the mix (demonstrated by the slowness of response to the tilting) should be much higher than milk. [It is possible to adjust the viscosity of the mix if it is clearly unsatisfactory, but the adjustment rarely comes out to be entirely uniform so it is best to get a satisfactory mix at the first shake up. If the mix is too runny, it is possible to thicken it by adding one heaped teaspoon of flour by gentle pouring onto the mix, closing the jar, reshaking it, and examining it again. This can be repeated until a satisfactory mix is obtained on inspection. If the mix is too thick (and usually has then some unmixed lumps of flour), it can be thinned by adding 25 ml cold water to the jar, reshaking it, and examining it again. There is a temptation to add larger quantities at each step, but the temptation should be avoided because one is having to find the correct mixture ratio within a small range of tolerance, and with larger quantities it is easy to jump right over the range, e.g. from too thick and unpourable to too runny, or vice versa.]

Anticipating cooking the pancakes in a non-stick pan, I recommend that about 25 ml of vegetable oil should be added and well shaken into the mixture.

By this stage, perhaps with a little practice to determine whether your flour needs extra sifting to avoid lumps, you should be able to achieve a good mix with a minimum of utensils used in the process—even the jug used to measure the 175 ml milk is partly washed by being used to measure the 225 ml cold water!

The pancakes are cooked readily in non-stick pans. I recommend about a 7-inch base-diameter pan, which should not be pre-heated. The mix can be poured in to give a thickness of about 1/4 inch. The viscosity of the mix should be so high that this requires the pouring edge of the mixing jar to be trailed around in a spiral or zig-jag pattern over the pan face. The rate of heating is important. In ideal circumstances, bubbles form in the mix and a few may break out at the upper face of the pancake before the strength of the pancake at the pan face is sufficient for the pancake to be turned over. At this point the pan face of the pancake is light gold. If the viscosity of the mix is too low many bubbles may escape, resulting in a less foamy pancake. If the heating is too rapid, the pan face discolours to brown and forms a crust before many bubbles have become visible from the top. If the heating is too slow, more time is required for the pan face to cook sufficiently to achieve strength to allow turning, and in the course of this longer first-face cooking time more bubbles escape, again resulting in a less foamy pancake.

Cooking on the second face requires only half the time for cooking on the first face.

Most persons find pancakes to be too dry to eat without embellishment. A popular New England addition is maple syrup. This can be prepared directly in climates where the winter is cold enough to give significant periods below the freezing point. In very early spring one can drill a hole into each maple tree and insert a metal channel with an open end protruding beyond the bark of the tree and flared downwards to allow the sap to drip into a collecting bucket. The sap that accumulates is collected daily and taken to a 'sugar house' if you have a farm (I take mine to my home kitchen) and boiled until only about 5 per cent of the original volume remains, and tested for taste. The season for producing good syrup is only 2–3 weeks for each tree, after which the tubular metal spike is removed and the hole patched.

Even if you do not have home-made (or store-bought) maple syrup there are several other embellishments possible. Molasses, marmalade or jam are popular. Some embellishments can be embedded in the pancake while it is being cooked. For example, apple can be shaved into thin segments and dropped into the mix soon after the latter has been put in the pan; about 1/3 of an apple per pancake gives a distinct sweetening and added moisture to the pancake (cooked apple products, such as apple sauce, are not as satisfactory). It is necessary to prepare the apple shavings before beginning to cook the pancake, as there is insufficient time once cooking has begun. Other small or sliced fruits can be introduced into the body of the pancake similarly. Blueberries are another favourite in New England.

A modified form of 'southern pizza' can be made with this pancake mix. This type of pizza has a thicker, softer crust than the pizza more commonly found commercially. Start by pouring a basic pancake mix into a pan and begin cooking it. Take small vegetables, such as peas or cut green beans (even directly from frozen packets), and spread carefully into the pancake mix. The vegetables will sink slowly into the mix, and should be spread out fairly uniformly. Most particularly, they should not be placed in clumps, as these weaken the pancake and it may tear later when being removed from the pan. Check the progress of cooking of the pan face of the pancake by turning up the edge of the pancake periodically with a spatula. When the pan face is light gold, cook the other face either by flipping the pancake or by putting it under a grill. When the second face is lightly cooked, pull the pancake out, place strips of cheese on it, and return it to the grill. When the cheese begins to melt, pull it out again and add items to your taste (e.g. thin-sliced mushrooms) and cover with a tomato sauce (the type that is used as a base for spaghetti sauce); return under the grill for 45 seconds, and serve.

Scientific footnote: Data on the viscosity of suspensions of solids in liquids can be found in R J Farris 1968 Prediction of the viscosity of multimodal suspensions from unimodal viscosity data *Trans. Soc. Rheol.* **12** 281–301.

Peter Bradshaw

CONVECTIVE CAKE AND UNSTABLE TOAST

A small boy I knew many years ago preferred raw cake mixture to cooked cake. He has more recently had this continuing taste legitimized by recipes in which a thin cake or pudding mixture is partly cooked, so that the top part of the mixture is cake-like and the bottom part provides a sauce. There is an interesting non-linear effect. A hot spot in the mixture 'rises' in both senses: the self-raising flour reacts more quickly (or in some recipes the air in the egg whites expands more) so that the mixture in the hot spot expands and it rises into a region of higher temperature, accelerating the heating process.... Examples are Denver Chocolate Pudding, also called Chocolate Fudge Pudding or Chocolate Upside-down Pudding and the Baked Lemon Pudding also called Lemon Surprise Pudding or Lemon Delicious Pudding. All these have in common that the end product has a cake crust on top and a creamy sauce at the bottom.

'UPSIDE-DOWN' LEMON PUDDING

Ingredients
  4 oz (120 g) caster sugar
  2 oz (60 g) butter
  ½ oz (15 g) flour

2 eggs
1 lemon
8 fl oz (225 ml) of milk

Cream together the sugar, butter and grated lemon rind. Beat in the egg yolks, add alternately the flour and milk then the juice of the lemon and finally fold in the beaten egg whites. Bake in a moderate oven (350°F = 175°C) till golden brown, about 40 minutes.

'UPSIDE-DOWN' CHOCOLATE PUDDING

Ingredients *(for the cake mixture)*

3 oz (90 g) self-raising flour
3 oz (90 g) caster sugar
3 oz (90 g) butter
4 Tbsp (30 g) cocoa
2 eggs
1–2 Tbsp milk
$\frac{1}{2}$ tsp vanilla essence
2 Tbsp (30 g) finely chopped walnuts

Mix the eggs and vanilla essence and beat into the creamed sugar and butter. Then fold in the flour–cocoa mixture and walnuts and add enough milk for a medium soft consistency. Ladle into a 9″ diameter or 8″ × 8″ buttered pie dish. Then pour on top the sauce prepared by mixing:

3 Tbsp (20 g) cocoa
6 Tbsp (3 oz = 90 g) brown sugar
12 fl oz (350 ml) of water or coffee.

Bake for about 40 minutes in a moderate to hot oven (380°F = 195 °C).

Toast as it browns presumably absorbs radiated heat at a greater rate, which should make the brown parts blacken faster. This impeccable theory does not seem to prevent the production of acceptably uniform toast. Perhaps the toast is heated mainly by conduction, but in that case one would expect the top part of the toast to brown much more quickly (in a conventional electric toaster) than the bottom part, which again is not confirmed by experiment.

D J Crisp

WHICH FIRST?

I frequently tell my tea-table friends that there are good scientific grounds for pouring the milk first when making a nice cup of tea. It is general practice to serve *unboiled* milk with tea since boiling denatures the proteins in milk and changes the flavour. Unboiled milk has a further advantage in that the undenatured milk protein binds the tannin and thus neutralizes its bitter taste that most people dislike.

Now if you pour the hot tea first and then add the milk some of its protein becomes denatured thus imparting a 'boiled milk' taste to the tea and becomes ineffective in removing the tannin's astringency. If you pour the cold milk first the proteins do not become denatured, the taste is that of fresh milk and much of the tannin is rendered tasteless before the cup is filled with hot tea.

Although I know of no experimental data to verify this principle it makes good table talk and establishes a reputation for scientific erudition.

P B Fellgett

CYBERNETICS AND ROUX SAUCE

1. *Introduction*

In his 1948 book (*Cybernetics: or Control and Communication in the Animal and the Machine* (MIT)) Norbert Wiener established the modern discipline of cybernetics, and defined the subject as concerned with control, communication, information and feedback. These are not disjoint concepts, but different facets of the same underlying principle. In the ultimate analysis, all control involves feedback, feedback control requires communication in

35

both directions, what is communicated is information, and the useful application of information implies control. The four concepts can be summed up by saying that cybernetics is concerned with interaction; in other words that the whole is not the sum of the parts but the sum of the parts and their interactions.

Control, communication, information, feedback and interaction are all prominent in cuisine. There are various kinds of interaction involved; between the cook and the ingredients, between the ingredients in the cooking, and finally the interaction on the palate.

2. *Recipes*

Recipes are communication; or should be. Often they rely heavily on local feedback. The following is scarcely an exaggeration of what may be called a universal recipe.

> *Into a clean dish, place the dry ingredients and add the liquids until the right consistency is obtained. Turn out into suitable containers and cook until done.*

Note first the *macro label* 'clean dish'. The writer of the recipe presumably does not suppose that the reader will use a dirty dish. The reference to a clean dish is not intended to give information; it merely labels what follows as a recipe. The rest amounts to an instruction to use feedback; in other words, 'get it right'. One hardly needs a recipe to tell the cook this.

However, the most dreaded element in a recipe has yet to be mentioned. It may be illustrated from a recipe for a fish soufflé. Having specified the critical point in beating the eggs, it said 'meanwhile have ready some *brandade de morue*' which (starting from salt cod) takes a night and day to prepare.

Real recipes are a quite different *poissonière*. They fall into two classes. One is the folk recipe, like bouillabaisse for which Elizabeth David (*French Provincial Cooking* 1969 (Penguin) p. 345) says 'you will never get the same instructions twice'. What matters is the idea, to be interpreted freely and always excellent if the interpreter knows his or her business. The other kind of recipe differs from the first as jazz does from classical repertoire. It is the product of a master and at first reading its implications may be no more obvious than they are from the score of J S Bach's 'Brandenburgs' or Beethoven's op. 130. It must be obeyed to the letter, but with interpretative skill certainly not inferior to that needed for improvisation on a theme. It is only then that the magic becomes apparent; a magic of interaction revealed by the communication of the recipe.

3. Cooking

The verb *to cook* has an equivocal connotation in a number of languages. In English we speak of 'cooking the books', and in French an adulterated wine is described as *cuisiné*. Properly, however, cooking refers to bringing about interaction between ingredients by the aid of heat. There is interaction also in the way heat is applied, whether by radiation as in roasting or by conduction as in stewing, whether suddenly so as to create a large temperature gradient as in deep-frying or slowly as in daube, and also whether the application of heat is accompanied by aqueous or fatty liquids.

The actual changes induced by heat mostly take place quite rapidly, as *minute* steak illustrates; cooking times are largely times for the heat to penetrate to the centre, which is why meat thermometers are useful and why microwave heating can speed cooking. A traditional formula of the kind 'twenty minutes to the pound and thirty minutes over' is a folk example of piecewise linear approximation (see Appendix). The application of heat in cooking itself interacts with mechanical processes, which is why knives, choppers, mincers, grinders, mortars etc. are as important a part of the *batterie de cuisine* as the pots, pans, stoves and ovens.

The interaction between starch and water underlies much cookery. Starch is insoluble in cold water but in hot water the starch grains are broken down, may be partly hydrolysed and a colloidal solution formed. The effect is seen in a striking form in the interaction between flour of various kinds and either plain water or egg. Performed in one way, this would yield a gum more suitable for paperhanging than for ingestion, whereas done differently and exploiting the mechanical properties of gluten, it leads to the multifarious joys of pasta.

Another interaction fundamental to cookery is the formation of aqueous—fat colloids in the emulsion sauces mayonnaise, hollandaise and béarnaise (whether or not garnished with love). The

37

traditional methods of avoiding or correcting 'curdling' by adjustment of pH and back-mixing are empirical versions of what is now understood systematically in colloid science.

Perhaps the most striking interaction is that which gives us the whole range of roux sauces. The ingredients are so simple, just flour, butter and milk or stock. Yet the result, caused by the starch – water interaction in the presence of fat and natural emulsifiers, far exceeds the sum of the parts; very cybernetic!

4. *Interaction in Eating*

After the ingredients have interacted in cooking, they are presented to the palate of the eater. The interactions that then occur are partly idiosyncratic to the individual and partly culturally conditioned, but many have considerable universality.

Even the simplest components of a meal interact, like the way in which raw tomatoes (preferably of Mediterranean type) go with olive oil and pepper. A combination I particularly like, although others may not agree, is kipper (oak-smoked and undyed) for breakfast followed by marmalade and toast, all with high-roast black coffee. These are special cases, but an almost ubiquitous aspect of eating is the desirability of having a suitable balance of either salt in savoury dishes or sugar in sweet ones. Salt and sugar are also important as preservatives, but even here what was originally done to preserve may come to be liked for its flavour, as with bacon or jam. The historical importance of the taste of salt is recorded in the Old Testament—Job VI : 6; and in the New—Mat. V : 13.

The fundamental property of a linear system is

$$\langle \text{effect of A} \rangle + \langle \text{effect of B} \rangle = \langle \text{effect of (A + B)} \rangle.$$

Interaction is represented by crossterms such as (AB) due to non-linearity. Perhaps I have a particularly non-linear palate because I seem to be sensitive to crossterms. In particular I detest sweetness in any dish supposed to be savoury. This practically excludes me from having gammon or duck in restaurants because of the inevitable pineapple or orange respectively. I also find many manufactured foods such as soups or sausages distressingly sweet. This trait causes particular problems in eating-out in the USA, since American cuisine pays little regard to crossterms. If

Americans like A and like B they seem to accept (A + B), and some will do things as strange to my palate as eating marshmallows with beef.

The interaction between food and wine is a source of much innocent pleasure, as well as not a little pretentious nonsense when 'rules' are over-elaborated on a basis of social fashion. Sequence and temperature intensify the interaction. Most wine customs are rational and predictable, such as older or fuller wines following younger lighter ones, sweeter following drier, red usually following white, white served cool and the red *chambré*, dry white with fish and red with roasts. Some are less obvious, such as Sauternes or *Trockenbeerenauslese* with melon, or red wine with mackerel.

Wine also interacts with the glasses from which it is drunk; the incurving of a tulip, goblet, copita or balloon slows diffusion of the volatile aromatics. Glasses for white wine or sherry have stems or bases designed to protect the contents from the heat of the hand, while those for red or brandy can be cupped in the hand with the opposite intention. The tall flute for sparkling wine is equally functional in showing-off the bubbles, in contrast to those flat catering 'champagne glasses' which minimise the sparkle.

5. *Classical Cuisine*

Emphasis on good natural ingredients simply prepared does not necessarily imply that importance is not attached to crossterms (think of Italian country cooking) but it is arguably in classical French cuisine that interactions are most elaborately exploited.

The traditional *grande cuisine* is a highly developed cybernetic system in which the *gros bonnet* exercises control of the *brigade de cuisine* through *chefs de partie* in turn controlling and organising the work of the *commis*. The kitchen interacts with the restaurant or hotel with orders being called and confirmed by feedback from the *chefs de partie*. All depends on the *mise en place*, the making ready of ingredients, stocks, sauces, vegetables, fish and meats which can be put together in almost endless combinations to fulfil whims of the diner.

Inevitably this wonderfully sophisticated organism is expensive, and has tended to be replaced by what we may call 'International Deep Freeze and Microwave Cuisine' in which these excellent technological devices are abused to give the illusion of *grande cuisine* without any of its artistry. If those who eat with their mouths must pay through the nose, they ought at least to have what they are paying for. Perhaps economic feedback from disgruntled patrons will turn more restaurants back to better things.

Appendix

Suppose that the time for the central temperature of a joint, or other food being baked, to rise by a given proportion of its final value depends only on the linear size of the object, its volume thermal capacity and its thermal conductivity. Denoting the dimensions of time, length and thermal energy by T, L and J respectively, the dimensional equation is then

$$T = (L)^a (JL^{-3})^b (JL^{-1}T^{-1})^c$$

and the solution $a = 2$, $b = 1$, $c = -1$. The cooking time therefore depends on L^2, i.e. $W^{2/3}$ where W is the weight of the food. This result is also to be expected from the physical argument that the heat needed to raise the temperature by a given amount is proportional to W, the area it must penetrate to $W^{2/3}$ and the length of the thermal path to $W^{1/3}$, giving a time proportional to $W^{1 + (1/3) - (2/3)} = W^{2/3}$.

This function can be approximated, see figure, by the straight line $0.654 + 0.466W$. Scaling the slope to the traditional '20 minutes to the pound' the intercept is 28 'minutes over' and the error is less than 5 minutes over a 5 : 1 range of weight.

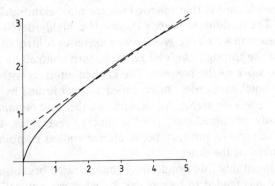

John Philip

PARSIMONIOUS BUT CREATIVE GASTRONOMY

La découverte d'un mets nouveau fait plus pour le bonheur du genre humain que la découverte d'une étoile.

Anthelme Brillat-Savarin

In the past I have expressed admiration for, and described personal attempts to practise, the principle of *scientific laziness*. I have said things like, 'Unnecessary work profoundly depresses people (like me) who are naturally lazy. We lazy people admire science most when it achieves maximal insight with minimal means, but we tend to think poorly of the use of elaborate methods, and of much energy and resources, to achieve uninteresting or even irrelevant results.' But today's earnest audiences (and readers) seem ill-equipped to cope with irony, so it is now prudent to talk instead about the principle of *scientific economy*. I continue to believe in this principle (whatever we call it), of which G I Taylor was a notable exemplar. Any reasonable application of it must disqualify a great deal of current research. The sheer ugliness and diseconomy of much research must lead many persons of taste and lively intelligence to turn away from what is represented to them as science.

Ludwig Mies van der Rohe's adage 'Less is more' expressed a similar principle of economy in architecture; but, alas, there also the principle seems to have become lost in a swamp of mindless eclecticism.

In gastronomy, however, it remains respectable to seek for economy and simplicity. The injunction, 'Waste is a grievous sin, which fills the heart of the honest man or the good cook with horror', directed to a young Tunisian cook, is to the point for all of us. And Escoffier's laconic dictum, '*Faites simple*', informs all serious gastronomy. Some of the following observations touch on creativity, serendipity, and physics, all of them somehow linked to the gastronomic parsimony I admire.

Parsimony with Time

In my (mid-Victorian) childhood in mid-Victoria, the cooking of a meal seemed a day-long labour. Even after the wood stove was supplemented by a gas stove, preparations for the 1 PM Sunday dinner after morning church began at 8 AM and things were put in the oven by 9 AM. I, however, demand quick results from cooking. I seek to keep the time and trouble of both preparation and cooking to a minimum.

Physical Equipment

Thanks to physics and technology, making a meal seldom takes us more than 90 minutes, and most take under the hour. In matters of culinary equipment, the refrigerator (with freezer) and the electric food mixer (with its attendant engines) are invaluable on the large scale; and our hand-powered *moulin à fines herbes* (mostly for garlic, parsley, sage and mint) is a small-scale marvel. On the hot-plates, pressure cookers work wonders. The convection oven helps, but, above all, the microwave oven saves time superbly. Its great virtue is the even heating: one puts the thermal energy where one wants it. One is no longer forced to rely on conduction to get the heat into the centre of the food. (The microwave is, of course, useless where gradation from surface to centre is a desired attribute of the dish.)

The Shape and Size of What is Cooked

The shape and size of what is cooked (be it bird, cake, sausage or vegetable) affects the cooking time. I offer an elementary illustrative example. The interested reader may pursue the matter further, possibly helped by OUP's mathematical bestseller of all time, *The Conduction of Heat in Solids* by Carslaw and Jaeger.

We limit ourselves to oven cooking by radiation and convection. At time $t = 0$ we place the food at uniform temperature into the hot oven, which we suppose capable, for $t > 0$, of maintaining the total external surface of the food at a constant higher temperature. Our concern is that the parts of the food most remote from the surface be adequately cooked. Purely for illustrative purposes, we here declare the food cooked when, at every point, its temperature increase is at least one-half the temperature increase at its surface. We call the time at which this happens $t = t_*$, the *cooking time*.

We consider four shapes for the food: the *slab*, a rectangular parallelepiped with sides in the ratio $1:5:5$; the *log*, a circular cylinder with diameter to length ratio $1:5$; the *hollow sphere* with ratio of internal to external radii $1:2$; and the *solid sphere*. For each shape we require the *dimensionless cooking time*, $\tau_* = \varkappa t_* V^{-2/3}$, where $\varkappa$ is the thermal diffusivity of the food and V its volume.

The mathematics of heat conduction gives the following values of τ_*: slab 0.011, log 0.020, hollow sphere 0.028, solid sphere 0.054. If $\varkappa = 1.3 \times 10^{-7}\,\mathrm{m^2\,s^{-1}}$, we find for $V = 1$ litre that the cooking time for the slab is just 14 minutes, for the log 26 minutes, for the hollow sphere 36 minutes, and for the solid sphere a whole 69 minutes. Note that according to our (too simple) criterion, cooking time for a given shape increases as the square of its characteristic length; so doubling the volume lengthens cooking time by 59%.

On Stuffing Poultry

The solid sphere mimics a stuffed bird, and the hollow sphere an unstuffed one. If $\varkappa$ for bird and stuffing are equal, the stuffed bird (by our simple criterion) needs twice the cooking time.

It is scarcely surprising that, all too often, the stuffing comes out as a repulsive oily (and possibly half-cooked) porous mass. (The temperature gradient drives into the central sponge of the stuffed bird the greasy juices that benefically drain from the unstuffed one.)

The remedy is simple, if unromantic. Bake your stuffing separately in its own small dish. The result is crisp and delicious, and takes little time. Very little indeed if you parboil ingredients such as onion and garlic, reserving the liquid for your sauce.

On Baking Vegetables

There is a long history of putting vegetables to cook around your roast: this takes time and the result can be greasy and half raw. It is quicker and cleaner to part-cook your vegetables in olive oil in the deep fryer first. Drain and replace the basket two or three times (to seal the surfaces) before you complete cooking by baking in the oven. It is best to use a separate dry dish, except when you are roasting a good piece of beef, minimally brushed with olive oil, and sitting high on a grid. Then you may crowd the vegetables on the floor of the meat dish, finally draining and crisping if need be.

This works marvellously well for potatoes, sweet potatoes, pumpkin (a delicious *human* food in Australia and New Zealand) and parsnips.

Sauce of the House

It is a great time-saver to have versatile staples on standby in the refrigerator. For us one such item is the Sauce of the House. This recipe is an updated version of that handed down to my wife Frances from her Manx great-grandmother Gawne.

200 ml milk
200 ml vinegar
20 ml Worcestershire sauce
3 large eggs
50 g polyunsaturated margarine
20 g raw sugar
8 g powdered mustard

Melt the margarine in saucepan over low heat. Add the other ingredients, already blended. Stir until it thickens without boiling. Store in a glass jar in refrigerator. Use as is, or make quick variants. Add finely chopped capers and gherkins for tartare sauce. Add tomato and chilli sauces for another seafood sauce. Add more mustard for a mustard sauce.

The Genesis of Recipes

Who except a few physicists will contest Brillat-Savarin's aphorism that discovering a new dish does more for human happiness than discovering a new star? In my view the acid test of a good cook is this: Can he foresee accurately the outcome of a new recipe? There is a singular pleasure when the result is just what you knew it would be. Few recipes spring from the void without antecedents. Most evolve through a long history. One applauds, nevertheless, the sampler in the New Orleans kitchen affirming

I love to cook
Without a book.

44

Cheese Potatoes

Serendipity, sometimes stemming from parsimony, may lead to recipes that are, at least, new to their author. My family had sailed by P & O from Long Beach for Australia. I had a day or two more at Caltech before I was to head home via Eastern US and Europe. The larder was almost bare, but there were potatoes, garlic and cheese to use up. Whence came the following recipe.

Pressure-cook thinly sliced potatoes until they come up to pressure. Turn off. Arrange layers of potato in lidless casserole, covering each layer with grated cheese and minced garlic, finishing with a layer of thinly sliced cheese. Bake in oven at 150°C.

The potatoes are almost cooked when they reach the oven, so this excellent dish takes very little time. Variants include adding a little milk; and treating sweet potato and pumpkin in the same way, either solo or in conjunction with potatoes. We much prefer this to *gratin Dauphinois*, and it takes a great deal less time and trouble.

Camembert Scones

Another serendipitous outcome of parsimony. Beyond a certain date, Camembert can be really past it. This is no occasion for despair, but rather an opportunity to make these unbelievably light and tasty scones.

To 100 g of ancient Camembert (both the runny centre and the aged crust) add 2 eggs and 100 ml of milk. Beat together rapidly in a mixer. Add self-raising flour to make the dough. Roll out and cut scones on a board. Bake in the oven at 220°C.

This works almost as well with old Brie, Stilton and Mersey Valley (a good sharp creamy Tasmanian cheese).

Fish and Marmalade

A quick, simple and delicious variant on fish baked in foil, customarily moistened with butter, white wine or lemon juice, is to paint filleted fish with a (not-too-sweet) marmalade. Also use marmalade as a variant sauce on fish cooked in other ways.

Irish Stew à la Rue de Montreuil

I hoped to include here the story of the evolution of our recipe for Irish stew, which serendipitously reached its apogee when I was called on to cook Sunday lunch in Paris. But I have exceeded already the space allocated by our stern Editor, so I must reserve that tale for another occasion.

Michael Hart

AN IMPOSSIBLE RECIPE

Well, almost! I read about it once, but a recent search of 137 cook books in my local public library failed to locate it.

In brief, we will learn how to prepare mussels florentine, or, if you prefer, mussels on spinach with cheese sauce. The dish can be an hors d'oeuvre, served in individual ramekins or a more substantial lunch-time snack when a casserole dish can be pressed into service. The exotic but cheap ingredient, mussels, stars in most cook books. Quantities are invariably specified in units other than those in which they can be purchased locally. Fresh spinach is not marketed satisfactorily because it deteriorates too rapidly after harvesting; you should grow your own. In any case, the two prime ingredients have orthogonal seasons (at least in the country where most Fellows of the Royal Society still live!). The third principal ingredient, cheese, often the centre of heated and informed debate, is here merely a foil for the other two. However, the dish would not be the same without it. This snack has such a compelling combination of taste, smell and texture that the secret techniques of experimental science must be called into play to make it possible outside its rare natural season. This requires a detailed knowledge of how and when to cheat but *above all* when not to cheat.

Apparatus

One ramekin (4 13/64″ diameter) per person or 9×10^{-3} m^2 of casserole dish per person.
A large number of saucepans and other kitchen utensils.
One pair of heavy duty rubber gloves.
The ingredients.

Main Programme

The structure of this recipe software breaks many of the rules of computer programming, but it is possible in practice because cooks can undertake several tasks in parallel. Two instructions, e.g. GOSUB and CONTINUE to the next program line are often simultaneous and the RETURN from a subroutine task may happen at unpredictable times in cooking.

T minus 48 hours: CONTINUE and GOSUB 'M'.

T minus 30 minutes: CONTINUE and GOSUB 'B1'.

T minus 15 minutes: CONTINUE and GOSUB 'S'.

T minus 10 minutes: CONTINUE and GOSUB 'B2'.

T minus 5 minutes: Make a 25 mm deep layer of spinach in the bottom of the ramekins or casserole dish. Cover with a close packed monolayer of mussels, and pour on béchamel sauce to half the depth of the mussels. Sprinkle with coarse grated cheese to just obscure the mussels from view.

T minus 2 minutes: place under the grill. Wait until the cheese has melted and just browns.

At approximately T minus zero:—sprinkle with grated Parmesan cheese, decorate with a sprig of parsley and serve.

Later on:

GOSUB 'P.S.'

GOSUB 'N'

END

Subroutines

'B1'   Make about 1 to 2 fluid ounces per person of béchamel sauce. Surely no recipe is necessary. If the usual recipes are too troublesome, RETURN to the main programme. Else RETURN at T minus 5 minutes.

'B2'   If you are already preparing béchamel sauce, RETURN. Otherwise, you have five minutes in which to blend hot butter and flour with milk in the ratio of 1 : 1 : 5 and to add seasoning. At T minus 10 minutes the question of weight per cent versus volume per cent does not arise. Unless you confess, your guests need never know. If they are in the kitchen now you will probably not arrive at T minus zero anyway. RETURN as soon as possible.

'M'   Buy, clean and feed the mussels. Allow about $\frac{1}{2}-\frac{3}{4}$ lb mussels per person in ramekins or $1\frac{1}{4}$ lbs each as a lunch-time snack. A single grain of sand ruins the entire meal for some guests. All cook books tell you to scrub and soak the mussels several times, but fail to recognise that diners do not eat the sand which is *on* the shell but object to the sand which was *inside* the shell. Remove barnacles, limpets and seaweed with either a blunt knife or a sharp knife. Contrary to popular belief, it does not matter which since both will be blunt afterwards.

Feed the mussels for two nights with a tablespoon of oats (or any other fashionable fruitless breakfast cereal). On the day, wash the mussels thoroughly and discard any which can be opened easily. Cook the rest over a boiling mixture of the usual ingredients. These might include white wine *and* cream (as in *Muscheln mit Wein*), or white wine *then* cream (as in *Moules à la Marinière*), but both are too rich for our needs. Try instead:

> *275 ± 1 ml dry cider (not cyder), actually 1 small can*
> *An equal amount of water*
> *A finely sliced red onion of about 57/64 inch in diameter*
> *A small handful of chopped parsley*
> *One medium sized bay leaf per person, but not more than 5 in total*
> *A few black peppercorns*

The mussels are best cooked in a very large covered saucepan. They should be contained in a wire basket so that they can be shaken every minute for about ten minutes. Remove the basket of mussels, GOSUB 'R' and remove those mussels which are open from their shells. Discard the rest. Place the shelled mussels in a sieve and wash and reheat them in the hot cooking liquor which you have remembered to save.

RETURN to T minus 5 minutes.

'N'   Next time will be better. GOTO T minus 48 hours.

'R'   Put on the gloves and RETURN. Unless you have heavy duty rubber gloves available, you will not finish by T minus zero. Computers often find their task impossible when they first read their software!

'S'   Prepare and cook the spinach. Allow about 3 ounces of leaf spinach per ramekin or 5 ounces per person in the casserole. Tear the leaf from the coarse stalk during washing but do retain sufficient stalk, in 3 cm lengths at the start of the season, reducing to 1 cm lengths later, since the texture contrast between the spinach bed and the other ingredients is important. Cook in a saucepan without added water, for about ten minutes, adding salt to taste. Drain, wash once in the boiling water which will undoubtedly be available about now, and squeeze dry. RETURN to T minus 5 minutes.

'P.S.' As in normal cook books, some essential advice has been omitted. For example, the grill should already be hot at T minus 2 minutes, and no guest may interact with the chef between T minus 5 minutes and T minus 2 minutes. T minus 10 minutes to T minus 5 minutes is also quite hectic (especially if the chef fails to RETURN from subroutine 'R'). RETURN.

Presentation

The quantities given will fill one ramekin per person as an hors d'oeuvre or can be used in a casserole dish for a lunch-time snack with fresh bread (Eurobread *please*, not British) and a dry white wine.

References

There are hundreds of cook books which do not contain this recipe. I regret that I cannot cite the author who introduced me to it. INSPEC appears unable to help me, but what might the keyword be?

Postscript

I mentioned earlier that it is rarely possible to make this dish with adequately fresh ingredients in the United Kingdom. Make it once in a good September and you will find the following 'scientific' advice indispensable for a repeat performance.

'Cheat 1' Use 'beet' instead of 'leaf' spinach. A longer autumn season opens and, provided that last year's plants grow quickly but do not run to seed too rapidly, a new spring season can be achieved.

'Cheat 2' Frozen spinach is almost invariably too finely chopped and pureed, even when it is called 'coarse'. However, at least one supermarket chain sells very coarse young spinach which is good enough.

'Cheat 3' I have scarcely mentioned the cheese. Don't waste money on the traditional cheeses which are grated, melted and toasted and don't overcook that which you use during the final two minutes (unless you prefer a rubberised intruder-proof cover on this dish). As a contribution to the farm policy and its unfortunate results, I recommend any mild Euro-Cheddar, provided that it is past its expiry date.

'Cheat 4' There is no cheat for live mussels.

James Beament

THE SCIENTIST DEFEATED BY DOUGH

Shortly after we were married in 1962 my wife, who was already a good basic cook but no scientist, asked me to explain the principle of yeast and baking powder because she wanted to try her hand at a pizza. I did so, adding that while I appreciated it might have been the only way primitive man could get bubbles of gas into a matrix, carbon dioxide was quite soluble in water. It was surprising when it was so finely distributed that enough remained as gas to aerate the mixture, but that was why you had to catch the dough at the right moment. Meringue, which she had found easy to make with one of the machines we had been given as a wedding present, was far more stable because it was based on air bubbles, and that ought to be a much more reliable way of doing things. A couple of days later at supper she produced a mouth-watering pizza from the oven. But neither the ordinary cutlery, the carving knife or the bread knife would make any impression on it. Being a realist she said it had better go on the compost heap to which I unthinkingly replied 'But it says in the 'Gardener's Treasury' you shouldn't put anything in compost that you can't break with a spade.' Our marriage survived, but I ceased to offer any scientific advice on cooking from then on, while she has developed into a magnificent cook.

Many years later in my Department, which has enormous experience of cereal growing and plant breeding, we grew a new variety of bread wheat for a well-known multi-national. Bread wheats are characteristically lower yielding but this one appeared to have Green Revolution potential, provided the fertiliser levels were right. We harvested it and sent it to the professionals to mill it and make some bread. A week later the baker rang us to ask if the Department could lend them a chain-saw. I come to the conclusion that man has carried out an infinite number of trial-and-error experiments over the ages to arrive at delicious food, and that investigating cooking would be like far too much else of modern

science—explaining why what does happen does so, without making the slightest difference to the fact that it does. If there was the least chance it would improve food, I would support such research, but every bit of modern 'scientifically manufactured' food I've tasted fails against the standard of the traditional equivalent.

Where research—and education of the medical profession—is really needed is investigating food allergies and their relationship to cooking. We know why some beans are lethal unless they are cooked, but why are cooked bananas almost as poisonous to some people who can enjoy them raw? Why do tinned tomatoes produce acne but not raw ones? Why does cooking destroy the cause of migraine in some cucurbits but not others? Why does rape honey have no effect on people who are hypersensitive to sinigrin? These are the questions to which scientific answers would be useful.

F Graham-Smith

THE GLITCH TEST FOR EGGS

A non-destructive test for distinguishing between fresh and hard-boiled eggs depends on the dynamics of rotation. Spin the egg on a smooth surface, stop it momentarily and release it. If it is fresh, the interior will still be spinning and the egg will rotate again.

I use this as a lecture demonstration illustrating the behaviour of pulsars, which are very condensed stars with a solid crust and a liquid interior. Unlike the insides of eggs, the liquid is a superfluid which can rotate for a period of days at a different rate from the crust. Occasionally part of the fluid and the crust are suddenly coupled together and there is a discontinuity in the rotation of the pulsar. This is known as a 'glitch': hence the name of the egg test.

Joshua Lederberg

ON COOKING EGGS

For some years I have remarked to students that we could (almost)
explain the chemistry of boiling an egg; frying was beyond us.

From a letter dated 16 September 1986

Richard Gardner
with the help of Rosa Beddington

ON BOILING EGGS

My cooking skills are very modest and extend little beyond the preparation of soft- and hard-boiled eggs. I naively thought that disclosure of this information to the Editor of this Anthology would secure my exclusion from the present venture. His response, however, was to draw my attention to the above communication which he had received from Dr Joshua Lederberg.

He then asked me whether, as a proficient egg-boiler, I considered this was indeed the case, and went on to raise the question of the temperature attained by the yolk and white at various times following immersion of eggs in boiling water. I was compelled to confess my total ignorance regarding these weighty matters. However, I did on reflection become intrigued about the thermal aspects of the process as a result of observing the egg-eating habits of Matthew, my 2-year-old son. Whilst normally tackling cooked food with caution in case it is too hot, Matthew quickly adopted the practice of dispatching the yolk of his 4-minute eggs without pause, using either a spoon or fingers of toast (often, inexplicably, termed 'soldiers'). Although he also likes the white, he invariably leaves it for later consumption. This suggests that the yolk either remains significantly cooler than the white during soft-boiling, or loses heat much more rapidly thereafter. In order to shed further light on this question, we decided to obtain a continuous record of the temperature of both components of the egg during the process of boiling.

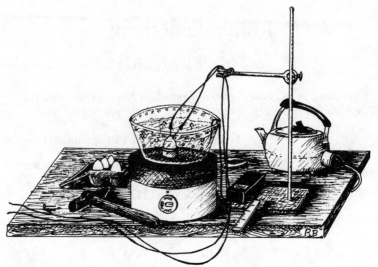

Figure 1   (Drawn by Rosa Beddington.)

Materials and Methods

Medium size hen's eggs purchased from a supermarket were used throughout the investigation. All the equipment employed, apart from the two-pen recorder, is illustrated in figure 1. It included a Pyrex bowl, a small electric hot-plate, and two thermocouples inserted into $1\frac{1}{2}''$ long 21G (0.8 mm outer diameter) disposable hypodermic syringe needles. Each egg was placed blunt end uppermost in a metal cup and the hammer then used to make make small holes in the shell with a pin through which the thermocouples could be inserted in the yolk and white, respectively. Once the thermocouples were in place and connected to the pen recorder, the egg was lowered into the bowl of already boiling water on the hot-plate by gripping the rim of the cup with pliers. Following final adjustment of the position of the thermocouples, their leads were clamped in a retort stand. On completion of the recording, each egg was allowed to cool, shelled, and then sliced perpendicular to its long axis with a razor blade in order to verify the location of the thermocouples.

Results

Recordings were made on two separate occasions. A total of 3 eggs was used on the first, No. 1 being employed in a trial run in which a thermocouple was inserted in the yolk only. Some problems were encountered with the pen recorder in this run, notwithstanding which an intriguingly low rate of rise in temperature was observed. Over-enthusiastic use of the hammer rendered egg No. 2 unsuitable for recording. In the case of egg No. 3, both the yolk and white were penetrated successfully with the thermocouples, and the pen recorder functioned in an exemplary way. Unfortunately, because of shortage of time, the recording had to be stopped at $16\frac{3}{4}$ minutes when, unlike the white, the yolk was still well below the temperature of the water.

On the second occasion, one egg (No. 4) was successfully penetrated with two thermocouples and recording continued until both white and yolk had attained 100°C. This run is illustrated in figure

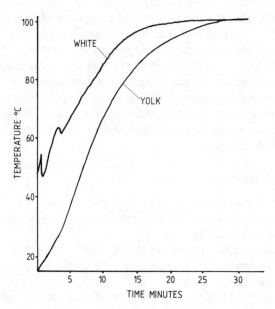

Figure 2 The first of the two fluctuations early in the temperature record for the white occurred during adjustment of the position of the thermocouple. The second was also seen at approximately the same juncture in egg No. 3, and may therefore be related to some internal event such as onset of coagulation of the white. This possibility remains to be explored.

2. It can be seen from the graph that the temperature of the white rose to 50°C within 2 minutes, was above 60°C by 4 minutes, and had reached 100°C by 18 minutes. In contrast, the temperature of the yolk rose much less abruptly, initially reaching only about body temperature by 4 minutes, and requiring a full 27 minutes from the time of initial immersion of the egg in boiling water to reach 100°C.

Discussion

A very marked difference in temperature of the white and the yolk of eggs has been found shortly after their immersion in boiling water. In the case of the white, there is an initial period of approximately $1\frac{1}{2}$ minutes during which the temperature rises very rapidly, followed by a much more gradual increase to 100°C. No such initial rapid rise is seen in the yolk, although its rate of increase in temperature actually exceeds that of the white after a few minutes. It would therefore seem that the white acts as a reasonably effective insulator in reducing transmission of heat to the yolk both before and after it has coagulated. As Matthew soon discovered, one practical consequence of this is, that while there is no risk of burning one's mouth on the yolk of a soft-boiled egg, it is indeed prudent to treat the white with circumspection. By the same token any micro-organisms lurking in boiled eggs are more likely to survive in the yolk than the white. Finally, it is important to note that eggs immersed in water which is then brought to the boil may well behave differently.

Acknowledgments

The fine thermocouples used in these experiments were fabricated by Mr Graham Read of the Clarendon Laboratory, Oxford and we are greatly indebted to him.

We also wish to express our thanks to Professor Nicholas Kurti of the Department of Engineering Science for his persistent and insistent interest in this project and for providing the eggs (4) and a Pyrex dish, to Dr Simon Haynes for offering us hospitality in his research room and for the loan of a two-pen recorder, to Dr Jonathan Hodby and Mr Clive Stayt for explaining to us the mysteries of the numerous switches of the two-pen recorder and to Professor Patrick Sandars, Head of the Clarendon Laboratory, for placing the general facilities of his Laboratory at our disposal.

Leon Mestel

THE CASE OF DE SITTER[†] RICE

The current fashion in cosmology is to apply particle physics theories to the early history of the Universe. Such a combination has given birth to the inflationary scenario where the Universe undergoes a rapid period of accelerated expansion. However, not only the Universe and the economy inflate!

A famous cosmologist, who shall remain nameless, inadvertently discovered inflation in the kitchen. Once he volunteered to cook the

† The Dutch Astronomer, Professor W de Sitter was a pioneer in establishing the concept of the expanding universe.

evening meal whilst his wife went out. On her return, she found most of the available saucepans filled with rice and naturally asked what had happened. The famous cosmologist said that he was cooking rice, a fact that was plain to see. It turned out that our culinary cosmologist, not realising that rice absorbed water and expanded, used the same volume of rice as that of potatoes. As a result, the rice began to appear over the edge of the saucepan; the cosmologist decanted the excess into another saucepan. Still more rice appeared over the edge of the saucepan...and so the saga continued.

Geoffrey Eglinton

TIME AND THE COOK

What *do* we mean when we speak of 'cooking'? Rendering the food we eat into a form that we consider 'cooked'?—such a definition encompasses everything from accidental alteration to the preparation of elaborate gourmet meals. Most food preparation, from washing and chopping, to prolonged heat treatment ('cooking') has a basic aim rooted in history, and probably even pre-history, of making the food less dangerous to eat, i.e. sterilisation of bacterial content and/or the hydrolysis or decomposition of toxic materials. Denaturing proteins is part of the aim but we know now that the thermal susceptibility of proteins varies considerably. Hot spring microorganisms live in temperatures up to $95°C$, so presumably 'cooking' of hot spring microbial mats might be none too effective as a means of preparing them for eating!

The heating process must break down complex biopolymers of all types, releasing flavours that are attractive to the palate: there must be an enormous amount of chemistry going on in these situations that may well repay the efforts of future chemists/cooks. Commercial pressures have already fostered such activities. Thus, wine and spirit production is accompanied by a large analytical effort. Thousands of organic compounds have now been identified and followed through the development of good wines. However, the same cannot be said for the study of other foods, such as the famous Chinese '100-year-old' eggs! Other delicacies deserving of attention include those that are prepared by burying the raw food

in the ground and leaving it to decay (mature?!) over months or years
—the bog butter of Ireland, the *Lutefisk* of Scandinavia and other
tasty morsels of decay. Here, one is looking at the long end of the
time scale for 'cooking' but there are also those at the short end!
Thus, the pasteurisation of milk involves flash heating for seconds
at 135°C—more recent developments include sterilisation by filtra-
tion through Nucleopore, or similar, filters in microseconds.

The following recipe is an example of cooking on a long
time-scale.

NORTH SEA OIL (Fr.—L'Huile de la Mer du Nord).
506. INGREDIENTS.—10,000,000,000,000,000 kg of fine-grained,
Kimmeridgian clay, rich in decaying microscopic marine algae (5%
total organic carbon).

Mode.—Bury sediment extremely slowly, using more sediment,
to 3 km deep beneath sea floor. Meanwhile, warm steadily to
150°C, allowing the pressure to rise to 500 atmospheres (50
megapascals). Keep lid on tightly or oil will escape. Serve through a
pipe 4 km long.

Time.—150,000,000 years. The mature sweet oil begins to gather
after 50,000,000 years.

Average cost, ingredients and cooking alone, 0d. After production, $15 or more a barrel.

Sufficient for the whole population (1987).

Seasonable from late 1970s to *c.* 2000 AD.

Apologies to: Mrs Isabella Beeton *The Book of Household Management*
S O Beeton, 18 Bouverie Street, London, EC1[†]

[†] 'Most people associate Mrs Beeton's book with Ward, Lock & Tyler. However, the
original publisher was Sam Beeton who, in 1866 as a result of the collapse of a bank
from whom he had borrowed money, became to his astonishment the "Licensee in
Bankruptcy" of Ward, Lock & Tyler, Publisher.' (Quoted from Nancy Spain's book
Mrs Beeton and her Husband.)

Christopher Longuet-Higgins

HORS D'OEUVRES

Bisecting the Ham Sandwich

It is possible (F J Dyson, private communication 1937) to find a
plane *P* that will equitably bisect any spatial distribution, however

improbable, of bread, butter and ham: there are 3 conditions to be satisfied and 3 degrees of freedom available (l, m and n in $lx + my + nz = 1$). Only recently did I realize that one should aim the knife so that it passes through the centres of mass B_1, B_2 and H of the bread, the butter and the ham, respectively. (For any plane through a body's centre of mass will divide the body into equal masses.) Unfortunately for the peckish, this algorithm cannot be relied upon to deliver half-sandwiches of elegant form or manageable structure. For if the undivided sandwich is such that B_1, B_2 and H nearly coincide, then there is no predicting the orientation of the plane P; to ensure an absolutely just bisection it may well be necessary to slice the sandwich not with a vertical but with a horizontal slash, or worse still, a *nearly* horizontal one.

The Importance of having a Lid

How people manage with lidless frying pans I shall never understand.

(1)   With a lid an egg can be cooked on both sides at once, and there is no need to turn it over, with the concomitant risk to the integrity of the yolk.

(2)   A well designed lid transforms the pan into a 'self-baster'. (Actually the so-called self-baster no more bastes itself than the erstwhile 'self-filling pen' actually climbed into the inkpot; but no matter.) Hot cooking oil from the pan condenseth on the lid and droppeth as the gentle rain from heaven upon the food beneath, in a process that a chemist would describe as reflux distillation.

(3)   The lid protects the chef against spattering, spitting or sputtering, such as occur especially in the frying of tomatoes or other ingredients containing small globules of imprisoned water.

Why, then, do the manufacturers of frying pans not supply them with lids or, at least, offer for sale lids of graded sizes from which one may select one that precisely matches one's own favourite utensil?

The Art of Cake Arrangement

How often, when friends call on a Sunday afternoon, does a host not offer tea, only to discover that the store cupboard contains no more than a partly consumed round cake? (The reader may omit to answer this question.) On such an occasion a little applied geometry may help to avert social embarrassment.

Let α be the apical angle of any one such cake; by hypothesis $\alpha < 2\pi$. Divide the cake into n equal sectors, where n is the integer nearest to $6\alpha/\pi$. Take a clean doily and with the aid of a protractor and a pencil mark upon it n radial lines at angles of $2\pi/n$. Place the doily on a cake pedestal, and position each slice of cake so that its apical angle is exactly bisected by one of the pencilled radii. The pleasing symmetry of the resulting arrangement will more than compensate for any possible shortfall in the value of n—unless n is zero, in which case the cake should be fed, in small places, to the visitors' dog.

In Praise of Clingfilm

How, in the bad old days, did one wrap up morsels of cheese, seal bowls of soup and store slices of cold meat? (Again, do not feel bound to answer.) The physics of clingfilm intrigues me; does its surface carry a negative charge, or what? Perhaps some readers of this anthology will know and will attempt to provide enlightenment.

A S V Burgen

IS THERE A CASE FOR PERMITTING THE IRRADIATION OF FOOD?

In the very year that Becquerel discovered radioactivity, it was first suggested that it might be used to kill micro-organisms in food and later patents were granted for this use. Serious study of this possibility followed the availability of large radioactive sources of ^{60}Co and ^{137}Cs after 1945. Extensive studies on food irradiation were carried out in Britain and the US in this period and later international evaluations were undertaken by FAO, WHO and IAEA, including important joint experimental studies in Karlsruhe.

Radiation, whether by x-rays or gamma-emitting radioisotope sources, generates radicals in the material which are generally very short-lived and react with the food, notably with DNA in micro-organisms and in surviving cell nuclei. In the first case they cause DNA damage that prevents the generation of daughter organisms; in the second case, the damage to DNA prevents changes in the food, which might follow enzyme induction, such as sprouting and ripening. The radicals do, of course, affect other food constitutents, unsaturated fats are oxidised, giving the equivalent of rancidity, and various proteins and carbohydrates are altered. However, there is little evidence of unique products, that are not also produced, for instance, in cooking or simple storage. For this reason it is not feasible at present to produce a test showing that irradiation has occurred.

Because of the random nature of the effects on micro-organisms, very large doses of radiation are needed to sterilise food, but much smaller amounts will reduce the viable organisms to, say, one percent of the pre-irradiation level, and this would have an important effect on the potential of any organism to cause disease.

Rather smaller doses will inhibit sprouting in potatoes and intermediate doses will delay ripening of fruits such as strawberries.

What are the potential uses of food irradiation? Firstly, there are a few foods that are currently quite heavily contaminated with bacteria and are responsible for an appreciable incidence of gastro-intestinal upsets; these are particularly chicken and certain shellfish, shrimps and prawns, even though they have been processed in an entirely satisfactory manner; spices are also often heavily contaminated. Irradiation therefore has the potential for considerable improvement in food hygiene.

The use of irradiation for extending the shelf life of soft fruits has a commercial rather than a hygienic potential; the spoilage of potatoes by sprouting in storage is a serious economic loss and could be prevented by very low levels of radiation. Not all foods are suitable for irradiation mainly because of flavour changes, and the uses mentioned are the main ones seen at present.

The public reaction to food irradiation has been almost uniformly hostile. Radioactivity has a very sinister connotation and there is a widespread assumption that the food is rendered radioactive. In fact, the induction of radioactivity by photons of up to 10 MeV is extremely small and mostly of such short life that the levels at point of sale would be a minute fraction of the natural radioactivity in the food (mainly due to ^{40}K), let alone the total radioactivity from our environment.

A second objection is that while radiation kills bacteria it has little effect on bacterial toxins. There is the possibility therefore that a food heavily contaminated with bacteria may be made acceptable in terms of viable organisms and yet remain hazardous in terms of toxins. This would really only be true if the food were eaten uncooked, as for instance oysters would be. This would be a food which should not be accepted for irradiation. The third objection is that irradiation causes some loss of vitamins in the food; this is true but it is so unlikely that a major part of the food intake will be irradiated that it is not a serious consideration at the present time.

The Advisory Committee on Irradiated and Novel Foods reported last year that they saw no toxicological hazard or special nutritional or microbiological problems in the irradiation of food. The report is at present awaiting a decision from the Government. A similar study is under way in the European Community and their report should be available soon.

Monty Finniston

A CHALLENGE TO INVENTIVE COOKS AND CATERERS

With the possible exception of Europe in the 19th century, the art of cooking has never seemed to me to have been the subject of great experiment. Taken over a week, meals in most households today vary little and menus even in the most highly thought of restaurants have a sameness about them; and this applies to the dishes of particular foreign countries—France, Italy, China or India—whose cooking may attract as a change from home feeding but would pall from sameness if constantly served. From someone like myself who is far from being a gourmet but likes his food made from good raw materials plainly cooked and not smothered with conventionally appropriate sauces, creativity in cooking is unlikely to be found. There is, however, one area of development which I would like others to try out for my benefit.

Most courses consist of dishes which are distinctly separated from each other. In the restaurant one would be faced with a menu which would start with a pâté, melon or mixed fruit or a smoked fish (salmon or haddock); this would be followed by a soup, in turn followed by a meat or fish dish and this in turn by cheese, fruit or other dessert concoction. And then coffee, although why this is the preferred drink to end a meal is not evident. Is there no other new alternative?

What I would like to see is more experimentation with the mix, as has been tried (and successfully) in many, but still too few, cases. As an example, why not try having many more meats or fish together with fruit? There are some standardised courses which do just this: duck à l'orange, chicken Maryland, pork with apple, fish Veronique and probably many others; or cheese, e.g. Parmesan, added to, not mixed, with soup or other mixtures of separate foods which can be identified on the plate. I am not suggesting mixed dishes as new forms of fast food, but rather as offering different tastes to be enjoyed in parallel rather that sequentially—the fifth generation of food presentation rather than outmoded past menus. Sauces of mixed content are not a substitute. It may be that associating different natural raw materials in cooking is not subject to scientific determination but perhaps there are some guidelines. Or is cooking an empirical art?

And while I am on the subject why should desserts in the main be cold or at room temperature? Why not more hot desserts of which the pudding in various forms used to be popular, but which for weight reasons has gone out of fashion. There must, however, be some slimming hot desserts waiting to be created.

Finally as to methods of heating for cooking, with the advent of the microwave I do not foresee, nor does there seem further requirement for, new or more elaborate forms of heating. Plasmas and lasers do not meet any need and at any rate are inappropriate.

Konrad Bloch

FOLKLORE AND FOOD SELECTION: MYTH OR WISDOM?

Without any knowledge of the science of nutrition, cultures in various lands have evolved dietary practices best fitted for survival in their natural environments. Modern science has now shown that in a number of instances intuitive selection of special dietary ingredients or practices may bestow physiological effects that are beneficial to health. Here are a few examples.

How to Prevent Pellagra

In rural areas of Mexico and other Central American countries corn meal, the dietary staple, is traditionally prepared by grinding the grain with limestone before baking the tortillas. These generally poor people enjoy good health on this sparse regime. Yet what appeared to be exactly the same diet caused a serious disease called pellagra (*pelle agra*, rough skin) among the poor in the Southern United States and in pockets of Northern Italy during the early part of this century. During the 1920s and '30s one vitamin after another was discovered, among them nicotinic acid or niacin, a component of the coenzyme nicotinamide adenine dinucleotide or NAD for short. Niacin, added to the diet of hominy grits or polenta, promptly restored the health of those affected with pellagra. Why the Mexicans and their neighbours do so well without supplementing their corn meal with a source of niacin was long an intriguing question. The answer emerged only recently: the tradition of grinding corn in the presence of limestone creates an alkaline milieu favourable for the action of an enzyme that liberates niacin from NAD. Though NAD as such is present in corn it is not absorbed from the gut into the bloodstream and is therefore wasted by elimination. Of course the Mexicans and their regional neighbours were unaware of the sophisticated biochemistry they were practising and one wonders who taught them the limestone technique. It is still a mystery why this knowledge never crossed the border into North America.

Kefir, Yoghurt, Koumiss, 'Sour milk'

Is the modern infatuation with yoghurt a health food fad? The answer is both yes and no. Ever since the domestication of animals man faced the problem of how to prevent fresh milk from spoiling, especially in warm climates. The Caucasian kefir, the koumiss of the Tartars (from mare's milk), the yoghurt of the Turks and the German '*Sauere Milch*' are all products of bacterial fermentation. Lactobacilli added to milk either as a pure culture (*Lactobacillus bulgaricus*) or in olden times inadvertently as an aerial contaminant, sour the milk by producing lactic acid from the milk sugar lactose. All other milk nutrients, proteins, fats and vitamins are preserved. But only in modern times when adults began to consume milk in large quantities, especially in the United States, has it been realized that fermented milk has an added benefit for certain population groups. Some Caucasians, about 10%, the majority of Africans and American blacks (50–70%), and nearly all Asians cannot tolerate milk. As adolescents and adults they lack the enzyme lactase that converts the milk sugar lactose to harmless sugars. In individuals afflicted with this inborn error of metabolism the consumption of more than a glass of milk will cause severe diarrhoea. Infants of all human races possess the lactose-destroying enzyme and therefore tolerate whole milk but may lose it if they belong to the races mentioned.

For those who are milk-intolerant but like the taste of fresh milk, supermarkets now sell what tastes like the real stuff but has been freed of the offending milk sugar by treatment with lactase.

Garlic

Travellers to various parts of the world should be prepared for many dishes heavily seasoned with garlic. The strong scent and pungent flavour of garlic (*Allium sativum*) does not appeal to everyone but if you have no choice, try to overcome your aversion and take solace in the notion that garlic is good for your health. Folklore has it that garlic is beneficial for the circulatory system; that it provides protection against stroke, coronary thrombosis and atherosclerosis. There is growing evidence that garlic indeed lowers blood cholesterol and hinders aggregation of platelets, i.e. the clotting of blood. Chemists have now isolated the active principle from garlic bulbs and have shown that the pure substance alone, called ajoene (from 'ajo' the Spanish for garlic), duplicates the salutary effects of garlic powder or extracts. What is remarkable, and came as a surprise, is that ajoene is totally odourless. In the future one may therefore enjoy garlic's health benefits without running the risk of offending the delicate sense organ of one's companion.

Similar beneficial effects have been attributed to onions but here the chemical basis has yet to be discovered.

As an aside for those who love gardening as well as cooking I quote from *Old Wives Lore for Gardening* (Maureen and Bridget Boland 1976 (Bodley Head)): 'A single clove of garlic planted beside each rose is guaranteed absolutely to keep greenfly from the plant.'

For those interested, here is some selected reading matter: *The Fanatics Ecstatic Aromatic Guide to Onions, Garlic, Shallots and Leeks* by M Singer (1981); *The Book of Garlic* by L J Harns (1974); *Garlic Therapy* by J Watanabe (1974).

Peppers

Among the common pungent condiments, pepper, whether black, red or white, is probably the most widely used, especially and most generously in tropical and semitropical regions. All peppers, the black variety, cayenne, chilli and paprika are species of the tropical *Capsicum* family. Why are peppers so popular? Because they enliven dishes that are otherwise bland or even hide the off-flavours of meat that is too far gone? Perhaps so but recent research adds one element to pepper's gustatory properties. The pungent principle in all species of the *Capsicum* family has now been isolated. Named capsaicin, this chemical causes hypothermia—shown so far in animals only—probably by stimulating receptors at the hypothalamic cooling centres. Perhaps it is not too far-fetched to speculate that the popularity of pepper derives in part from the bodily comfort it produces—another example of intuitive wisdom.

Section III Technological Know-how and Culinary Art

Stephen Hales (1677–1761)

AN ACCOUNT OF SOME TRIALS TO CURE THE ILL TASTE OF MILK, WHICH IS OCCASIONED BY THE FOOD OF COWS, EITHER FROM TURNIPS, CABBAGES, OR AUTUMNAL LEAVES ETC. ALSO TO SWEETEN STINKING WATER†

This method of blowing showers of air up through liquors will be of considerable use in several other respects, as well as in distillation, as appears by the following trials, viz.

I have been informed, that it is a common practice, to cure the ill taste of cream from the food of cows, by setting it in broad pans over hot embers or charcoal, and continually stirring it, till scalding hot, and till cool again. But when I attempted to do this much sooner, and more effectually, by blowing showers of air up through it, I soon found it to be impracticable, by reason of its very great degree of frothing up. The ill taste must therefore be got out of the milk, before it is set for cream; which, I have been told, has been practised, and that with some benefit, by giving the milk a scalding heat, without stirring it.

May 22. I ventilated some ill-tasted, new unheated milk of a cow, which was purposely fed with crow-garlick mixed with cut grass. After 15 minutes ventilation the taste was a little mended; in half an hour's blowing it was something better. At the hour's

† From *Phil. Trans. R. Soc.* 1755 **49** 339.

end it had the same taste but was sensibly better than the unventilated milk. I was disappointed of an opportunity to repeat the experiment with crow-garlick milk, with a scalding heat: it would then probably have been soon perfectly aired; as it is reasonable to believe from the event of the following experients, viz.

August 23, four quarts of ill-tasted new milk, from a cow, which had fed eighty-four hours on cabbage leaves only, and drank during that time very little water, were put into a leaden vessel, eight inches in diameter, and thirty inches deep. The leaden vessel was heated in a large boiler, and set into a vessel of hot water; thereby to give the milk a scalding heat, and also keep it hot. In ten minutes ventilation it was perfectly cured of its ill taste; and after standing twenty-four hours in a broad pan, there was a thick scum, which was half cream and half butter, free from any ill taste; the skimmed milk was not sheer or thin: so here is a method to make good butter from ill-tasted milk.

The froth of the milk was so great, by reason of a too brisk ventilation, as to make it froth over the vessel, which was thirty inches deep; if it had not been kept down, by constantly lading and breaking the very large bubbles of froth. But when the ventilation is more gentle, the froth has risen but three inches from six quarts of milk which was nine inches deep. The cabbage milk was but six inches deep. I repeated the like operation the same day, with the evening milk of the same cow; but giving it only a heat that I could bear my fingers in, for a little time; with this degree of heat, after forty-five minutes ventilation, the milk (though much better tasted), yet was not so completely cured as the former milk. Hence we see how necessary heat is, to volatilize the rancid oil (which gives the ill taste) to such a degree as to cause it to fly off by ventilation.

It was observed, that what was milked from this cow a week after she had done eating the cabbage, had an ill taste.

I have not as yet had an opportunity to try to cure, in the same manner, the ill taste of milk, which is occasioned by cows feeding on autumnal leaves, or turnips, they having probably eaten this autumn the fewer leaves, on account of the plenty of grass, occasioned by much rain; which has hitherto prevented turnips from being rancid, which are observed to be most so when they shoot out in the spring. As opportunities offer I purpose to make trials, which I conclude others will also do, which will probably be attended with the same good effects as that on the cabbage milk.

But though the ill taste of milk from feeding on cabbage leaves was thus effectually cured by volatilizing with heat and dissipating by ventilation the rancid oil, yet the bitter taste of a strong infusion of chamomile floweres in six quarts of water was not sensibly abated by an hour's ventilation of it, while scalding hot.

I am informed, that in Devonshire†, they set the pans of milk on trivets, making fires under them, to give the milk, gently and gradually, a scalding, but not a boiling heat, which would disturb the rising cream; and then set it on the floor in the milk-house to cool, where in twelve hours it has a thick scum, partly butter and partly cream. The skimmed milk is very thin and sheer; and the cream in great plenty and delicious, except that it gets a smoaky taste, which it is apt to do; and which might probably be prevented by having a range of as many stoves as there are pans of milk to be used at one time; all to be warmed by one fire, either at one end, or the middle of the flue or funnel in the brick-work, which conveys the smoke and heat under the stoves. And as the pans nearest to the fire will soonest have their due heat, on their removal to bring the farthest and coolest pans nearest the fire; and instantly covering the uncovered stoves with proper covers to prevent the heat and smoke from coming out; by this means the milk would all be soon heated, with any kind of fuel, and that with much less in quantity than in the common way.

And the more effectually to prevent the smoke from coming at the milk, it may be well to have the broad outer rim of the pans turned perpendicularly downwards, three or four inches, that it may enter deep into a circular groove of sand; and if it shall be needful, the sand may be wetted in order the more effectually to prevent the passage of the smoke. I thought of this method about fifty years since, on tasting the smoaky butter in Somersetshire. By the same means the poor might save much fuel in boiling the pot, especially in summer, when a fire is wanted only for boiling the pot.

† This is an early printed recipe for clotted cream.

When any pans are to be removed from the stoves, the ascent of the smoke through the uncovered stove may be prevented by first closing the flue near the fire, by an iron sliding shutter or register.

Milk might thus most commodiously be heated to a scalding heat with little fuel, fit for ventilation, in a vessel of a proper depth, set in the same manner as the pans in a stove, to secure it from smoke, with bellows fixed properly near it. By this means there would be little trouble or expense in curing ill-tasted milk by ventilation.

May 14th, merely to see what the event would be, a gallon of new milk just from the cow was ventilated, for an hour and half, which produced six ounces of butter; and though it was ventilated half an hour longer, yet no more butter was made; it was whitish, wanting both the colour and taste of good fresh butter.

I am credibly informed, that in the places famous for making the best fresh winter butter they set the pot of cream in warm water, so long as till it has acquired that small degree of sourness, which it very soon has in warm summer weather, which gives it an agreeable flavour. And in order to give it colour, they grate a well-coloured carrot into a little milk, which, as soon as stained, is strained from the carrot through a sieve and then mixed with the cream.

It is found by experience, that the quantity of cream is increased, by putting into the milk a little warm water in winter and cold in summer; which being thereby in some degree thinned, the cream is thereby more easily disentangled, so as more freely to ascend to the surface of the milk.

I ventilated three gallons of stinking Jessopswell purging water. On first blowing, the smell of the ascending vapour was very offensive, which offensiveness abated much in five minutes: In eleven minutes the smell was much better: In twenty minutes the water seemed sweet both in smell and taste; and not sweeter at the end of forty-five minutes, fifteen or twenty minutes will probably suffice.

July 20th, three gallons of stinking sea-water were ventilated; in five minutes it was much sweetened, and no ill smell in the ascending air, though at first it was very offensive: At the end of ten minutes it had a small degree of ill taste; after twenty

71

minutes no ill taste or smell. It frothed near a foot high during part of the ventilation: this from the bitumen etc.

Some sea-water, which was made to stink with flesh and isinglass being put into it, was not made perfectly sweet, not even by a ventilated distillation, and an hour's more ventilation after it was distilled; so that putrefaction with animal substances is not easily completely cured by ventilation.

When the water was 27 inches deep in the leaden vessel, no air could be blown up through it by the force of the bellows; But at 18 inches depth the air could freely be blown up in showers, thro' the water; when therefore it is requisite to blow up through great depths of water, the bellows may be worked with a lever, as smiths bellows are worked.

As it is found by experience, that the milk and butter of cows, which drink stinking water, has a very bad taste, this plainly shews, that the water retains its putrid quality, when mixed with the blood. Whence it is much to be suspected, that the stinking water, which is drank in ships, by retaining its putrid quality, even when mixed with the blood may thereby promote that putrid distemper the scurvy, as well as some other distempers. And much more does the putrid close air in ships, which is mixed with the blood from the lungs, promote putrid and other disorders. By the same means also pestilential infections are taken in: For as the salutary properties of good air are conveyed by the lungs, so are also the malignant qualities of bad air.

Thus also the putrid water in marshy aguish countries, may be a cause of agues, as well as the putrid air, which they breathe; which, as well as the putrid water, may probably carry some of its putrid quality into the blood through the lungs. This method therefore of sweetening stinking water, by blowing showers of air up through the stinking water of some aguish places, may be beneficial.

Live fish may well be carried several miles, by blowing now and then fresh air up through the water, without the trouble of changing the water: for this ventilation will not only keep the water sweet, but also enrich it with air, which is necessary for the life of fishes; with which air they supply their blood, by breathing the water, thin spread, between their gills; but stinking water will kill fish.

I have found that much of the heating oil may be got out of

tar-water, by blowing showers of air up through it when scalding-hot, for 15 or 30 minutes, the longer the better; the less volatile, and more salutary acid remaining.

[*STEPHEN HALES (1677–1761) is described in the* National Dictionary of Biography *as a physiologist and an inventor. Educated at Corpus Christi College, Cambridge he became a fellow of the College in 1703, was elected an FRS in 1718 and was awarded the Royal Society's Copley Medal in 1739. (He was the fifth Copley Medallist.) He was also a founding member of the Society which was to become The Royal Society of Arts. In physiology he worked on the anatomy and nutrition of plants and on blood pressure. His inventions included the use of ventilation to purify the air in ships, prisons, granaries, etc. and to remove obnoxious smells and tastes from liquids. He also pioneered bottled mineral water!*]

Brian Mercer

POTATOES, MESHED AND FRIED
(Fr. *Pommes Frites Netlou*)

Recipe according to British Patent No. 836555 (with assistance from Mrs Beeton's *Book of Household Management* 1912 edition, recipe numbers 1569 and 1575).†

Ingredients.—1 lb of potatoes, 1 oz of butter, 1 or 2 tablespoon-fuls of milk, salt.

Method.—Peel and steam the potatoes over a saucepan of boiling water, mash them well with a fork. Heat the butter in a stewpan, add the milk, stir in the potato, and season to taste with salt. Beat well with a wooden spoon.

Saw a 12″ wooden school rule into two equal lengths. Cut V-shaped notches at $\frac{1}{4}$ inch spaces into one edge of each of the two pieces of rule. Abut the notched edges together and hold firmly over the discharge nozzle of a kitchen mincing machine. Place the

† If the 1912 edition is not available recipes 1142 and 1145 of the facsimile 1st edition may be consulted.

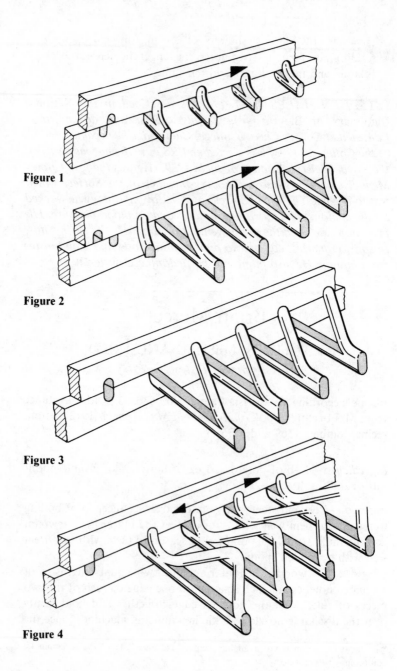

Figure 1

Figure 2

Figure 3

Figure 4

mashed potato into the hopper of the mincing machine and turn the handle. As the potato is extruded through the notches, reciprocate the two rules as shown in figures 1, 2, 3 and 4. Ensure that the edges of the rule are held firmly together during reciprocation.

The method will create a potato net or net-like structure having mesh strands and intersections, characterised in that the intersections are each composed of an integrally extruded mass and the mesh strands are divisions from the said intersections, the whole net being an integral extruded entity.

Cut the potato mesh into $1\frac{1}{2}$ inch squares. Make some oil or dripping quite hot in a saucepan, put in the potato mesh pieces, and fry to a nice brown. When they are crisp and done take them up, drain them on a paper before the fire, and serve very hot, after sprinkling them with salt. These are delicious with rump steak.

Time.—About half an hour. *Average Cost.*—11p per 1b.
Sufficient for 3 persons. *Seasonable* at any time.

(Another Method)

Ingredients.—10,000 tonnes of linear low-density polyethylene granules containing 2% carbon black. For this recipe the rule must be made from steel and cut into two halves with a hack-saw. The V-shaped notches should be filed into one edge of each of the two pieces of rule. The barrel of the mincing machine should be heated to $200°C$. It is strongly recommended that the cooks wear asbestos gloves.

Method.—Place the polyethylene granules in the hopper of the mincing machine and turn the handle. Reciprocate the rules as described in the previous recipe and allow the extrudate to pass through a large saucepan of cold water to quench the molten polymer. Continue the operation 24 hours each day.

Regrettably, this recipe produces a tasteless and somewhat indigestible product. However, it can be used for soil stabilisation, renal dialysis, crop harvesting and many other applications. If it were possible to refine the method it could be licensed in thirty countries and possibly create a completely new international industry.

Peter Fowler
with the Help of Rosemary Fowler

CLEANING SILVER

Until recently in our household, when silver was to be cleaned and polished it involved the use of proprietary fine abrasive slurries. They worked, and one's cloth showed the evidence with black marks! Equally, in the long term perhaps, the silver did too because on older items the hallmarks are often worn. More recently, bottled solutions proved useful for removing tarnish on forks and spoons, perhaps with the same effects.

The method we ourselves now use for cutlery and other small items which can be immersed in water is as follows. Line the bottom of a suitably sized plastic box with aluminium foil. Sprinkle with about a dessertspoonful of salt and fill with hot water. Lay a few items to be cleaned in the solution so that each item touches the foil. Hey Presto—they are clean in a remarkably short time. Remove, wash, and dry.

This is a particularly labour-saving method if occasionally incorporated into the washing-up routine. Washed items can spend a short time in the salt solution before being returned to the washing-up water and dried.

The fact that each item has to touch the foil for there to be any cleaning effect whatsoever shows conclusively that the removal of the tarnish involves electrolysis. The tarnish is often silver sulphide which is readily formed when silver forks and spoons are used with eggs or green vegetables, especially Brussels sprouts. The removal of the sulphur is accompanied by a smell of H_2S. We believe that the silver in the tarnish is returned to the items.

Another method is to use washing soda with aluminium foil and very hot, near boiling, water. A vigorous reaction occurs involving the solution of the foil and the emission of hydrogen. Nascent hydrogen is said to be involved, and certainly it does not matter in the slightest if electrical contact is made. Leaving the silver in the solution for too long deposits a slight white film on it. If this does occur it is easily removed in the washing and drying stage.

We hope that our preferred method will be proved right in the long term, that our silver survives without slowly being lost, that it stays looking nice not requiring much effort to keep it so, even through we eat sprouts, eggs, and other foods which provide plenty of tarnish.

We are indebted to Sir Charles Frank for suggesting the salt electrolysis method to us. He felt that it would work.

R McNeill Alexander

A DISSECTION GUIDE TO ROAST LAMB

The lamb on your plate was once a living sheep. The meat was the muscle it used, when it ran or jumped. You will be puzzled how to carve a joint if you do not know its structure, and the structure is far more interesting if you understand how the animal used it.

Look first at a lamb chop (figure 1(*a*)). The long curved bone (hidden by the intercostal muscles) is a rib. The lump of bone at the thick end is half a vertebra. The strip of fat along the upper edge of the chop is the subcutaneous fat, the layer of fat that lies just under the skin. It is well developed in domestic mammals (including ourselves) but thin and patchy in most wild ones: a gnu chop would be much leaner than a lamb chop.

The eye of the chop is a slice of the longissimus muscle, the biggest muscle in the whole body. It runs lengthwise along the back, just above the joints of the backbone (figure 1(*b*)). When it

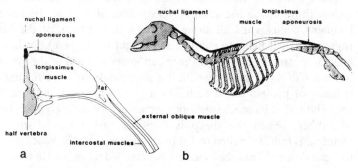

Figure 1(*a*) A lamb chop and (*b*) a diagram showing some of the structures in a sheep's back.

77

shortens it straightens the back, an action that is particularly important in taking off for a jump. It is also used in galloping, which involves bending the back at one stage of the stride and straightening it at another.

You might suppose that the fibres of the longissimus muscle would run lengthwise along the back, in the direction of the muscle's pull. A vertical cut through the eye of the chop will show that they do not: they run obliquely, in an arrangement described as 'pennate'. They start on the ribs and run upwards and backwards to connect to an aponeurosis (a sheet of tendon). When they shorten they pull the aponeurosis forward, straightening the back or even making it bow upwards. If the fibres ran lengthwise along the muscle in a 'parallel-fibred' arrangement the muscle would consist of a relatively small number of very long fibres. It could shorten a lot (because the fibres were long) if its situation allowed, but it could not exert much force. The position of the longissimus does not allow much shortening so it is better to have a pennate muscle made of a larger number of shorter fibres, which can exert more force.

The narrow strips of lean in the chop are the intercostal muscles, which connect adjacent ribs, and the external oblique muscle, which runs from the ribs back into the wall of the abdomen. There are two layers of intercostal muscles, one arranged so that its contractions expand the rib cage and one to contract it. These movements play a part in breathing, but movements of the diaphragm are also important. The external oblique is one of the muscles that support the abdomen, fighting the flab.

There is another tiny detail of the chop that I find fascinating, a yellow thing at the top corner. This is the tail end of the nuchal ligament, which runs all along the neck to the back of the head (figure 1(b)). It helps to support the weight of the head but has to be able to stretch so that the sheep can lower its head to the ground to feed. Cut it out and play with it if your meal is not too formal. It is made of protein but it feels like a piece of rubber. Laboratory tests show that its mechanical properties are exceedingly like those of rubber. When the sheep is standing with its head up, the ligament is taut, stretched to 1.3 times its slack length. When it puts its head down to feed the ligament is stretched more, to 1.8 times its slack length.

The nuchal ligament has rubber-like properties that are little

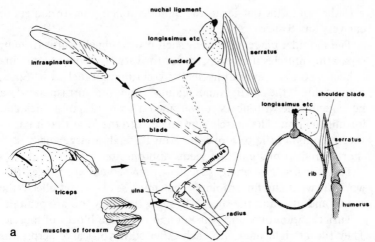

Figure 2(a) A shoulder of lamb, drawn from an X-ray picture, with slices cut from it. (*b*) A diagrammatic section through the shoulder region of a sheep.

affected by cooking. Tendon and aponeurosis are much less extensible in the raw state, much more like string, but cooking converts them to gelatine, changing their properties dramatically.

There is a lot to be seen in a simple chop, but look now at something more complicated. Figure 2(*a*) shows a whole shoulder of lamb, a joint for a party rather than an ordinary meal unless you have a big family. I took an x-ray picture to show the bones inside the joint. The foot has been cut off at the wrist so we see the bones of the forearm (radius and ulna) and upper arm (humerus), and the shoulder blade. The bulging fat-covered side of the joint lay immediately under the skin of the shoulder, and the flat side lay against the ribs.

You will probably cut your first slices across the outer side of the upper arm. The two big pieces of lean in the slice are two of the three heads of the triceps muscle, the biggest muscle of the fore leg. It connects to the ulna at the back of the elbow and its job is to straighten the elbow, or to prevent it from bending under the weight of the body. The slices cut across it more or less at right angles to its fibres. Carving across the grain of meat so that there are no long fibres in the slice is generally recommended, but you cannot do it

79

with the rest of the outside of the shoulder unless you are content to cut very small slices.

The shoulder blade has a bony shelf projecting outwards from it, separating muscles that swing the leg forward from ones that swing it back. You can avoid this shelf by cutting parallel to it. Slices from behind the shelf come mainly from the infraspinatus, a pennate muscle with fibres converging on both sides of a thick and inedible tendon. The muscle runs so close to the joint that it has to shorten only a little to move the joint through a large angle, so a short-fibred, pennate design seems appropriate.

The forearm has small, succulent, dark-coloured muscles that work the wrist and finger joints. They must be carved parallel to the radius and ulna and the slices will show that they too are pennate.

Turn the joint over and you will find two main blocks of muscle. They run at right angles to each other so if you carve across the fibres of one you will cut parallel to the fibres of the other. The longissimus muscle runs parallel to the backbone, with the semispinalis muscle (that continues forward into the neck) beside it. With them is a piece of nuchal ligament, far longer than you would find in a single chop. Cut it off the joint and pull on its ends and you will find out how extensible it is.

At right angles to these are the serratus muscles, connecting the shoulder blade to the ribs. Think of the legs as pillars topped by the shoulder blades. The sheep's trunk is suspended from these pillars with the serratus muscles serving as cables (figure 2(b)).

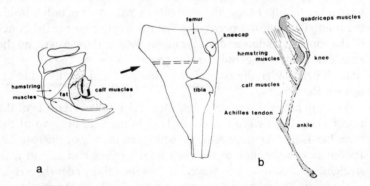

Figure 3(a) A half leg of lamb, drawn from an X-ray picture, and a slice cut from it. (b) A diagram showing the principal muscle groups of a sheep's leg.

Finally, look at a leg of lamb (figure 3). I used a half leg for the illustration because my wife and I felt rather sated after eating our way through the shoulder. It contains the knee joint and parts of the bones immediately above and below it: a whole leg would contain the whole of the femur, right up to the hip.

The knee is straight, as the joint comes to the table, because the carcass was hung up by its heels after slaughter. The slice in figure 3(a) is from behind the knee, where two of the principal muscle groups of the leg overlap (figure 3(b)). These are the hamstring muscles (the main muscles of the back of the thigh) and the muscles of the calf. The hamstrings are big muscles with long parallel fibres. They swing the leg back, doing a lot of the work when the animal accelerates or jumps. The calf muscles are pennate, with short muscle fibres attaching to tendons which are shown black in figure 3(a). At the lower end of the calf, the tendons of these muscles are bundled together to form the Achilles tendon, which is attached to the heel (figure 3(b)).

Tendon has very good elastic properties. It stretches only a little but, because it is strong, it can store a lot of energy. The catapults used by the ancient Romans for hurling rocks into besieged cities used springs made of bundles of tendons. The Achilles tendon of the sheep, and some of the tendons in the fore leg, are used as springs, enabling the animal to bounce along as if its legs were pogo-sticks. This saves energy, when the sheep runs. A perfect ball in a frictionless world could bounce along for ever with no further input of energy, and even in the real world bouncing mechanisms can be economical of energy.

I have written only about sheep, but cattle and pigs have very similar structure. Most of what I have written about lamb applies also to beef, pork and bacon. I hope that it will add interest to your meat.

Benjamin Thompson,
Count Rumford (1753–1814)

ON THE
CONSTRUCTION OF KITCHEN FIREPLACES
AND KITCHEN UTENSILS;
TOGETHER WITH
REMARKS AND OBSERVATIONS RELATING TO THE
VARIOUS PROCESS OF COOKERY,
AND
PROPOSALS FOR IMPROVING THAT MOST USEFUL
ART †

[*After a lengthy discourse on fuel conservation in which Count Rumford concludes that, for example, 100 lbs of beef can be boiled by burning 4 lbs of dry pinewood or $2\frac{1}{4}$ lbs of pit-coal, he turns his attention to the question of what temperature is needed to cook meat.*]

My principal design in publishing these computations is to *awaken the curiosity of my readers*, and fix their attention on a subject which, however low and vulgar it has hitherto generally been thought to be, is in fact highly interesting, and deserving of the most serious consideration. I wish they may serve to inspire cooks with a just idea of the importance of their art, and of the intimate connection there is between the various processes

† From the *Collected Works of Count Rumford* edited by S C Brown (1969) Vol. III pp 55–384 (Cambridge, MA: Harvard University Press).

in which they are daily concerned, and many of the most beautiful discoveries that have been made by experimental philosophers in the present age.

The advantage that would result from an application of the late brilliant discoveries in philosophical chemistry, and other branches of natural philosophy and mechanics, to the improvement of the art of cookery, are so evident and so very important that I cannot help flattering myself that we shall soon see some enlightened and liberal-minded person of the profession take up the matter in earnest, and give it a thoroughly *scientific* investigation.

In what art or science could improvements be made that would more powerfully contribute to increase the comforts and enjoyments of mankind?

And it must not be imagined that the saving of fuel is the only or even the most important advantage that would result from these inquiries: others of still greater magnitude, respecting the *manner* of preparing food for the table, would probably be derived from them.

The heat of boiling water, continued for a shorter or a longer time, having been found by experience to be sufficient for cooking all those kinds of animal and vegetable substances that are commonly used as food; and *that degree* of heat being easily procured, and easily kept up, in all places and in all seasons; and as all the utensils used in cookery are contrived for that kind of heat, few experiments have been made to determine the effects of using *other degrees of heat*, and *other mediums* for conveying it to the substance to be acted upon in culinary processes. The effects of different degrees of heat in the same body are, however, sometimes very striking; and the taste of the same kind of food is often so much altered by a trifling difference in the manner of cooking it, that it would no longer be taken for the same thing. What a surprising difference, for instance, does the manner of performing that most simple of all culinary processes, *boiling in water*, make on potatoes! Those who have never tasted potatoes *boiled in Ireland*, or cooked according to the Irish method, can have no idea what delicious food these roots afford when they are properly prepared. But it is not merely the *taste* of food that depends on the manner of cooking it: its nutritiousness also, and its wholesomeness,—qualities still more

83

essential if possible than taste,—are, no doubt, very nearly connected with it.

Many kinds of food are known to be most delicate and savoury when cooked in a degree of heat considerably below that of boiling water; and it is more than probable that there are others which would be improved by being exposed in a heat greater than that of boiling water.

In the seaport towns of the New England States in North America, it has been a custom, time immemorial, among people of fashion, to dine one day in the week (Saturday) on *salt-fish*; and a long habit of preparing the same dish has, as might have been expected, led to very considerable improvements in the art of cooking it. I have often heard foreigners, who have assisted at these dinners, declare that they never tasted salt-fish dressed in such perfection; and I well remember that the secret of cooking it is to keep it a great many hours in water that is *just scalding-hot*, but which is never made actually to boil.

I had long suspected that it could hardly be possible that *precisely* the temperature of 212 degrees of Fahrenheit's thermometer (that of boiling water) should be that which is best adapted for cooking *all sorts of food*; but it was the unexpected result of an experiment that I made with another view which made me particularly attentive to this subject. Desirous of finding out whether it would be possible to roast meat in a machine I had contrived for drying potatoes, and fitted up in the kitchen of the House of Industry at Munich, I put a shoulder of mutton into it, and after attending to the experiment three hours, and finding it showed no signs of being done, I concluded that the heat was not sufficiently intense; and, despairing of success, I went home rather out of humour at my ill success, and abandoned my shoulder of mutton to the cook-maids.

It being late in the evening, and the cook-maids thinking, perhaps, that the meat would be as safe in the drying-machine as anywhere else, left it there all night. When they came in the morning to take it away, intending to cook it for their dinner, they were much surprised to find it *already cooked*, and not merely eatable, but perfectly done, and most singularly well-tasted. This appeared to them the more miraculous, as the fire under the machine was gone quite out before they left the kitchen in the evening to go to bed, and as they had locked up the kitchen when they left it and taken away the key.

This wonderful shoulder of mutton was immediately brought to me in triumph, and though I was at no great loss to account for what had happened, yet it certainly was quite unexpected; and when I tasted the meat I was very much surprised indeed to find it very different, both in taste and flavour, from any I had ever tasted. It was perfectly tender; but, though it was so much done, it did not appear to be in the least sodden or insipid,—on the contrary, it was uncommonly savoury and high flavoured. It was neither boiled nor roasted nor baked. Its taste seemed to indicate the manner in which it had been prepared; that the gentle heat, to which it had for so long a time been exposed, had by degrees loosened the cohesion of its fibres, and concocted its juices, without driving off their fine and more volatile parts, and without washing away or burning and rendering rancid and empyreumatic its oils.

[I repeated Rumford's experiment for a Friday Evening Discourse I gave at the Royal Institution in London in 1969. A 2 kg leg of lamb was placed in a slow oven and the temperature of the joint was recorded by two thermocouples embedded in hypodermic needles, one measuring the temperature 5 mm under the surface and the other in the centre. The figure (from Proc. R. Inst. *1969 **49***

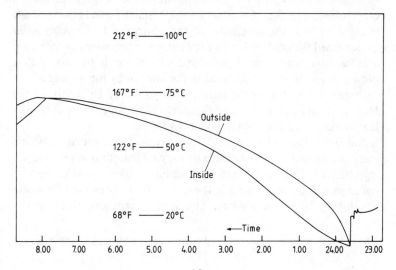

451) shows that the temperature never rose above 70°C and the members of the audience who tasted the result (it was a cold joint) agreed with Rumford's enthusiastic judgement.]

Nicholas Kurti

THE HYPODERMIC SYRINGE IN THE KITCHEN†

Originally, I was going to call this article 'Pravaz–Rynd–Wood Cookery', but it sounded both obscure and pretentious. It is true that when, a couple of years ago, I asked my Oxford colleague Dr A H T Robb Smith, a physician actively interested in both history and gastronomy, about the origins of the hypodermic syringe he gave me the names of those three doctors as having been involved in the development of the instrument. However, I soon discovered that, at least as far as culinary applications are concerned, the story is not quite so simple.

Some Historical Remarks

First of all, who was the inventor of the 'syringe', i.e. a 'cylindrical tube with nozzle and piston into which liquid is first drawn by suction and then ejected in a fine stream used in surgery, gardening etc.' (*Concise Oxford Dictionary* 1964)? Blaise Pascal (1623–1664) is credited with the invention of this instrument (*Encyclopaedia Britannica* 15th edn) which he used for his experiments on pressure and vacuum. The syringe, equipped with a nozzle but not with a needle, seems to have been used in the kitchen by the middle of the 18th century. Certainly, as pointed out to me by Dr Robb Smith, Hannah Glasse, in *The Art of Cookery* (1747) uses a syringe to give her 'Syringed Fritters' their fanciful shapes.

But a 'syringe' is a far cry from 'hypodermic syringe', which ends in a pointed, hollow needle of varying lengths and permits the injection of fluids deep into a material. I asked several medical colleagues about its origin but it was not until I consulted Dr Robb Smith that I had the answer. This is not surprising since on the

† From Oxford Symposium on Food and Cookery, 1984 and 1985 *Cookery: Science, Lore and Books (Proceedings)* 1986 (London: Prospect)

continent, especially in France, the hypodermic syringe is usually associated with the name of Dr C G Pravaz of Lyon, and in Hungary until the 1930s it was generally referred to as the 'Pravaz-syringe' (*fecskendö*).

Dr F Rynd working in Dublin developed his hypodermic syringe to remove blood from the vein to analyse if for sugar content. Dr C G Pravaz, working in Lyon, developed his instrument independently of Rynd in 1851 (published in *Comptes Rendus de l'Académie des Sciences* 1853 p 88) to inject iron perchlorate into the artery for the treatment of aneurism (morbid dilation of an artery). The needle, which moves inside a tube, is a '*trois-quarts très fin en or ou en platine*'—and once again it was Dr Robb Smith who told me that this must be, as indeed it is, the French for 'trocar', a needle with a three-facetted point.

Finally, Dr Alexander Wood (*secundus*) in Edinburgh, unaware of the work of Drs Rynd and Pravaz, developed his hypodermic syringe and was, probably, the first, at least in Great Britain, to administer painkilling drugs by subcutaneous injection.

The 'Culinary Injector'

As far as culinary use goes, Pravaz, Rynd and Wood jointly deserve the credit for conceiving and developing an instrument which, apart from its great medical and surgical importance, can make significant contributions to culinary art. Although 'hypodermic syringe' is a perfectly legitimate designation of this implement, irrespective of its end-use, it has strong medical associations and perhaps the expression 'culinary injector' might be adopted when referring to the kitchen utensil. It is preferable to 'flavor injector', the name under which ordinary, disposable hypodermic syringes are marketed in the US—partly because this name is probably protected, but, more importantly, because the aim is not always to impart a flavour to the preparation.

Three or four syringes in size between 2 ml and 20 ml form a useful addition to one's *batterie de cuisine*. The needles should be about 1.5 mm in diameter—they will pass puréed jam and thick sauces—and have lengths between 20 and 60 mm. Although 'disposable' plastic syringes are adequate for most uses—they last for several years—it is advisable to have at least one glass syringe with a metal or glass plunger. The pistons of the plastic syringes tend to swell and stick if they are used with greasy fluids, e.g. melted butter.

The First (?) Published Recipe Involving a Hypodermic Syringe

I first came across the mention of a *'Gigot de Mouton Pravaz'* in an article in André Simon's *Wine and Food Quarterly* some time in the 1940s. About 25 years later I mentioned this fact in a letter to *The Times* (6 March 1973) and as a result I received from Dr Robb Smith a reprint of his article 'Doctors at the Table', published in *The Journal of the American Medical Association* (**224**, No 1, 2 April 1973), an amusing and learned account of the contributions of the medical profession to gastronomy. The article ends with the recipe for *'Gigot de la Clinique'* taken from Bernard Guégan's *Le Cuisinier Français* (Paris, 1934). This dish was the creation of a country surgeon and the Baronne Pierlot who communicated the recipe to Guégan and had to bribe the surgeon's cook to obtain it. I give the recipe in Dr Robb Smith's translation.

A week in advance place the leg of mutton in a marinade, called Samaritan's Balm, as it is a mixture of wine and oil—old Burgandy, Beaune or Chambertin and pure olive oil of Provence—to which one should add the usual seasoning together with a touch of ginger and cayenne, grated nutmeg, a handful of bay leaves and half a spoonful of sugar (this acts like musk in perfumery, to fix the various ingredients). Turn the leg of mutton in this marinade once or twice a day. The essential part of the receipt is to take a large hypodermic syringe containing burnt brandy and orange juice and inject it three or four times into the meat. This initial injection is not repeated, but afterwards the marinade is injected with the syringe three or four times a day. At the end of a week, the leg of mutton is perfect, embalmed with aromatic herbs, which have penetrated the flesh, so that it is transformed into venison of unbelievable and exquisite quality. Roast it and serve with a classic sauce chevreuil to which is added just before serving, two spoonsful of hare's blood.

The Culinary Injector Used to Help or Replace Marinading

Marinading is an ineffective and wasteful way to introduce liquids into large joints. Not having seen any experimental results on the speed of penetration of a marinade I carried out the following simple experiment with a 20 mm thick circular slice of leg of lamb 100 mm in diameter. I put the meat into blue-coloured white wine, its top sticking out of the 'marinade' by about 1 mm so that the marinade could penetrate it only from the sides and the bottom. I could observe the rate at which the blue colour moved towards the inside and noted that in the first 36 hours it penetrated only about 10 mm. In other words, for a completely immersed 20 mm thick slab of meat total penetration would have taken about 36 hours which equals one and a half days. For a 30 mm slab it would have been about 3 days, for 40 mm 6 days, for 60 mm 13 days. These figures, however, must be taken with more than a pinch of salt, since much depends on the type of meat, the nature of the marinade, the temperature and other factors. The figures nevertheless indicate that, in the case of *large* joints, injecting the marinade at points about 20 mm apart can greatly accelerate the process. Also, much less marinade is needed and this can be of importance if expensive ingredients are used.

If the object of the marinade is not just to impart a flavour but also to stimulate chemical, in particular enzyme, reactions it may happen that the reaction time is longer that the normal penetration time. Then injection is of no great advantage, unless one speeds up the reaction velocity by increasing the temperature.

The Culinary Injector as an Aid to Tenderising

'Hanging' meat is a way to allow the naturally occurring enzymes to do the tenderising. It is, however, possible to accelerate the process by 'injecting' enzymes into the meat and at the same time imparting new flavours.

It is quite possible that the use of pineapple with ham or pork originated in the chance observation of its tenderising effect on the meat. Indeed *fresh* (but not tinned or otherwise sterilised) pineapple juice contains a powerful proteolytic (protein dissolving) enzyme bromelin, similar to papain, found in papaya fruit and papaya leaves. I give below two recipes which give satisfactory and even pleasing results, but a word of caution and a word of advice is necessary. It is not possible to give exact quantities and exact timing, since much depends on the ripeness of the pineapple, on the quality of the meat and on the temperature at which the process is carried out. And do not tenderise unless it is necessary. It is a mistake to try to improve some high-quality raw material if nature has done it for you.

PORK CHOPS 'PRAVAZ'

4 chops, about 170 g (6 oz) each
70 ml fresh *pineapple juice*
4 slices of fresh pineapple, 5 mm (3/16 in) thick
120 ml (4 fl oz) double cream
150 ml (5 fl oz) soured cream
1 egg yolk
Lard
Sweet paprika
Lemon juice to taste

Inject 10 ml of pineapple juice into each chop, 6–8 evenly distributed pricks on each side. Leave them standing at ordinary temperature for at least two hours, then fry them slowly in lard. When brown, remove them from the pan, keep warm and braise the pineapple slices in the lard. When cooked arrange them on the serving dish and place a chop on each. Pour off the fat from the pan, add 30 ml pineapple juice to loosen and dissolve the residue from the chops, add the previously mixed double and sour cream, and lemon juice if it is too sweet, bring to simmering point, stir in a small teaspoon of sweet paprika and thicken with the egg yolk. Pour over the chops and serve.

GAMMON WITH PINEAPPLE

A well-cured and well-cooked gammon joint needs no embellishment or tenderising, but for a tough joint the following recipe might be worth trying.

Soak the joint in cold water to reduce saltiness. Inject *fresh* pineapple juice, about 40 ml for every 500 g, and leave standing for 6–10 hours in a warm place. Start baking it in a slow oven (about 140°C) so that its temperature rises very gradually, taking one to two hours for the centre of the joint to reach 45°C. (The temperature at the centre can be recorded easily with a thermocouple anchored in a hypodermic needle, stuck in the joint and connected to a millivoltmeter.) Finish cooking in a hot oven.

If you find the joint, or part of it, has been over-tenderised, the offending bits can be turned into a pâté. They are usually so soft that no further mincing or pounding is necessary. Just mix thoroughly with butter and add seasoning according to taste.

The Use of the Culinary Injector for Distributing Ingredients Fairly Uniformly Within Pieces of Meat

CHICKEN RYND (a more meaningful name for Chicken Kiev)

Chicken Kiev is usually made by placing a piece of garlic butter mixed with parsley inside a chicken breast, covering it with egg and breadcrumbs and frying it. If well made, the result is pleasing, but it often happens that when you attack it with your knife it retaliates by squirting hot garlic butter on you and then leaves you with dry insipid meat. Thanks to Dr Rynd (and Drs Pravaz and Wood) the following alternative can be recommended.

Remove the skins from chicken thighs and inject them with the following concoction: melt some slightly salted butter (about 10 g per thigh), add finely chopped parsley and garlic (the more the better) and leave standing in a warm place (preferably 30°C) for about 12 hours. The top of a gas boiler, a radiator, an airing cupboard or standing in warm water are possibilities. Decant the butter, pressing out as much as possible of the butter and juice from the garlic–parsley mixture. (A garlic press, or fine sieve might be used.) For the injection the chicken pieces should be cold and the butter 40–50°C. Suck the butter into a *glass* (see above) syringe through the needle and immediately make one or two 2 ml injections. By now the needle will have become cold and blocked with solid butter. Suck some more butter into the syringe and repeat the process. The advantage of injecting into the cold chicken pieces is that the butter immediately solidifies and cannot exude from the meat.

Coat the pieces in pancake batter, roll in breadcrumbs and fry in hot oil, about 5 minutes on each side. Finish cooking in a warm oven (200°C) for about twenty minutes.

János Szentágothai

MARINADING BY INJECTION

Curing or marinading by injection of salt solutions or various alcoholic fluids such as wine, beer, vinegar etc., containing various spices is more widely used in culinary practice than is generally believed. Such procedures are usually kept secret and exact prescriptions are almost never given, probably also because they have in most cases never been experimentally tested with appropriate controls.

During my childhood we lived in a large country house in one of the distant suburbs of Budapest, where we fattened our own pigs, poultry etc. and had professional butchers just to kill the pigs, clean them and cut the carcasses down to their major pieces. All other work, including smoking, was done by our kitchen staff. In Hungary this was practised in almost every household, even in the less affluent ones, and my mother was most accomplished in the use of all possible recipes, which were abundant in Hungary and highly differentiated according to the several regions and nationalities living there, all of whom had their specific technologies, many of them unique in producing most excellent flavours. Having witnessed and participated in these activities from early childhood I was motivated later to keep up this practice in our own household.

When I was professor of anatomy at Pécs University during the years 1946–1963 it was the general practice in many families of the professors' 'collegium' to agree with one of the local farmers that they would fatten at least one pig, previously selected from their stock. The pig would be killed some time during the winter and the whole procedure of marinading the hams and pieces of bacon and of preparing the sausages was performed either on the farm or, in the case of the more fastidious families, the carcasses were brought to the professors' houses, especially to the more spacious houses, so that all these procedures could be carried out at home. There were still private butchers who could be hired to give a hand in this work and to smoke the material in their smoke-houses. We occasionally competed, with chosen connoisseur colleagues as judges, to find out whose sausages, hams etc. had the best flavour. As an anatomist I did not need, of course, any professional help to dismember the carcasses and separate the various cuts or pieces of meat and other organs for further processing.

In order to be on the safe side, especially when the weather was not sufficiently cool—for prior to the late 1950s there were no electric refrigerators, let alone deep freezers, for private households—I very often used intra-arterial injections of prepared marinading fluids, especially for hams intended to be smoked and kept for gradual consumption as '*prosciutto crudo*' over the whole year. The distal parts of the legs had, of course, to be removed one or two days after the injection. One had to be very careful with this procedure lest the ham became too salty; no such danger was involved in the conventional procedure of applying the marinade only by submerging the hams or chunks of bacon in the marinading fluid. The injection of marinading fluids by a syringe either into the arteries or simply into the tissues is an excellent procedure, but the details of this technique have to be learned by experience.

REFLECTIONS ON THE INTRA-SAUCE

Lady (Isabelle) Vischer in her excellent book *Now to the Banquet* (London: Victor Gollancz, 1953) describes how 'A French colonial doctor, who resided a long time in Morocco and who was an artist in cookery and a most fastidious lover of food, invented whilst in Africa a sauce, which later became the celebrated feature of a restaurant under the name of Intra-sauce. The doctor gave intravenous injections of alcohol, permeated by a very learned combination of thyme, mint and sometimes aniseed, to lambs and pigs. This perfumed their flesh without doing any harm to the animals, and the sauce, the 'Intra-sauce', extracted from the juices of the roasts was, as a friend of mine who tasted it many times told me, Lucullan. I possess the menu of a dinner given one day by the Societé de Pathologie Exotique, in honour of the celebration of their 25th anniversary, on which figures as the principal dish: *Baron de Mouton Marocain à l'Intra-sauce*.

Most physicians, even anaesthetists, do not have any experience about what concentration of alcohol could be injected intravenously without major harm or pain. 10% alcohol solutions would precipitate the proteins, so that local tissue damage and clotting of the blood would almost certainly occur. It might be tested experimentally whether with very slow injection into a larger vein and letting the injection fluid be immediately diluted, one might run up close to this concentration. I would assume that a fluid of physiological saline containing 1% of alcohol and sufficiently well distributed, or solved spices (extracts) could be injected (more correctly infused) into living animals without major harm. One would, though, have to calculate the eventual concentration of alcohol in the blood, because 0.3−0.4% approaches the lethal limit of alcohol poisoning. Since the total volume of blood is about one twelfth of the entire body volume, the amount of the injected fluid could be calculated approximately, although one would have to reckon with alcohol that is taken up by the body tissues, especially the intercellular tissue spaces, and that is metabolised during a slow infusion. It would be probably much simpler to take repeated samples of blood from a distant vein and let the infusion continue so that the blood alcohol concentration would be kept below 0.20−0.25%. A considerable amount of spices could then be gradually injected without causing too much discomfort to the animal. Eventually, the animal could be killed by exsanguination in a state of deep (alcoholic) anaesthesis. Very considerable effects in taste and flavour of the meat could certainly be achieved.

Alec Merrison

with the help of Andria and Benedict Merrison

THE DEFENSIVE COOK

Cookery intended to enhance the quality of life is well-documented and has an extensive literature (see, for example, A Brillat-Savarin 1826 *La Physiologie du Goût*.) This elevation of cookery to an art-form—and the desirability of doing so could be questioned—has nothing to do with the essential function of cookery, namely to take the raw materials which are to be transmuted into food by 'cooking' (a term which includes, for example, simple burial in the ground, the form of preparation of the Caribbean 'pepperpot') and making these raw materials both digestible and edible, perhaps sometimes on the very weakest of criteria.

This essential function of cooking describes virtually all the preparation of food which goes on in the world and might be termed *defensive* cookery. This underlines the fact that man[†] is surrounded by a hostile environment, has to survive in that environment and simply has not the time and effort available to practise 'art-form' cookery. This is not to demean or diminish this latter cookery; it is not a value-judgement; it is a simple statement of fact.

So, leaving to one side the desirability of art-form cookery, it is clear that man[†] individually and, indeed, collectively, must be capable of practising defensive cookery. This truth was somewhat rudely revealed to the senior author when during the 1939–45 war his mother was called up[‡] and he was left with the stark alternatives—to cook or to starve. The same truth was exposed to the junior[§] authors when they became aware of the odd fact that their parents, who include the senior author, seemed to be rarely at home. Although they put their views to the senior author and his wife, always with clarity and strength, and sometimes poetically[‖], there appeared to them to be little or, at least, no substantial change in the habits of their seniors so they too were forced into the practise of defensive cookery. When we use the word 'forced' we hope that it will not be inferred that we view the status of a defensive cook as unattractive or dishonourable. Indeed, we would regard that man who has not acquired the simple skill of a defensive cook as a plonker[¶].

Defensive Cookery—its Characteristics

It is characteristic of defensive cookery that it should take up little time or skill, that it will rely on materials easy to hand, and that the

[†] The word *man* embraces the word *woman*. This manner of proceeding was disputed by one of us but, most unusually, she bowed to the will of the majority.
[‡] That is to say, conscripted to serve His Majesty King George VI.
[§] The words 'senior' and 'junior' are used strictly to describe age. Again, no value-judgement is implied.
[‖] 'The world is too much with us late and soon. Getting and spending we lay waste our powers.'
[¶] A Somerset dialect word which, for the sake of the fastidious who may read our paper, we forebear to translate. A word, perhaps we should say, which springs to the lips of the junior authors, whose natural language is the vernacular, much more readily than to those of the senior author.

resultant dish will satisfy and, perhaps, greatly exceed the minimum criteria we speak of above. This is not to be read as meaning that we have little respect for the pleasures of the palate. On the contrary, we are very much of Dr Samuel Johnson's opinion that—'he who does not mind his belly will hardly mind anything else.'[†]

Rather than generalise further it seemed to us that we might best illustrate our theme by an example, or recipe, of defensive cooking. We recognise that what follows might well induce a sense of nausea in the more sensitive of our readers and we urge them to omit the reading of the following section.

What to do with 'Rubber' Chickens

Some explanation is in order. If our defensive cook wants to eat roast chicken then it is unlikely that he will want or, indeed, be able to put the time or money into a trip to Bourg-en-Bresse so that he might purchase a *poulet de grain*[‡]. It is much more likely that he will acquire his chicken from the bottom of a deep-freeze while perambulating in his local supermarket. It is this kind of chicken, to use the word generously, that we style a 'rubber' chicken. Our defensive cook, who will be a man of taste and experience, will regard the 'rubber' chicken as a challenge.

He will, after removing the giblets (if the chicken has escaped the EEC net), insert into the chicken a roughly-cut onion. He will then put the chicken onto a largish sheet of aluminium foil, put a small quantity of mixed herbs upon it and cover the chicken with rashers of streaky bacon. He will then cover the chicken with a smaller piece of foil, wrap it well with the bottom foil and cook at 200°C for $2\frac{1}{2}$–3 hours. He will remove the juices of the chicken at approximately hourly intervals; these, with fat removed, will form the basis for his gravy. The bacon will need cooking for only $1\frac{1}{2}$ hours and must then be removed from the chicken and put to one side. The rashers can be eaten as they are, or as bacon rolls (around the chicken livers, after further cooking), or they can be used for further defensive dishes.

Apart from the boiling of bones for soup or stock, the defensive cook will be able to get twenty person-meals from (say) a $5\frac{1}{2}$ lb

[†] Boswell *Life of Johnson*.
[‡] Unless, of course, he already lives in Bourg-en-Bresse.

(2.5 kg) chicken. One successful way we have used for using up the last scraps of the chicken is to make a pilaff from them.

But we will not give the recipe for this because we feel that we have already demonstrated well enough our principles, and we feel tolerably sure that if any of our readers who are not already defensive cooks can make the transition to being such then whatever they die of will not be starvation.

And this is the simple message we wish to convey in our paper: on acquiring the skills and the status of a defensive cook the earlier the better. Who, after all, would wish (at least for any length of time) to be regarded as a plonker?

Acknowledgments

It is with pleasure and gratitude that we thank Maureen Merrison whose contributions to this paper and in so many other ways are, sadly, too numerous to mention.

Benjamin Thompson, Count Rumford (1753–1814)

OF THE
EXCELLENT QUALITIES OF COFFEE
AND THE
ART OF MAKING IT IN THE HIGHEST PERFECTION†

Among the numerous luxuries of the table unknown to our forefathers, which have been imported into Europe in modern times, *coffee* may be considered as one of the most valuable.

Its taste is very agreeable, and its flavour uncommonly so; but its principal excellence depends on its salubrity and on its exhilarating quality.

---

† From the *Collected Works of Count Rumford* edited by S C Brown (1970) Vol. V pp 265–315 (Cambridge, MA: Harvard University Press).

It excites cheerfulness without intoxication, and the pleasing flow of spirits which it occasions lasts many hours, and is never followed by sadness, languor, or debility.

It diffuses over the whole frame a glow of health, and a sense of ease and well-being which is exceedingly delightful. Existence is felt to be a positive enjoyment, and the mental powers are awakened and rendered uncommonly active.

It has been facetiously observed that there is more wit in Europe since the use of coffee has become general among us; and I do not hesitate to confess that I am seriously of that opinion.

●　　●　　●

That coffee has greatly contributed to our innocent enjoyments, cannot be doubted; and experience has abundantly proved that so far from being unwholesome it is really very salubrious.

This delicious beverage has so often been celebrated, both in prose and verse, that it does not stand in need of my praises to recommend it. I shall therefore confine myself to the humble office of showing how it can be prepared in the greatest perfection.

There is no culinary process that is liable to so much uncertainty in its results as the making of coffee; and there is certainly none in which any small variation in the mode of operation produces more sensible effects.

●　　●　　●

Great care must be taken in roasting coffee not to roast it too much. As soon as it has acquired a deep cinnamon colour, it should be taken from the fire and cooled; otherwise much of its aromatic flavour will be dissipated, and its taste will become disagreeably bitter.

●　　●　　●

Before I proceed to describe the apparatus I shall recommend for making coffee, it will be useful to inquire what the causes are which render the preparation of that liquor so precarious; and, in order to facilitate that investigation, we must see what the circumstances are on which the qualities depend which are most esteemed in coffee.

Boiling hot water extracts from coffee which has been properly roasted and ground an aromatic substance of an exquisite flavour, together with a considerable quantity of astringent matter, of a bitter but very agreeable taste; but this aromatic substance, which is supposed to be an oil, is extremely volatile, and is so feebly united to the water that it escapes from it into the air with great facility.

If a cup of the very best coffee prepared in the highest perfection, and boiling hot, be placed on a table in the middle of a large room, and suffered to cool, it will in cooling fill the room with its fragrance; but the coffee after having become cold will be found to have lost a great deal of its flavour.

If it be again heated, its taste and flavour will be still farther impaired; and after it has been heated and cooled two or three times it will be found to be quite vapid and disgusting.

The fragrance diffused through the air is a sure indication that the coffee has lost some of its most volatile parts; and as that liquor is found to have lost its peculiar flavour, and also *its exhilarating quality*, there can be no doubt but that both these depend on the preservation of those volatile particles which escape into the air with such facility.

• • •

In order that coffee may retain all those aromatic particles which give to that beverage its excellent qualities, nothing more is necessary than to prevent all internal motions among the particles of that liquid, by preventing its being exposed to any change of temperature, either during the time employed in preparing it, or afterwards till it is served up.

This may be done by pouring boiling water on the coffee in powder, and surrounding the machine in which the coffee is made by boiling water or by the steam of boiling water; for the temperature of boiling water is *invariable* (while the pressure of the atmosphere remains the same), and the temperature of steam is the same as that of the boiling water from which it escapes.

But the temperature of boiling water is preferable to all others for making coffee, not only on account of its *constancy*, but also on account of its being most favourable to the extraction of all that is valuable in the roasted grain.

As it is well known that the heat of boiling water is not that which is the most favourable for extracting from malt those saccharine parts which it furnishes in the process of making beer, I thought it possible, though not at all probable, that some lower temperature than that of boiling water might also be most advantageous in preparing coffee; but after having made a great number of experiments, in order to ascertain that important point, I found that coffee infused with boiling water was always higher-flavoured and better tasted than when the water used in that process was at a lower temperature.

• • •

I have found, by the results of a great number of experiments, that *one quarter of an ounce* avoirdupois of ground coffee is quite sufficient to make a gill [†] of most excellent coffee, of the highest possible flavour and quite strong enough to be agreeable.

• • •

But this cannot be done unless the method which I use be employed for making the coffee.

In order that the advantages which will result from the adoption of that process may be perceived and estimated, it will be useful to give a short description of the method formerly pursued, and to explain the disadvantages which resulted from it.

Formerly the ground coffee being put into a coffee-pot with a sufficient quantity of water, the coffee-pot was put over the fire, and after the water had been made to boil a certain time the coffee-pot was removed from the fire, and the grounds having had time to settle, or having been fined down with isinglass, the clear liquor was poured off and immediately served in cups.

From the results of several experiments which I made with great care, in order to ascertain what proportion of the aromatic and volatile particles in the coffee escape and are left in this process, I found reason to conclude that it amounts to considerably more than half. This loss may easily be explained. It is

[†] Or, in metric measures, 7 g for 140 ml.

occasioned principally, no doubt, by the motions into which the liquid is thrown in being heated, and afterwards on being made to boil;

• • •

Now, when coffee is made in the most advantageous manner, the ground coffee is pressed down in a cylindrical vessel which has its bottom pierced with many small holes so as to form a strainer, and a proper quantity of boiling hot water being poured cautiously on this layer of coffee in powder the water penetrates it by degrees, and after a certain time begins to filter through it.

This gradual percolation brings continually a succession of fresh particles of pure water into contact with the ground coffee, and when the last portion of the water has passed through it every thing capable of being dissolved by the water will be found to be so completely washed out of it that what remains will be of no kind of value.

It is however necessary to the complete success of this operation that the coffee should be ground to a powder sufficiently fine, as has already been observed.

• • •

In order to convey distinct ideas of the different parts of the apparatus necessary in making coffee in the manner I have recommended, I have added a figure (see figure 1) which represents a vertical section (drawn to half the full size) of a coffee-pot constructed on what I conceive to be the very best principles. Its size is such as is most proper for making four cups of coffee at once. [†]

a is the cylindrical strainer, into which the ground coffee is put, in order that boiling-hot water may be poured on it: when this strainer is filled with boiling water (after an ounce of ground coffee has been properly pressed down on its bottom), the quantity of the liquid is just sufficient for making four cups of coffee.

b is the ground coffee in its place.

[†] Figure 2 shows a modern replica, which is 180 mm diameter at the base and 280 mm high. It makes 1.7 litres, or 14 of Rumford's one-gill cups.

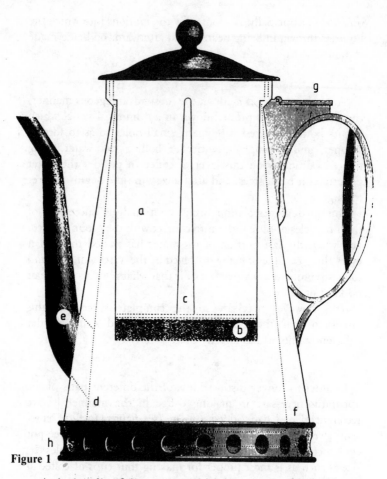

Figure 1

c is the handle of the rammer which is represented in its place.

d is the reservoir for receiving the coffee which descends into it from the strainer; and

e is the spout through which the coffee is poured out.

f is the boiler, into which a small quantity of water is put, for the sole purpose of generating steam for keeping the reservoir hot.

g is the opening by which the water is poured into the boiler or out of it: this opening has a flat cover, which moves on a hinge that is represented in the figure.

The boiler is of a conical form, and is enlarged a little at its upper extremity, in order to receive the cover which closes it above.

The reservoir and the boiler are fixed together above by soldering, so that the reservoir remains suspended in the boiler.

The cylindrical strainer is suspended on the upper extremity of the reservoir by means of a flat projecting brim, about two tenths of an inch broad.

h is the hoop, made of sheet copper, and perforated with a row of holes, on which the boiler reposes: a part of the bottom of the boiler is seen through these holes.

The reservoir is represented by dotted lines, in order the better to distinguish it.

The opening in the side of the boiler, by which the water enters it, is represented in the figure. This opening is covered by a part of the handle of the coffee-pot.

● ● ●

As coffee is very wholesome and may be afforded at a very low price, especially in countries which have colonies where the climate is proper for growing it, many public advantages would be derived from the general introduction of it among all classes of society.

One most important advantage, which on a superfical view of the subject is not very obvious, would most probably be derived from it. As coffee possesses in a high degree an exhilarating quality, it would in some measure supply the place of spirituous liquors among the lower classes of the people.

Those who work hard stand in need of something to cheer and comfort them; and it is greatly to be lamented that the strong liquors now used for that purpose are not only very unwholesome and permanently debilitating both to the mind and the body, but that their operation is accompanied by a peculiar species of madness which renders those who are under the influence of it very mischievous, and so lost to all sense of decency and propriety as to become objects of horror and aversion.

The pleasing flow of spirits that is excited by coffee has none of these baneful effects.

Instead of irritating the mind and exciting to acts of violence,

Figure 2

it calms every turbulent and malevolent passion, and is accompanied by a consciousness of ease, contentment, and good-will to all men, which is very different from that wild joy and unbridled licentiousness which accompanies intoxication.

Coffee is not only very wholesome, but when sweetened with sugar is very nourishing.

Sugar is supposed to be the most nourishing substance known. Its nourishing powers are even such that the use of it has been recommended in fattening cattle.

An ingenious young man, Doctor—, a physician who resided in London, made a long course of experiments on himself several years ago, with a view to determine the relative nutritive powers of those substances which are most commonly used as food by mankind; and he found that sugar was more nourishing than any other substance he tried.

He took no other food for a considerable time than sugar, and drank nothing but water; and he contrived to subsist on a surprisingly small quantity of sugar. If my memory does not fail me, it was no more than two ounces a day.

It is much to be lamented that this interesting young man should have fallen a sacrifice to his zeal in promoting useful science; but his health was so totally deranged by these experiments, which he pursued with too much ardor and perseverance, that he died soon after they were finished. All the resources of the medical art were employed, but nothing could save him.

As common brown sugar is quite as nourishing as the best refined loaf sugar, and as a great many persons prefer it for coffee, it appears to me to be extremely probable that coffee may be found to be one of the cheapest kinds of food that can be procured, and more especially in Great Britain.

Half a pint of the best coffee or two full cups may be made with half an ounce of ground coffee, which, if one pound avoirdupois weight of raw coffee can be bought in the shops for twelvepence sterling, will cost only *six sevenths* of a farthing; and , if a pound of brown sugar can be bought for one shilling, one ounce of sugar, which would be a large allowance for two cups of coffee, would cost only three farthings; consequently the materials for making half a pint of coffee would cost less than one penny.

As coffee has a great deal of taste, which it imparts very liberally to the bread which is eaten with it, and as the taste of coffee is very agreeable to all palates, and the use of bread greatly prolongs the duration of the pleasure which this taste excites, a very delicious repast may be made merely with coffee and bread, without either butter or milk.

The taste of the coffee predominates in such a manner that the butter would hardly be perceived, and might be omitted without any sensible loss. But I acknowledge that in my opinion the addition of a certain quantity of good cream or milk to coffee improves it very much. Milk, however, is not a very expensive article in Great Britain; and if the butter be omitted, which is by no means necessary (and is even unwholesome), a good breakfast of milk coffee might be provided for a very small sum.

What a difference between such a breakfast and that miserable and unwholesome wash which the poor people in England drink under the name of *tea*!

All the coffee that can be wanted may be had in the British colonies, and paid for in British manufactures; but tea must be purchased in China, and paid for in hard money.

These are circumstances which ought, no doubt, to have great weight, especially in such a country as England, where all ranks of society are equally sensible of the advantages of their distinguished situation, and equally anxious to promote the public prosperity.

• • •

But I must hasten to put an end to this Essay, which has already exceeded the limits to which I had hopes of being able to confine it. Being anxious that it might be read by many persons (as I thought that it would be very useful), I felt the necessity of making it as short as possible. I shall conclude with a few observations on the means that may be employed for rendering the use of coffee more general among the lower classes of society.

In the first place, the method of making *good coffee* must be known; and the utensils necessary in that process must be so contrived as to be cheap and durable, and easy to be managed.

It will be in vain that the laws are repealed which laid restrictions on the free use of coffee, as long as the great mass of the people remain ignorant of its excellent qualities; they will be little disposed to substitute it in the place of another beverage, to which long habit has given them an attachment.

As long as coffee shall continue to be made according to the method generally practised in England, I shall have no hope of its being preferred to tea; for its qualities are so inferior when prepared in that way that it is hardly possible that it should be much liked.

• • •

For very poor persons who cannot afford to buy a coffee-pot, I shall recommend a very simple contrivance, by means of which coffee may be made, and even in the highest possible perfection.

I have often made use of this contrivance in making my own breakfast, and I have not found the coffee to be in the least inferior to that made in the most costly and complicated machines.

This little utensil is distinctly represented in the ... [figure 3], which is drawn to a scale of half the full size.

The whole of this apparatus consists of a coffee-cup, which should hold about three quarters of a pint, and a strainer made of tin, which is suspended in it by its brim.

This coffee-cup should be cylindrical, and when employed in making one gill of good strong coffee should be three inches in diameter within, and three inches and a half deep. The lower part of the strainer is one inch and a half in diameter, and one inch deep; and the upper part of it two inches and nine tenths in diameter, and about one inch and a half in depth.

The water which is poured on the ground coffee should be boiling hot, the cup and the strainer having both been previously heated by dipping them into boiling water.

As the coffee will not be more than eight or ten minutes in passing through the strainer, it is probable that it will be quite as hot as it can be drunk after it has descended into the lower part of the cup; but, if it should be necessary to keep it hot a longer time, the cup may be placed in a small quantity of boiling water,

Figure 3

contained in a small saucepan or other fit vessel placed near the fire.

When all the coffee has passed into the lower part of the cup, the strainer may be taken away, and the cup may be covered with the cover of the strainer.

• • •

I shall conclude by a few observations on the means that may be used for preserving ready-made coffee good for a considerable time in bottles.

The bottles having been made very clean must be put into clean cold water in a large kettle, and the water must be heated gradually and made to boil, in order that the bottles may be heated boiling hot.

The coffee, fresh prepared and still boiling hot, must be put into these heated bottles, which must be immediately well closed with good sound corks.

The bottles must then be removed into a cool cellar, where they must be kept well covered up in dry sand in order to preserve them from the light.

By this means ready-made coffee may be preserved good for a long time, but great care must be taken not to let it be exposed to the light, otherwise it will soon be spoiled.

When wanted for use, the coffee must be heated in the bottle and before the cork is drawn; otherwise a great deal of the aromatic flavour of the coffee will be lost in heating it. And, in order that it may be heated in the bottle without danger, the bottle must be put into cold water, and this water must be gradually heated till the coffee has acquired the degree of heat which is wanted. The cork may then be drawn, and the coffee poured out and served up.

As good coffee is very far from being disagreeable when taken cold, and as there is no doubt but it must be quite as exhilarating when cold as when it is taken hot, why should it not be made to supply the place of those pernicious drains of spirituous liquors which do so much harm?

Half a pint of good cold coffee properly sweetened, which would not cost more than half a pint of porter, would be a much more refreshing and exhilarating draught, and would no doubt be incomparably more nourishing.

How much, then, must it be preferable to a dram of gin!

The advantages and disadvantages to agriculture and commerce which would arise from the introduction of a new beverage for supplying the place of malt liquors and ardent spirits distilled from grain must be estimated and balanced by those whose knowledge of political economy fits them for determining these most intricate and important questions.

Section IV Diet and Nutrition

Linus Pauling

HOW TO LIVE LONGER AND FEEL BETTER†

My feeling is that I do not have enough special information about cooking to justify my contributing to the anthology. I realize, however, that in fact I have been saying, in my lectures, that people should enjoy life, and in particular should enjoy eating. I recommend that people eat what they like except for cutting down on sugar, and in addition that supplementary vitamins be taken.

From a letter of 19 December 1986.

The availability of vitamins does not mean that you should not include fruits and vegetables in your diet. It is true that for more than eighty years science-fiction writers have been writing about a world of the future in which people would not eat ordinary food but instead would swallow a tablet or two each day. We have now gone part-way toward this goal in that the need to eat large amounts of fruits and vegetables in order to have enough vitamins to keep us alive has been eliminated. By taking a few vitamin tablets we can obtain not only the minimum requirement that may

† Excerpts from Linus Pauling's *How to Live Longer and Feel Better* 1986 (New York: W H Freeman) pp 23–24 and 30–31.

be furnished by the natural foods eaten in sufficient quantity but the optimum intake that puts and keeps us in the best of health. We may ask how much further modern nutritional science and molecular biology might take us. The answer is that our nutritional needs can never be met by a few tablets per day. A rather large amount of fuel is required to provide the energy to keep us warm and to run the biochemical processes in our bodies that permit us to function and to work. That requirement comes to about 2500 kilocalories of food energy per day. To obtain this much food energy, about one pound, dry weight, of starch or the sugar glucose must be ingested. What is more, the body requires certain fats it does not itself manufacture, and it must be supplied with protein to replace the protein of its principal working parts as they wear out in the course of a day. A diet of this sort is available, as will be discussed in the next chapter, and it consists of much more than a few tablets.

•　•　•

The various classes of foods—meats, fish, fruits and vegetables, grains and nuts, dairy products—all have value in providing protein, fat, carbohydrates, minerals, vitamins, and other valuable micronutrients, such as gamma-aminobenzoic acid, choline, lecithin and the ubiquinones. The amounts of these important constituents are different in different foods, and it is wise to have a varied diet, one that appeals to you, and to supplement it with the important vitamins and minerals in order to get them in the optimum amounts.

The servings of meat and fish must be kept small in order to keep the total protein intake down to the recommended amount, 0.8 g per kilogram body weight.

Ovolactovegetarians, who accept eggs and milk but not meat and fish, can keep in good health by taking supplementary vitamins and minerals. Strict vegetarians need to select the vegetable foods with care to insure that they have the proper intake of those vegetables that provide the essential amino acids that are present in only small amounts in most vegetable foods.

The intake of fat should be limited, but enough should be eaten to provide the essential fats.

Fruits, vegetables, grains and nuts should be eaten in a satisfying variety and amount. Fruits and vegetables provide some protein and fat, large amounts of carbohydrates, and also vitamins, minerals and other micronutrients. A high intake was needed in past centuries in order to provide the minimum amounts of these micronutrients, as well as carbohydrate for energy. In the new era of modern nutrition the optimum intakes of vitamins, more than can conveniently be provided by fruits and vegetables, are available in supplements, as discussed throughout this book. It is wise, nonetheless, to supplement the vitamin supplements with a good intake of fruits and vegetables.

John Loutit

AN EXPERIMENTAL PATHOLOGIST LOOKS AT FOOD

Recently there have been notable changes in the attitude of the public to food. First, there is increasing news value in the subject to satisfy a demand for greater technical excellence and variety, what we might call the Good Food Campaign, an artistic cult. Then there is the bio-medical aspect, the scientific counterpart.

Let us start with the latter. For a century nutrition has been a well recognised branch of physiology, quantifying the body's needs in energy (Calories) and identifying essential constituents of food, proteins, their size, shape and construction, fats, carbohydrates, vitamins and minerals essential for normal growth in infancy and adolescence and routine maintenance thereafter. Now specialists in other branches of medicine are getting in on the act. Cardiologists, epidemiologists and general practitioners who sign death certificates recognise more cases of coronary artery disease as a cause of death than say 50 years ago. With their own methods of investigation they find statistical associations with various factors which together form the modern lifestyle.

In the last decade the national diet has been identified as one such factor; extremists say the chief one. It is not only our problem in Britain but that of other advanced countries that 'have never had it so good'. Thus international bodies like the World Health Organisation, as well as national committees, have considered the relationship of national diets to coronary and other cardiovascular diseases. In Britain nutritionists as a Panel on Diet of the Department of Health and Social Security Committee on Medical Aspects of Food Policy reported in 1984 that this has been wisely discussed in scientific journals and more widely but less wisely by journalists. As an ordinary reader of the press and viewer of television I am frightened by these presentations which demand that we entirely change our eating habits if we wish to survive. When as an uncommitted scientist I read the Report of the Panel on Diet in Relation to Cardiovascular Disease, I find this an eminently cautious review. When it came to formulating recommendations for the general public, the Panel could be certain of only one thing, that obesity was a predisposing factor: thus reducing Calories and increasing exercise were required (maybe they overemphasised exercise: this promotes appetite and moderate exercise does not use up as many Calories as one thinks). Taste and appetite were not mentioned in the report. Other recommendations to the public were based not on compelling but on suggestive evidence that the British diet was unbalanced insofar as it contained too much saturated (S) to polyunsaturated (P) fatty acid and too much fat in relation to other ingredients. It would be better balanced by reducing intake of fat to provide not more than 35% of the calorific content and by increasing the P/S ratio to 0.45, i.e. replacing some animal fats, meat and dairy products, by fats of vegetable origin with the added benefit to guts of simultaneously increasing fibre or indigestible matter. The modified diet should not contain more simple sugars or common salt than hitherto.

The message that I get from the journalists expounding this gospel to the public is not this sensible advice. They imply that through 'healthy' eating one can attain immortalisation (whereas in fact a more balanced diet can merely delay some features of inevitable senescence). To this end they advocate eschewing meat and dairy products (with the loss of many desirable flavours), salt and sweets, instead to chew a vegetable diet, rabbit food. Our primate forefathers came down from the trees, developed opposable thumbs enabling them the better to pick up, observe and manipulate objects, i.e. to use tools, and became hunter–gatherers. We have a background of a million or so years evolving on a mixed diet. Can we in a generation profitably go back to the trees on a purely vegetable diet? Even agriculture has a history of barely

113

10,000 years. Some tribes for economic, religious or other reasons, practise strict or relaxed vegetarianism and with ethnic experience survive; but in changed circumstances they are liable to deficiency diseases. Will our novice vegetarians avoid in a sunless climate skeletal disorders from shortage of fat-soluble vitamins and calcium, or nutritional anaemias? Yes, but only if they are regimented in a professionally planned dietetic scheme.

Next let us look at our first point, food as an art form. Cook books lead the sales league for booksellers. Every 'quality' newspaper has its special columns and columnists on food and drink. BBC 2 and Channel 4 on television add visible demonstration to wordy exposition. Most performances, particularly in 'vision', are entertaining and instructive. Moreover, in print much nonsense may be perpetrated. Artists can be precious, prone to fetish. I well remember a reporter being taken out by the Arch Mandarin of the Good Food Campaign to buy materials (in Kensington) for a meal at which he would be host. The guide line was *Good Food must be fresh, never canned or frozen*. In the event purchases for starters were salami and ham (two very remarkable examples of fresh food, uncontaminated by the modern techniques of canning and freezing but hallowed by ancient methods for lengthening shelf life—salting, smoking and dehydration). The main course was filleted fish. My neck of the woods, and I suspect Kensington, has no direct flight of this morning's catch from Mevagissey—fish comes packed in ice in which it may have been for days or weeks. These fillets were cooked in remarkable fashion being placed on plates taken from an oven at its peak temperature: no guidance was given how to unstick one from the other. Finally the sweet course was a bought apricot tart.

Like the newspaper columnist I offer three recipes which appeal to me. One modern scribe informs me that now the order of precedence is colour, texture, taste. I have two demands only, smell and taste, and one reminder, food is not only for nourishment but enjoyment. I select materials that are not fresh but processed in some way. Salting and smoking give an extra flavour to fish and meat as well as prolonging shelf life—hence smokies and ham. Dehydration is similar; raisins are not a substitute for grapes but desirable in their own right and so are dried apricots. Canning may alter natural flavours but not, to my taste, of Cape gooseberries (*Physalis edulis*). I grew up with them in Australia as a backyard

114

crop and I miss them. I cannot find them in a natural state now in the largest superstores. Even canned they are difficult to find; they come from the Cape (S. Africa) and masquerade on labels as golden-berries; and if you write your menus in French, as *coquerets de Pérou*.

SMOKY PANCAKES

1 Smoky, about 6–8 oz
Batter—4 oz flour
    $\frac{1}{2}$ *oz cooking oil*
    1 egg
    6 fl oz half milk half water

Make pancakes in advance. Put all constituents in a blender: whizz until homogenised (this not only blends but aerates). Cook pancakes in the usual way—about 8—and store between layers of greaseproof paper.

Smokies, small haddock, have been hot smoked, i.e. cooked. Remove skin and dissect out bones. Tease out flesh into flakes.

Cheese sauce. This too can be made in advance. Extract flavour from skin and bone, covering them with milk and heating to a gentle simmer. Strain. Make roux with 1 oz margarine or butter, $\frac{3}{4}$ oz flour, the flavoured milk made up to 6 fl oz, 1 fl oz single cream and 2 oz grated cheese. Heat until just bubbling and thickened, then incorporate the fish.

Putting together. Spread the filling equally over the surface of each pancake. Roll up and align on a heat-proof plate. Dredge with more grated cheese and cook in the oven at 400° F (gas mark 6) for 10 minutes and serve.

HAM AND APRICOTS

2–3 lb of ham or bacon, e.g. slipper
6 cloves, herbs (e.g. bay leaf, rosemary)
Liquid honey or golden syrup.

Sauce. Soak 3 oz dried apricots for 12 or more hours, then simmer to softness, perhaps $\frac{1}{2}$ hour or more. Reserve 12–20 halves for decoration. Homogenise the remainder in gently warmed jellied stock.

Soak the bacon for 6–24 hours to remove salt. Dry and stick cloves into places whence later they are readily recoverable. Steam meat and herbs in steamer for 40 minutes. Remove the cloves and the rind. Transfer the piece to a roasting tin with fat and dry off the bacon for 10–15 mins at 400° F (gas mark 6). Then coat with syrup and attach halved apricots over surface: return to oven for 10 mins more only, to avoid over-caramelisation. Dish and keep warm. From the roasting tin remove any excess fat and blend the rest of the juice with apricot homogenate and stock as required.

CAPE GOOSEBERRY BAVAROIS (a party dish only—highly fatty)

14 oz tin Cape gooseberries
4 egg yolks
10 fl oz milk
4 oz. sugar
10 fl oz double cream
Powedered gelatin.

The tin will contain about 4 fl oz juice and 10 oz fruit. Separate and scatter a rounded teaspoonful of gelatin on the surface of the juice, allow to stand for some minutes to swell the gelatin. Then heat gently to solution.

Layer the berries on the bottom of a 1 litre pie dish, cover with the warmed juice; cool till set.

Make the custard with the egg yolks and sugar beaten till creamy, and added to the milk heated but not boiling. Heat gently stirring with a wooden spoon until the mixture thickens and the spoon no longer grates on the bottom of the pan but glides.

Separately add a heaped tablespoonful of gelatin to about 2 fl oz water, allow to swell and bring to solution with gentle heat. Stir this into the custard. In due course the mixture will begin to set. At this point add the cream, whipped until thick, and amalgamate with the custard. Pour onto the base of jellied berries and refrigerate. When set, it can be delivered by placing the pie dish gently onto hot water for 30 seconds or more as required to loosen the surface of the gel. Invert onto a serving plate and decorate if required.

Fred Dainton

SAMUEL BUTLER'S DICTUM

'The healthy stomach is nothing if not conservative. Few liberals have good digestions.'

Samuel Butler *Mind and Matter. Indigestion*

[*This quotation reminded me of Churchill's remark (probably apocryphal) when Lord Cherwell and Sir Stafford Cripps arrived simultaneously at a meeting after it had begun, 'Well, they have at last finished munching their lettuces'. To find out the truth about Churchill's remark I wrote to Professor R V Jones who replied that he did not know of it but referred me to the following quotation which may well have been the origin of the story.*]

W S Churchill (1874–1965)

A REFUTATION

The course of my remarks now reaches the President of the Board of Trade (Sir Stafford Cripps). Everyone knows the distinguished talents which the Right Hon. Gentleman brings unstintedly to the services of his fellow countrymen. No one has made more sustained exertions to contribute to the common pot and few take less out than he does. I have got my vegetarian too, my honoured friend Lord Cherwell. These ethereal beings certainly do produce a very high level and a very great volume of intellectual output, with the minimum of working costs in fuel.

W S Churchill in a debate on a motion of censure
6 December 1946 *Hansard* Vol. 416, Col. 2544.

Bernhard Neumann

A VEGETARIAN BREAKFAST DISH

The only cooking for which I might claim a nanoparticle of originality is a vegetarian paste (I am an ovo-lactarian vegetarian) which I make and spread on my breakfast toast.

Ingredients

Polyunsaturated (vegetable) margarine
Soy sauce
Garlic cloves
Spices as the fancy dictates
Tofu (inert) yeast
(all preferably salt-reduced or salt-free)

Method:
Use a rule of thumb to measure the quantities of the ingredients. Melt the margarine gently, add the other ingredients in the order in which they are listed and stir. Let cool, then refrigerate.

This is, from my point of view, a highly successful recipe, because nobody else will touch it (if a guest, out of politeness or curiosity, tastes it once, she or he comments that it is 'interesting', and never tries it again).

Lord Cherwell (1886–1957)

IN PRAISE OF LOW-EXTRACTION FLOUR

I notice that Belgium, Denmark, Norway and Czechoslovakia all get an 80% extraction of wheat or better for their bread; we are to go up to 85% wheat extraction. I know many food cranks prefer that. I believe some noble Lords even prefer it so I had better withdraw the expression 'food cranks'. Many people claim to prefer what I have heard called 'the bread of affliction' and think it wholesome. It may or not be so. I have not been convinced that it is more wholesome.

But I maintain that we have no right to force people to eat stuff they do not like because some of us think it wholesome. It has been imposed on people for the six years of war and now after they thought they had got rid of it they find this nasty, sour, grey bread imposed on them again and I find it one of the most lamentable concomitants of our meal-time.

Lord Cherwell in the debate on food supplies
20 February 1946 *Hansard* Vol. 139, Col. 786.

John Humphrey

CAMBRIDGE BONS VIVANTS

During my final year as an undergraduate at Trinity College, Cambridge, when I was doing part II Biochemistry and R L M Synge (later FRS and Nobel Prize winner for Chemistry with A J P Martin) was a research student in the Department, we shared the same tutor, A S F Gow. Gow was a member of the Family Dining Club. This consisted of himself, A E Houseman, Sir Stephen Gazelee (Librarian at the Foreign Office) and one other whose name I do not remember. It dined once a month, and the purpose was conversation and above all the enjoyment of food—but there were problems about discovering novel dishes. Dick Synge and I offered to use our knowledge of practical biochemistry (e.g. protein coagulation) to produce a novel meal, Gow accepted this and we were given the run of the Trinity College kitchens to prepare it. I forget exactly what we served up, but I think that it contained a soufflé made from pressed white fish juice, and the hepatopancreas of scallops cooked with grapes in a béchamel sauce. Anyway, it was good enough to earn Gow's grateful approval, and as a reward he presented us with *Le Code de la bonne Chère* by Edouard de Pomiane, a French Academician. This book contained many excellent recipes, and had been written to explain some of the scientific principles underlying cooking to young Frenchwomen who were too blasé to accept without question the empirical knowledge passed on by their forebears. It was out of print for many years, but I think that it was republished by Hachette.

To be honest, I have applied the principles of cookery in

practical scientific experiments more often than the other way round—except for using the microwave oven to advantage. However, I made one contribution. This was a reasonably pleasant fruit cake make without eggs, useful during World War Two, and oddly enough the recipe was given to Annette Benacerraf, wife of Professor Baruch Benacerraf (recently awarded a Nobel Prize for Medicine) and a niece of Edouard de Pomiane. Mrs Benacerraf was exquisitely sensitive to eggs—her lips would swell if touched by any food containing eggs—but she could eat this cake with impunity. I think that the recipe spread among her friends in the USA.

Alas, I no longer have the recipe nor have I been in a position to make experimental eggless cakes. The important thing was to add bicarbonate of soda at the right time. However, my wife supplied the answer in the form of a recipe already tried out.

EGGLESS RICH FRUIT CAKE

250 g flour, a pinch of salt
½ level tsp bicarbonate of soda
300 ml water
120 g mixed peel, chopped
60 g chopped, blanched almonds
60 glace cherries, cut up
500 g mixed dried fruit (currants, raisins, sultanas)
Grated rind of 1 orange and 2 lemons
250 g butter
1 large can sweetened condensed milk

Put the water with all ingredients except flour and bicarbonate into a saucepan and bring to the boil, stirring all the time. Lower the heat and simmer for 3 minutes. Remove from the heat and allow to cool. Grease and line the cake tin, 8-inch square or 9–10-inch diameter round. Sieve flour and salt into a large mixing bowl. Add the bicarbonate of soda to the cooled fruit mixture and stir quickly. Add to the flour and mix quickly together. Put into the prepared tin and spread evenly. Bake at 180°C (350° F) for about 3 hours. Cool for at least 5 minutes in the tin, then turn onto a wire tray until cold.

Benjamin Thompson
(Count Rumford) 1753–1814

OF FOOD; AND PARTICULARLY OF FEEDING THE POOR[†]

RUMFORDSCHE SUPPE

[*When Sir Benjamin Thompson (later Count Rumford) entered the service of Carl Theodor, the Elector of Bavaria, in the 1780s Munich was infested with beggars who 'having been bred from their very infancy in that profession were so attached to their indolent and dissolute way of living as to prefer it to all other situations. They were not only unacquainted with all kinds of work but had the most insuperable aversion to honest labour, and had been so long familiarized with every crime that they had become perfectly callous to all sense of shame and remorse' (See Editor's Note, page 6). He then set out to reform their morals by improving their living standards. He established workhouses (men, women and children over the age of five were expected to work 12–14 hours a day) and set up soup kitchens.*

Rumford's ideas about food and, in particular, food for the poor are set out in an essay of some 25,000 words. Copious extracts from the first two chapters will serve as a useful introduction to the central recipe of the soup which, to this day, is known in Germany as Rumfordsche Suppe *and it is even consumed on occasions, though undoubtedly in a less frugal form.*]

INTRODUCTION

IT is a common saying that Necessity is the mother of Invention; and nothing is more strictly or more generally true. It may even be shown that most of the successive improvements in the affairs of men in a state of civil society, of which we have any authentic records, have been made under the pressure of necessity; and it is no small consolation, in times of general alarm, to reflect upon

† From the *Collected Works of Count Rumford* edited by S C Brown (1970) (Cambridge, MA: Harvard University Press) Vol. V pp. 169–262.

the probability that upon such occasions useful discoveries will result from the united exertions of those who, either from motives of fear or sentiments of benevolence, labour to avert the impending evil.

The alarm in this country at the present period [November 1795], on account of the high price of corn, and the danger of a scarcity, has turned the attention to the public to a very important subject, *the investigation of the science of nutrition*—a subject so curious in itself, and so highly interesting to mankind, that it seems truly astonishing it should have been so long neglected; but in the manner in which it is now taken up, both by the House of Commons and the Board of Agriculture, there is great reason to hope that it will receive a thorough scientific examination. And, if this should be the case, I will venture to predict that the important discoveries and improvements which must result from these inquiries will render the alarms which gave rise to them for ever famous in the annals of civil society.

OF FOOD

CHAPTER I

Great Importance of the Subject under Consideration.—Probability that Water acts a much more important Part in Nutrition than has hitherto been generally imagined.—Surprisingly small Quantity of solid Food necessary, when properly prepared, for all the Purposes of Nutrition.—Great Importance of the Art of Cookery.—Barley remarkably nutritive when properly prepared.—The Importance of culinary Processes for preparing Food shown from the known Utility of a Practice common in some Parts of Germany of cooking for Cattle.—Difficulty of introducing a Change of Cookery into common Use.—Means that may be employed for that Purpose.

THERE is, perhaps, no operation of nature which falls under the cognizance of our senses more surprising or more curious than the nourishment and growth of plants and animals; and there is certainly no subject of investigation more interesting to mankind. As providing subsistence is, and ever must be, an object of the first concern in all countries, any discovery or improvement by which the procuring of good and wholesome food can be facilitated must contribute very powerfully to increase the comforts and promote the happiness of society.

That our knowledge in regard to the science of nutrition is still very imperfect, is certain; but I think there is reason to believe that we are upon the eve of some very important discoveries relative to that mysterious operation.

Since it has been known that water is not a simple element, but a *compound*, and capable of being decomposed, much light has been thrown upon many operations of nature which formerly were wrapped up in obscurity. In vegetation, for instance, it has been rendered extremely probable that water acts a much more important part than was formerly assigned to it by philosophers; that it serves not merely as the *vehicle* of nourishment, but constitutes at least one part, and probably an essential part, of the *food* of plants; that it is decomposed by them, and contributes *materially* to their growth; and that manures serve rather to prepare the water for decomposition than to form of themselves, substantially and directly, the nourishment of the vegetables.

Now a very clear analogy may be traced between the vegetation and growth of plants and the digestion and nourishment of animals; and as water is indispensably necessary in both processes, and as in one of them (vegetation) it appears evidently to serve as *food*, why should we not suppose it may serve as food in the other? There is, in my opinion, abundant reason to suspect that this is really the case; and I shall now briefly state the grounds upon which this opinion is founded. Having been engaged for a considerable length of time in providing food for the poor at Munich, I was naturally led, as well by curiosity as motives of economy, to make a great variety of experiments upon that subject; and I had not proceeded far in my operations before I began to perceive that they were very important, even much more so than I had imagined.

The difference in the apparent goodness, or the palatableness and apparent nutritiousness, of the same kinds of food, when prepared or cooked in different ways, struck me very forcibly; and I constantly found that the richness or *quality* of a soup depended more upon a proper choice of the ingredients, and a proper management of the fire in the combination of those ingredients, than upon the quantity of solid nutritious matter employed,—much more upon the art and skill of the cook than upon the amount of the sums laid out in the market.

I found likewise that the nutritiousness of a soup, or its power of satisfying hunger and affording nourishment, appeared always to be in proportion to its apparent richness or palatableness.

But what surprised me not a little was the discovery of the very small quantity of *solid food* which, when properly prepared, will suffice to satisfy hunger and support life and health, and the very trifling expense at which the stoutest and most laborious man may, in any country, be fed.

After an experience of more than five years in feeding the poor at Munich,—during which time every experiment was made that could be devised, not only with regard to the choice of the articles used as food, but also in respect to their different combinations and proportions, and to the various ways in which they could be prepared or cooked,—it was found that the *cheapest*, most *savoury*, and most *nourishing* food that could be provided was a soup composed of *pearl barley, pease, potatoes, cuttings of fine wheaten bread*, vinegar, salt, and water, in certain proportions.

The method of preparing this soup is as follows: The water and the pearl barley are first put together into the boiler and made to boil, the pease are then added, and the boiling is continued over a gentle fire about two hours. The potatoes are then added (having been previously peeled with a knife, or having been boiled, in order to their being more easily deprived of their skins), and the boiling is continued for about one hour more, during which time the contents of the boiler are frequently stirred about with a large wooden spoon or ladle, in order to destroy the texture of the potatoes, and to reduce the soup to one uniform mass. When this is done, the vinegar and the salt are added; and last of all, at the moment it is to be served up, the cuttings of bread.

The soup should never be suffered to boil, or even stand long before it is served up after the cuttings of bread are put to it. It will, indeed, for reasons which will hereafter be explained, be best never to put the cuttings of bread into the boiler at all, but (as is always done at Munich) to put them into the tubs in which the soup is carried from the kitchen into the dining-hall; pouring the soup hot from the boiler upon them, and stirring the whole well together with the iron ladles used for measuring out the soup to the poor in the hall.

It is of more importance than can well be imagined that this bread which is mixed with the soup should not be boiled. It is likewise of use that it should be cut as fine or thin as possible; and, if it be dry and hard, it will be so much the better.

The bread we use in Munich is what is called *semmel* bread, being small loaves weighing from two to three ounces; and, as we receive this bread in donations from the bakers, it is commonly dry and hard, being that which not being sold in time remains on hand, and becomes stale and unsalable. And we have found by experience that this hard and stale bread answers for our purpose much better than any other; for it renders mastication necessary, and mastication seems very power-fully to assist in promoting digestion. It likewise *prolongs the duration of the enjoyment of eating*, a matter of very great importance indeed, and which has not hitherto been sufficiently attended to.

The quantity of this soup furnished to each person at each meal, or one portion of it (the cuttings of bread included), is just *one Bavarian pound* in weight; and, as the Bavarian pound is to the pound avoirdupois as 1.123842 to 1, it is equal to about nineteen ounces and nine tenths avoirdupois. Now to those who know that a full pint of soup weighs no more than about sixteen ounces avoirdupois, it will not perhaps at the first view, appear very extraordinary that a portion weighing near twenty ounces, and consequently making near *one pint and a quarter* of this rich, strong, savoury soup, should be found sufficient to satisfy the hunger of a grown person; but when the matter is examined narrowly and properly analyzed, and it is found that the whole quantity of *solid food* which enters into the composition of one of these portions of soup does not amount to quite *six ounces*, it will then appear to be almost impossible that this allowance should be sufficient.

That it is quite sufficient, however, to make a good meal for a strong, healthy person, has been abundantly proved by long

125

experience. I have even found that a soup composed of nearly the same ingredients, except the potatoes, but in different proportions, was sufficiently nutritive and very palatable, in which only about *four ounces and three quarters* of solid food entered into the composition of a portion weighing twenty ounces.

But this will not appear incredible to those who know that one single spoonful of *salop*, weighing less than one quarter of an ounce, put into a pint of boiling water, forms the thickest and most nourishing soup that can be taken; and that the quantity of solid matter which enters into the composition of another very nutritive food, *hartshorn jelly*, is not much more considerable.

The *barley* in my soup seems to act much the same part as the *salop* in this famous restorative; and no substitute that I could ever find for it, among all the variety of corn and pulse of the growth of Europe, ever produced half the effect,—that is to say, half the nourishment at the same expense. Barley may therefore be considered as the rice of Great Britain.

It requires, it is true, a great deal of boiling; but when it is properly managed it thickens a vast quantity of water, and, as I suppose, *prepares it for decomposition*. It also gives the soup into which it enters as an ingredient a degree of richness which nothing else can give. It has little or no taste in itself, but when mixed with other ingredients which are savoury it renders them peculiarly grateful to the plate.

It is a maxim as ancient I believe as the time of Hippocrates, that *"whatever pleases the palate nourishes;"* and I have often had reason to think it perfectly just. Could it be clearly ascertained and demonstrated, it would tend to place *cookery* in a much more respectable situation among the arts than it now holds.

That the manner in which food is prepared is a matter of real importance, and that the water used in that process acts a much more important part than has hitherto been generally imagined, is, I think, quite evident; for it seems to me to be impossible upon any other supposition to account for the appearances. If the very small quantity of solid food which enters into the composition of a portion of some very nutritive soup were to be prepared differently and taken under some other form,—that of bread, for instance,—so far from being sufficient to satisfy hunger and afford a comfortable and nutritive meal, a person would absolutely starve upon such a slender allowance; and no great relief would be derived from drinking *crude* water to fill up the void in the stomach.

But it is not merely from an observation of the apparent effects of cookery upon those articles which are used as food for man that we are led to discover the importance of these culinary processes. Their utility is proved in a manner equally conclusive and satisfactory, by the effects which have been produced by employing the same process in preparing food for brute animals.

It is well known that boiling the potatoes with which hogs are fed renders them much more nutritive; and since the introduction of the new system of feeding horned cattle, that of keeping them confined in the stables all the year round (a method which is now coming fast into common use in many parts of Germany), great improvements have been made in the art of providing nourishment for those animals, and particularly by preparing their food by operations similar to those of cookery; and to these improvements it is most probably owing that stall-feeding has, in that country, been so universally successful.

● ● ●

These facts seem evidently to show that there is some very important secret with regard to nutrition which has not yet been properly investigated, and it seems to me to be more than probable that the number of inhabitants who may be supported in any country, upon its internal produce, depends almost as much upon the state of *the art of cookery* as upon that of *agriculture*. The Chinese perhaps understand both these arts better than any other nation. Savages understand neither of them.

But, if cookery be of so much importance, it certainly deserves to be studied with the greatest care, and it ought particularly to be attended to in times of general alarm, on account of the scarcity of provisions; for the relief which may in such cases be derived from it is immediate and effectual, while all other resources are distant and uncertain.

I am aware of the difficulties which always attend the introduction of measures calculated to produce any remarkable change in the customs and habits of mankind; and there is

127

perhaps no change more difficult to effect than that which would be necessary in order to make any considerable saving in the consumption of those articles commonly used as food, but still I am of opinion that such a change might with proper management be brought about.

There was a time, no doubt, when an aversion to potatoes was as general and as strong in Great Britain, and even in Ireland, as it is now in some parts of Bavaria; but this prejudice has been got over, and I am persuaded that any national prejudice, however deeply rooted, may be overcome, provided proper means be used for that purpose, and time allowed for their operation.

• • •

But without enlarging farther in this place upon these public kitchens, and the numerous and important advantages which may in all countries be derived from them, I shall return to the interesting subjects which I have undertaken to investigate, —the science of nutrition, and the art of providing wholesome and palatable food at a small expense.

CHAPTER II.

Of the Pleasures of Eating, and of the Means that may be employed for increasing it.

WHAT has already been said upon this subject will, I flatter myself, be thought sufficient to show that, *for all the purposes of nourishment*, a much smaller quantity of solid food will suffice than has hitherto been thought necessary; but there is another circumstance to be taken into the account, and that is the *pleasure of eating*, an enjoyment of which no person will consent to be deprived.

The pleasure enjoyed in eating depends first upon the agreeableness of the taste of the food, and secondly upon its power to affect the palate. Now there are many substances extremely cheap, by which very agreeable taste may be given to food, particularly when the basis or nutritive substance of the food is tasteless; and the effect of any kind of palatable solid food (of meat, for instance) upon the organs of taste may be increased almost indefinitely, by reducing the size of the particles of such food, and causing it to act upon the palate by a larger surface. And if means be used to prevent its being swallowed too soon, which may be easily done by mixing with it some hard and tasteless substance, such as crumbs of bread rendered hard by toasting, or anything else of that kind, by which a long mastication is rendered necessary, the enjoyment of eating may be greatly increased and prolonged.

The idea of occupying a person a great while, and affording him much pleasure at the same time, in eating a small quantity of food, may perhaps appear ridiculous to some; but those who consider the matter attentively will perceive that it is very important. It is perhaps as much so as anything that can employ the attention of the philosopher.

The enjoyments which fall to the lot of the bulk of mankind are not so numerous as to render an attempt to increase them superfluous. And, even in regard to those who have it in their power to gratify their appetites to the utmost extent of their wishes, it is surely rendering them a very important service to show them how they may increase their pleasures without destroying their health.

If a glutton can be made to gormandize two hours upon two ounces of meat, it is certainly much better for him than to give himself an indigestion by eating two pounds in the same time.

I was led to meditate upon this subject by mere accident. I had long been at a loss to understand how the Bavarian soldiers, who are uncommonly stout, strong, and healthy men, and who, in common with all other Germans, are remarkably fond of eating, could contrive to live upon the very small sums they expend for food; but a more careful examination of the economy of their tables cleared up the point, and let me into a secret which awakened all my curiosity. These soldiers, instead of being starved upon their scanty allowance, as might have been suspected, I found actually living in a most comfortable and even luxurious manner. I found that they had contrived not only to render their food savoury and nourishing, but, what appeared to me still more extraordinary, had found out the means of increasing its action upon the organs of taste, so as actually to argument and even prolong to a most surprising degree the enjoyment of eating.

This accidental discovery made a deep impression upon my

mind, and gave a new turn to all my ideas on the subject of food. It opened to me a new and very interesting field for investigation and experimental inquiry, of which I had never before had a distinct view; and thenceforward my diligence in making experiments, and in collecting information relative to the manner in which food is prepared in different countries, was redoubled.

In the following chapter may be seen the general results of all my experiments and inquiries relative to this subject. A desire to render this account as concise and short as possible has induced me to omit much interesting speculation which the subject naturally suggested; but the ingenuity of the reader will supply this defect, and enable him to discover the objects particularly aimed at in the experiments, even where they are not mentioned, and to compare the results of practice with the assumed theory.

The Recipe

[*Rumford gives two recipes. The main ingredients of Soup No. I are pearl barley, peas and bread while in Soup No. II the quantities of pearl barley and peas are halved and replaced by about twice the amount of potatoes; I give the recipe for Soup II which Rumford prefers.*

	Quantity (lb)	in 1800 £	s.	d.	in 1988 £
Pearl barley	71 ⎫				
Peas	66 ⎬	0	11	3	25
Potatoes	230 ⎭				
Bread	70	0	10	2	17
Salt	20	0	1	2	1
Vinegar	47	0	1	5	4
Water	983				
	1487	1	4	0	47
Add fuel (88 lb Wood or 50 lb Coal)		0	0	2	1
		1	4	2	48

This quantity was supposed to feed 1200 people, i.e. the prime cost per person comes to 0.24d. or 1 farthing at 1800 prices or 4p at 1988 prices.

Rumford adds labour costs as well as depreciation and maintenance of kitchen furniture which increases the cost by about 10%. At today's prices an increase of 50% would seem more realistic, but even so the daily cost of feeding a Munich beggar comes to only 6p, a very modest sum.

However, the calorific value of the daily soup ration comes to only 1000 kilocalories, less than half of the generally accepted minimum.

The prices given above refer to Munich and Rumford calculates that in London his soup would be twice as expensive.]

Section V Alcohol

TWO OPPOSITE EFFECTS OF DRINK
Benjamin Franklin (1706–1790)

[*The following extract is from Franklin's* Autobiography *and refers to his stay in London in 1725.*]

... I left Palmer's to work at Watts's, near Lincoln's Inn Fields, a still greater printing-house. Here I continued all the rest of my stay in London.

At my first admission into this printing-house I took to working at press, imagining I felt a want of the bodily exercise I had been us'd to in America, where presswork is mix'd with composing. I drank only water; the other workmen, near fifty in number, were great guzzlers of beer. On occasion, I carried up and down stairs a large form of types in each hand, when others carried but one in both hands. They wondered to see, from this and several instances, that the *Water-American*, as they called me, was *stronger* than themselves, who drank *strong* beer! We had an alehouse boy who attended always in the house to supply the workmen. My companion at the press drank every day a pint before breakfast, a pint at breakfast with his bread and cheese, a pint between breakfast and dinner, a pint at dinner, a pint in the afternoon about six o'clock, and another when he had done his day's work. I thought it a detestable custom; but it was necessary, he suppos'd, to drink *strong* beer, that he might be strong to labor. I endeavored to convince him that the bodily strength afforded by beer could only be in proportion to the grain or flour of the barley dissolved in the water of which it was made; that there was more flour in a pennyworth of bread; and therefore, if he would eat that with a pint of water, it would give him more strength than a quart of beer. He drank on, however, and had four or five shillings to pay out of his wages every Saturday night for that muddling liquor; an expense I was free from. And thus these poor devils keep themselves always under.

Samuel Pepys (1633–1703)

[*In 1667 Parliament set up a Committee to investigate irregularities in the management of the Navy. The accusations were serious and on 28 February 1668 the Commons decided that the Principal Officers of the Navy should be ordered to answer those accusations the following week at the Bar of the House. Pepys literally locked himself into his office for the next days preparing his defence, and this is how he describes the dreaded day.*]

With these thoughts I lay troubling myself till 6 a-clock, restless, and at last getting my wife to talk to me to comfort me..... So I up and to my office, ... and so I did huddle up the best I could some more notes for my discourse today; and by 9 a-clock was ready and did go down to the Old Swan, and there by boat, with T. Hater and W. Hewer with me, to Westminster, where I found myself come time enough and my Brethren all ready. But I full of thoughts and trouble touching the issue of this day; *and to comfort myself did go to the Dog and drink half a pint of mulled sack, and in the Hall did drink a dram of brandy at Mrs. Howletts, and with the warmth of this did find myself in better order as to courage, truly*. So we all up to the Lobby; and between 11 and 12 a-clock were called in, with the Mace before us, into the House; where a mighty full House,..... and full of expectation of our defence and what it would be, and with great praejudice. After the Speaker had told us the dissatisfaction of the House and read the report of the Committee, I began our defence most acceptably and smoothly, and continued at it without any hesitation or losse but with full scope and all my reason free about me, as if it had been at my own table, from that time till past 3 in the afternoon; and so ended without any interruption from the Speaker, but we withdrew. And there all my fellow-officers, and all the world that was within hearing, did congratulate me and cry up my speech as the best thing they ever heard, and my fellow-officers overjoyed at it.

Samuel Pepys The Diary 4–5 March 1668.

Stafford Cripps (1889–1952)

A VERY BENEVOLENT CHANCELLOR

The receipts from the duties on the cheaper kinds of table wines, those taxed as 'light wines imported in cask', have fallen off very sharply in the last few months. I propose to make a substantial reduction in these duties and I hope that this will, in due course, bring about an increase in consumption which will not only benefit the Exchequer but will also assist our trade with France and with the wine-producing countries of the Commonwealth. I propose therefore to make a reduction of 12s. a gallon equivalent to 2s. a bottle forthwith. I have been able to make an arrangement with the trade whereby there will be some light French wines in particular on sale retail in the near future at 8s. a bottle the present cheapest being about 12s. bottle.

Sir Stafford Cripps,
Budget statement April 1949 Hansard Vol. 463 Col. 2092

[*The duty on wine imported in bottle remained the same at 4s. 7d. a bottle. For wine imported in cask it was reduced by 2s. to 2s. 7d. per bottle. This welcome tax change, coming from an austere, teetotal Chancellor of the Exchequer was greeted with surprise. I was told that, in addition to the reasons given in his speech, Sir Stafford Cripps wanted to encourage in this way British wine shippers to exercise their skill and use local labour to bottle not only cheap but also high-quality wines.*]

Michael Faraday (1791-1867)

PALM WINE[†]

... Some palm wine has lately been brought into this country from Cape-Coast Castle, under the direction of Captain Bagnold. This fluid, when fresh, is of the colour and consistence of milk; it is very sweet, is not inebriating, and is drank as a luxury by the natives and Europeans. When exposed to the air for a few hours it becomes slightly acid, and very intoxicating. That which Captain Bagnold possessed, and which he gave me for examination, had been obtained by tapping from the tree, Jan. 1, 1818, and it was first opened in London, April 1819.

It came in a stone-bottle, badly corked, but sealed up. When the bottle was opened it had a smell like that of fermenting beer, and the atmosphere within the bottle contained so much carbonic acid that, poured into a glass, it extinguished a taper within it. The wine was a thin, milky, aqueous fluid. It was very sweet and somewhat acid; it acted readily on litmus paper, and contained both carbonic and acetic acids. When the wine was placed on a filter, it slowly passed through perfectly pellucid, leaving the white insoluable part on the filter. This, when heated in a tube, gave off abundance of ammonia, and appeared to be vegetable albumen; the clear fluid was rendered opaque, by the addition of alcohol, and the precipitated matter, on separation, was found to be gum.

Eight ounces of the wine were taken as from the bottle, and carefully distilled with a little pounded marble, until 4-5ths had come over, and this, made up to the original quantity by pure water, gave an alcoholic solution of specific gravity, 993.7, at $55°$ Fahr. equal to 4.7 per cent of alcohol, by Gilpin's Tables.

The portion left in the retort was separated from the marble, and evaporated until like a syrup; alcohol was then added, which formed a sweet brown solution, and left an insoluble matter, which, dried at $212°$, weighed 20 grains. It was partly soluble in water, and resembled a mixture of gum and albumen.

† From the *Quarterly Journal of Literature, Science and Arts* 1819 Vol. 7. p. 387. (Courtesy of the Director of the Royal Institution.)

The alcoholic solution deposited some very minute crystals, which were supertartrate of potash, and then, being evaporated at 212° to dryness, gave a hard brown cake, weighing 167 grains, which was principally sugar. An accident prevented any experiments on the quantity of salts contained in this portion of the wine, and, with the exception of a very minute quantity, no more was to be obtained.

Samuel Curran

THE IMPORTANCE OF SMELL

Humans are endowed with five senses and it appears to many like me, involved closely in science for the best part of a lifetime, that we do comparatively little to recognise the major role that our senses, and especially that of smell, play in everyday life. Having made that point it is relevant to go on to stress the fact that as a Scot I am perhaps too prone to enlarge on the blessings that Scots have bestowed on mankind, not all of them in science and engineering. It is possible that I am guilty from time to time of exaggerating the value of the role that they have played. Be that as it may the fact remains that Scotch whisky has proved a blessing in many situations throughout history although a minority would contend that *in toto* it had been more of a curse than a help. Most doctors would speak in favour of it so I am going to assume that what I want to expound will be of interest to many more than those who enjoy a 'dram' for its own sake. The overall attributes of the dram have certainly merited careful scientific study. It seems to me the matter of smell has been rather neglected.

As a Scot I contend that we have far too little scientific knowledge of the most world-famous drink. So I come to my main point. I admit that I have no inside information about the goals of those responsible for bringing to market the outstanding product of Scotland but I am a regular customer of some distillers and I have what would appear to be grounds for a complaint to lodge with them. It is a clear memory of mine that research done under the auspices of the US Navy, soon after the Second World War, showed the various well known drinks in their pecking order as regards purity of the alcohol content. It struck me when I read the results of the research that the US Navy work had been realistic and that the results deserved a good deal of publicity. Briefly the work proved that a good quality vodka was just ahead of Scotch whisky in freedom from the undesirable traces of 'heavy' alcohols in the ethyl alcohol, traces that produce hang-over and even worse in the way of side-effects of drinking. Scotch and vodka, together with first quality gin, were far in front of a long series of other alcoholic drinks. The Navy were in a position to give informed advice to seamen about how to indulge themselves. The work could and should have been widened in scope to examine the many sad effects on consumers of the trace constituents of the explored range of popular drinks. Thinking on this study it seems safe to assert that the vapours that give the characteristic odours to such drinks as Scotch and vodka will be present only in minute amounts. This deduction is all the more reasonable as general information shows that the sense of smell is remarkably acute and often less than one part per million is effective in giving rise to the smell of a substance.

It is certainly not clear that those in charge of whisky production have given thought to the smell of their product. However, the consumer is often obliged to take smell on his or her breath into consideration. Often when a glass of scotch and soda or something similar would fit the bill the drinker thinks of duties or engagements ahead and decides that a drink less revealing of the consumption of alcohol would be more in keeping with the occasion. So a less favoured tipple is chosen. It is a pity if smell becomes the controlling factor in choice, especially if Scotch with little or no smell could be provided through science.

Since my interest in the purity of drinks was stimulated some forty years ago our ability to identify compounds of all kinds has grown dramatically. It seems certain that the smell of whisky is attributable to a minute trace of some heavy vapour in the drink and as scientists we would begin work by identifying that vapour. This could prove to be an arduous task but in no way too difficult to resolve. I recall my pleasure when during my years with the UKAEA we managed in 1956 to put a large double-focusing mass spectrometer in operation and found we were in a position for the first time to identify a range of large heavy molecules (molecular weight around 240) even when the amounts of the substances available were very small indeed. The sensitivity was excellent, indeed such that large organic molecules contaminating the nominally pure samples of transuranic elements of very nearly the same mass could be distinguished from the atoms. At the present day the neat compact time-of-flight mass spectrometer can do much the same as the large sophisticated machine and yield a thoroughly sound analysis of compounds containing heavy organic molecules. By applying one of them we might well manage to locate the molecule or molecules responsible for the not too acceptable smell of whisky. It would then be necessary to find an easy way to remove the offending constituent and finish with Scotch that did not smell in a fashion that most people dislike.

It must be stressed that many would still persist in asking for the Scotch which they have come to prefer even with its smell and possibly in fact to some extent because of its smell. The more fastidious would, however, almost certainly switch their allegiance to the smell-free type of Scotch that is visualised here. Doubtless also a considerable number of new consumers would begin to swell the ranks of those whose favourite drink was Scotch but who had refrained from becoming attached because of smell. One can think of many who want to avoid a smell on their breath and among the many are most of the female sex. So Scotch could well start to appeal to a new range of customers.

There will be those who say that the essential nature of some of the excellent Scotch whiskies would be lost in removing even the tiny amount of material that gives rise to the characteristic odour. It is really hard to believe this but success in the research outlined here is necessary in order to establish the truth. Surely it is time to do much more with a matter as important as the smell of a world-famous national drink. Removal of a small blemish in the totality of the attributes of Scotch is no unimportant achievement. We note in passing that the value of exported whisky is around one billion pounds sterling per year. I trust that the suggested programme will be pursued and crowned with success. A drink of record popularity could well result!

I should refer to a special personal reason for interest in research on Scotch. The older one gets the more a help to the circulatory system is appreciated and for hundreds of years the excellence of Scotch in this respect has been recognised. Many very elderly people know the kind effects of a dram on the declining capability of the human body and it is good to think they might in future years enjoy a stimulant without all and sundry knowing they have indulged themselves. The research has its important social side! We have to demonstrate that the erudite branches of science take note of human needs.

Peter Maitlis
with the help of Marion Maitlis

MULLED WINE WITH A KICK IN IT

Marion is a great believer in the healing and comforting powers of the Capsicum. Originally cultivated by the Indians in tropical America, the name is believed to derive from the Greek 'kapso'—to bite. It refers to the pungency of some peppers, especially those from which cayenne and tabasco are obtained. The essential ingredient, capsaicin, can be detected by our taste buds at a level of one part in fifteen million. Pure capsaicin is very unpleasant and irritates the skin and the eyes, but in the dilute form found in nature it is widely used in cooking because of its pungency. It has also been used as a folk-remedy for flatulence, and is reputed to give relief from rheumatism, lumbago, and neuralgia, when applied in an ointment.

We like to make Mulled Wine with Kapso, a bite or a kick, in it. This is what we usually do. We put 4 cups (800 cm^3) of red wine (and if it is of reasonable quality, so much the better), 2 cups of orange juice, and half a cup (100 cm^3) of brandy into a good-sized saucepan. We add a medium-sized lemon cut into slices, half a cup of sugar (100 grams), one bay leaf, 6 cloves, 2 sticks of cinnamon, and half a teaspoonful of allspice. Now we add our secret ingredient which makes all the difference: a small amount of cayenne pepper, about enough to cover the tip of a knife (10–20 milligrams). We stir the mixture vigorously with a wooden spoon while it is slowly heating on the stove, and then we keep it just below boiling for ten minutes. This allows all the flavours to be extracted into the brew without losing too much into the vapour. We serve it very hot, in heat-resistant glasses, preferably with a handle that you can hold onto. Hopefully you will need something to hold onto.

It is a good idea to use a small amount of cayenne the first time you try this so that you can judge your tolerance and that of your guests. Then increase the amount as you like. When applied to wine and taken in moderation and in slow sips we find it a cure for most ills.

John Postgate

TWO APERITIFS

Two of my recipes are for aperitifs. The first was devised shortly after the end of the Second World War when drink of any kind was not easily come by, in collaboration with my father, the late Raymond Postgate, whom many will remember as founder and long-time Editor of the *Good Food Guide*. Although he was a historian and writer, he became known around 1950 to 1970 as an gastronome and wine expert. I well recall the afternoon when we composed it together, a bottle of 'British Wine of Port Character', some vanilla essence and some anonymous quinine bitters assembled on his kitchen table at Finchley, North London. We were mixing them and tasting, mixing and tasting, seeking something comparable to the genre of French aperitifs which includes Dubonnet, Byrrh and Cap Corse. Our wives were out shopping; when they returned we offered them the results of our research with somewhat inebriate pride—for there was little of the port-type left in our bottle. We were mildly offended by the coolness of their response, but over subsequent years the recipe repeatedly justified itself as an economical and acceptable aperitif, often requested by my own regular guests. Actually, my father took against aperitifs in later life, preferring to offer a plain or sparkling white wine, so I present the recipe as he might have approved it shortly after we had worked out the proportions, with my own tested modifications in the notes section.

POSTGATES' CORSICAN APERITIF

Take 1 bottle of British Ruby or Tawny wine, sometimes marketed as 'of Port character' [1]. Add 2 to 4 drops of quinine bitters [2]. Insert a vanilla pod [3] and leave to steep in the bottle at room temperature for at least 3 weeks [4]. Decant from the pod (which can be re-used) and serve with ice, with a slice of lemon, or straight.

Notes

[1] Gratifyingly, the cheaper the British wine, the better. Real port and Cyprus port-type work less well.

[2] A thimble of Campari, not available at the time of our researches, is ideal.

[3] Nonsense. Use 2–3 drops of vanilla essence and skip the decanting. My parent was rather against essences.

[4] Chemists will find this difficult to believe, but 3 weeks at domestic room temperature transforms it from vanilla-flavoured port into a drink with its own character. I've kept it for six months longer without further improvement.

My second recipe is for a derivative of my own, based on British white port-type wine; it is not only a good cheap aperitif but goes down well for elevenses with cake. Much favoured by my late mother-in-law, it is appropriately named:

SOLACE

Take 1 bottle of British white port-type wine [1], add a thimble of Campari followed by about 2 cm^2 of zest of an orange (the thin orange skin with as little pith as is feasible) [2]. Stand for 2 days about the house, decant from the orange, store corked. It needs no further maturation; serve straight or with ice.

Notes

[1] Again, the cheaper, the better.

[2] Orange essence will not do—it makes it surprisingly nasty.

Finally, a vegetable dish which I fondly believe is my own invention, but who knows? It owes something to a passing interest of my father's in Elizabethan recipes but is completely bogus in that it has no mediaeval origin known to me. However, it is very good and goes well with roasts, particularly pheasant or, I imagine, cockatrice.

[*For this dish see the Recipe section on page 220.*]

Denys Wilkinson

THE BRIGHAM YOUNG

A few years ago my wife and I were marooned for several days in a private lodge near the head of the Weber Valley in the Uinta Mountains of Utah by an unusually heavy and unseasonal snow fall. (The little-known Uintas, which rise to over 13,000 feet, are the only significant mountain range of the United States that runs E–W rather than N–S. I mention this so that you might acquire something of academic as well as of spiritual value from my little piece.)

We were fortunate in that the lodge in which we found ourselves was that of our genial hosts, our old friends Professor and Mrs Eastman Hatch of Utah State University (of which I am most happy to be an honorary alumnus, sharing the platform at my investiture with Dr Bob Hope, but that is another story). We were also fortunate that, perhaps surprisingly for Utah but consonant with the liberal emancipation of our hosts, the lodge was superbly stocked with a vast and impressive range of spirituous fluids.

Now, dedicated academics such as myself and Professor Hatch cannot be deprived of access to their normal sources of intellectual ferment without seeking replacement in the form of whatever alternative intellectual activity might be approached through whatever resources might alternatively present themselves; in this case, the spirituous fluids. Professor Hatch and I, advised and abetted by our respective wives Anne and Helen, fell to a competition for the invention of new contributions to what in the ambivalent circle of Utah's social life is referred to as the 'attitude adjustment period'.

I won. That is not to say that Professor Hatch's brilliant innovations were not of the highest calibre nor that my own several that failed to receive the highest accolade were not also superior to the majority of the turbid and turgid offerings that one conventionally encounters. But I won. My winning invention I named, honouring the *genius loci*, the Brigham Young. The naming and inaugural ceremony, as the blizzard was slackening, was not accompanied by the expected splitting of the heavens and the descent of flaming brimstone and treacle in equal proportions but that was presumably because even the heavens were momentarily stunned.

But what, then, is the Brigham Young? My aim throughout my academic life has been to strive for elegant simplicity: the Brigham Young is simply a mixture of tequila and tabasco. (Note immediately that the glass should, under no circumstances, for sentimental or other misguided reasons, be given a salt-encrusted rim.) The proportions are critical: one tablespoon (US measure) of tequila to one drop (standard) of tabasco. It is important to secure mixing by a stirring-related rather than by a shaking-related mechanism since aeration is highly undesirable. Thorough mixing is quite difficult to achieve in a sufficiently gentle way. It is my belief that an even superior mode, rather than one of homogeneous mixing, would be into a finely layered sub-division of the ingredients so that the impact of the tabasco would effect its own rhythm or, at least, metre. It was my intention to consult G I Taylor on this important development in fluid dynamics but, alas!, that was not to be. I hope to be able to report the results of these continuing alcoholo-dynamical researches in subsequent editions of this book.

The only other technical remark is that the drink should be extremely deeply chilled (263 K) and that it is best that the drinker be also.

Knut Schmidt-Nielsen

PHYSICS IN THE KITCHEN AND APPLEJACK IN THE CELLAR

What is the connection between making applejack in Minnesota, Norwegian dried codfish and port? Closer links than you might think, considering barriers to free international trade.

Perhaps I should explain. When I grew up in Norway there was a trade agreement with the Portuguese, who needed dry codfish for their favourite dish, bacalao. The Norwegians in return got cheap port, which could be used to get wonderfully drunk, and the whole thing could be arranged as a barter deal without any use of money, which neither country had enough of to spend on the good things in life. This was in the late 1920s when I was in middle school and surreptitiously began to be interested in alcohol.

Next piece of information. Grapes can't grow in Norway, it is too cold, but the Norwegians make wine anyway, from rhubarb. It doesn't taste too bad, it is sweet, and is fermented to an alcohol concentration where the natural fermentation will stop because the yeast is inhibited by the increasing alcohol concentration, about 12 or 13%. There is only one manufacturer of rhubarb wine in all of Norway, and he would love to fortify the wine with added alcohol, the way sherry and port are fortified, but this is illegal in Norway. This is to the disadvantage of the consuming public, the drunks, that is, who would prefer a bit more kick for their money. So they buy cheap port instead, and get a cheap drink and a bad hangover.

Third piece of information. My father was a professor of organic chemistry with a specialization in what was called technical organic chemistry, including food technology. He had an all-consuming interest in food with a substantial emphasis on its enjoyment. It belongs to the story that he was also very knowledgeable and quite inventive.

For some reason unknown to me, my father was consulted by the manufacturer of rhubarb wine, and he made the brilliant suggestion that the alcohol concentration in the wine could be increased by freezing out some of the water. Adding alcohol was against the law, but the law said nothing about removing water. Clever idea, but the law makers were concerned about the trade agreements and selling codfish to a country that didn't have money to pay for it. If people stopped buying port (and drinking it, I presume), the codfish would pile up in Norway and the Portuguese wouldn't have bacalao to enjoy. Solution, change the law, and freezing wine became illegal. End of preamble, and now for the applejack.

When I moved to Duke University in 1952 after half a dozen years in the United States, I encountered apple cider and the difference between sweet cider and hard cider. Lots of apples are grown in the mountains of North Carolina. But hard cider is not for sale anywhere because of its alcohol content, while sweet cider is in every grocery store. A little yeast, accidental or not, could remedy this situation, and this is exactly what happened to me.

One day when we discussed hard cider the way research students usually discuss the merits of home brewed beer, one of them asked

Figure 1 Silenus meets Norvegicus.

if I had ever tasted applejack. I never had, but my curiosity was piqued. He explained, yes, he had an uncle in Minnesota who used to make applejack in the winter. He put a jug of hard cider out on a cold winter night and the water would freeze to ice. When I insisted on more detailed information, he became sadly vague, no, he said never seen it himself, but it was exactly as he said.

I continued my inquiry to find out about the details of the procedure. Another helpful soul knew how, his grandfather in Wisconsin etc., etc., on a cold winter night etc., but his memory failed miserably when it came to technical details. This went on for some time, everybody knew what was done in the good old days, but nobody had tried, or even seen it done, or knew any tricks of the trade.

I might not have believed any of these stories of grandfathers and uncles and cold winter nights, were it not for childhood memories of the consequences of trade agreements and codfish and port. What had been made unlawful in Norway was undoubtedly well founded in reality and should be given serious consideration.

Decision. I put a gallon jug of hard cider outside on a cold night, feeling certain that the alcohol content would protect the glass from breaking when the contents froze. The temperature fell to well below minus ten Celsius, and in the morning the cider was as clear and unfrozen as ever. I later understood why a second night was equally unsuccessful, the heat capacity of a gallon is too great to reach a sufficiently low temperature in a few hours. More time was needed.

At that lack of success I turned to modern technology and put the jug in the freezer. At minus twenty freezing proceeded, but I didn't get the expected chunk of clear ice and some concentrated fluid—the whole mass was frozen to a thick slush of tiny ice crystals. I gradually learned (1) that a strong and powerful liquid can nevertheless be poured off, and (2) if the jug is left for a longer time in the freezer, some recrystallization takes place and the crystals will be larger. Conclusion: be patient!

When you have turned the frozen jug upside down and have seen the unfrozen concentrate slowly drip into a suitable receptacle, you know that you finally have reached that elusive goal, you have produced real genuine applejack. You taste a few drops of the valuable liquid, you are mortified by the hot, raw, burning taste. No pleasure, totally undrinkable.

What to do with undrinkable pride? Let it sit in the cellar to be 'aged' as all good wine and brandy must! Several months later it tastes the same, barely altered if at all. Next remedy: think! what is done with good cognac and whisky? It is aged in charred oak barrels. But my measly little pint of valuable fluid would barely be enough to moisten the inside of a barrel. Even if I had a small keg, it would just absorb most of my precious liquid and leave me only drops.

Think again! If I cannot put my applejack into the barrel, turn the problem around and put the barrel into the applejack. Easy, a few sticks of white oak from a log of firewood and a piece or two of fresh charcoal from the fireplace. Several weeks later the stuff was quite drinkable, although no great pleasure. This was in 1967, and the bottle is still around in 1987, it tastes like well aged, smooth brandy with a clear apple nose and a complex finish. Conclusion: turn the barrel inside out, and then you need time, time, and more time. You may ask why the old bottle is still around if it is so good. Simple again, other batches have been produced, and some have been excellent.

I have learned more over the years, as I have gained in age and experience. Don't use baker's yeast for the fermentation, wine yeast is better, and never, never let apple cider ferment by its natural yeasts. Horrible end product, even the research students wouldn't drink it. In the beginning of the fermentation cycle it tastes quite good, but this is not when you want to drink it. You would miss out on the real stuff. Advice: use a good white wine yeast; a Chardonnay yeast is fine.

Next piece of advice: don't be impatient, let the hard cider sit and mature for a few months, and use a bubbler to keep it well protected from air and oxygen, until the fresh, yeasty taste is gone. It is like any good wine, except Beaujolais Nouveau, it improves with time. If you now make applejack from the aged hard cider, it will not be so bad after all, and you start the further aging process with a much finer raw material. Result: an even finer end product. Conclusion: use good yeast and take your time, ample time.

More advice: the sticks of oak should be from a freshly split but aged log. This gives the applejack a fine oaky flavour, but it also makes it a little astringent because of the tannins extracted from the wood. (The charcoal I have given up on, I don't think it makes much difference.) The remedy is to mix some eggwhite into half a

147

cup or so of the oaked applejack and add it to the jug. The whole batch turns ugly and murky. After a few months of sitting untouched, the muck has settled to the bottom and the liquid above is brilliantly clear with the bitter tannins firmly bound to the egg albumin and sequestered in the thick layer of sediment at the bottom. Next problem, separate the clear fluid from the sediment without stirring up the gunk—not as easy as it looks. This is *your* problem.

Final advice: if it is legal in your country, take advantage of a physiologist's experience in the kitchen and enjoy some applejack in your cellar.

Postscript

The production of strong alcoholic beverages by freezing has a long and illustrious history. The Editor has called my attention to the perhaps most scholarly historical discourse on the subject, an article by Dr Joseph Needham, the distinguished biologist and historian, and his collaborators. Dr Needham has kindly given me permission to quote from the article, which deals with the history of distillation as practised in China.

Lu Gwei-Djen, Joseph Needham and Dorothy Needham

THE COMING OF ARDENT WATER

(Excerpts arranged by Knut Schmidt-Nielsen, from AMBIX **19** 69–112 (1972))

Dr Needham quotes from early records that Kao-Chang presented 'frozen-out wine' to the Imperial court about the year 520, most probably on a number of successive tribute visits. Much later, towards the end of the 14th century, when distillation had been known for centuries (perhaps since the 6th century), freezing was used to test liquor. People used to go to the high mountains and leave their spirits out to freeze. Strong alcohol solutions would not freeze, but if diluted and adulterated with sharp herbs they would.

The earliest description in Europe known to Needham and his

collaborators is by Paracelsus (1493–1541). About 1620 Francis Bacon (1561–1626) wrote: 'Paracelsus reporteth, that if a glass of wine be set upon a terras in a bitter frost, it will leave some liquor unfrozen in the centre of the glass, which excelleth *spiritus vini* drawn by fire.'

Somewhat later, in 1661, Robert Boyle (1627–1691) reported on the experiences of Dutch men who wintered in Novaya Zemlya: 'There was scarce any unfrozen Beer in the barrel; but in that thick Yiest that was unfrozen lay the Strength of the Beer, so that it was too Strong to drink alone, and that which was frozen tasted like Water ....'

Naturally, if the frozen part of the beer tasted like water, the process could be used in reverse, that is, to obtain pure water from frozen ice. Securing drinking water from the sea by this method seems to have occurred first to the Danish physician Thomas

Figure 1 Freeze-fortified beer, a Dutch discovery on Novaya Zemlya.

Bartholinus in the same year that Robert Boyle wrote about the frozen beer. Boyle himself recommended the method to sailors in cold latitudes, and Captain Cook supplied fresh water to his crew by melting sea ice in 1773.

Evidently, the method of separating water from fermented beverages became widely known and used. Needham quotes information from Professor Stephen Mason about the place of applejack in Canadian folklore: 'That was the country where grand-dad always left half a dozen casks of cider in the snow and ice during winter-time; then at Christmas a tube would be inserted and the liquor drawn off. The excisemen supposedly turned a blind eye on this.'

We must hope that today's excisemen will be equally generous if someone should fall for the temptation to put a small jug of hard cider in his freezer, just to test the validity of a scientific principle.

[*It was not till the 1970s that cider and perry lost their privilege of being the only alcoholic drinks in the UK with no excise duty levied on them. In about 1948, encouraged by this fact, I thought of doing some Canadian applejack experiments in Oxford using artificial cold. I was under the impression that our laws only forbade the possession of stills and the production of spirits by distillation without a licence and that, provided one did it only for one's own consumption, the enrichment of alcohol by freezing was permissible. I consulted a distinguished lawyer, the late Dr W T S Stallybrass, Principal of Brasenose College, Oxford, and he advised me that I would be within my legal rights in doing this, but, fearing that the Board of Excise might get wise to this trick, enjoined me to make forthwith a few bottles for his personal use before it was too late. I did not pursue the matter at that time and it was not until I began preparing a public lecture that I looked into the question again and found that Dr Stallybrass was alas wrong and that the relevant provisions of the Spirits Act of 1880 were amended by the Finance Act of 1921, and as a result the manufacture of spirits by any process, not only by distillation, became prohibited except by licence. My guess is that the Board of Customs and Excise realised by the early 1920s that the refrigeration industry and its domestic applications had become something to be reckoned with.*]

150

Section VI Ingredients— Standard and Exotic

P G H Gell

THE BANQUET OF ATREUS

In a world where starvation, especially protein starvation, is almost the norm, it is significant that, as far as one can discover, no group of humans whatever has adopted the regular practice of eating its own kind, cooked or uncooked, as a normal form of nourishment, though it is not uncommon among 'primitive' man as a form of religious ritual. Among other mammals it is common enough for recently delivered females to eat their young when threatened, as a method of protecting them, or of males to eat the young fathered by a rival male for, according to Dawkins (R Dawkins 1976 *The Selfish Gene* (Oxford University Press)), perfectly good dynastic reason, while, from timber wolves to caged mice, the sick and incompetent are regularly killed and eaten. But no mammal at least makes a habit of eating its own species as a normal nutritional resource, though frogs and fish may do. In the human race the tabu on anthropophagy is extremely strong, even surviving the compulsions of hunger, fear and approaching death. It is true that there are accounts in the literature of small groups under conditions of extreme stress eating their own dead (P P Read 1974 *Alive: the Story of the Andes Survivors* (Lippincott, Philadelphia); D Tuzin 1983 *Cannibalism and Arapesh Cosmology: A Wartime Incident with the Japanese* (EC)† pp 61–71), but these accounts are always associated with signs of extreme horror caused by the breaking of a stringent tabu.

We do have of course many literary descriptions of anthropophagy in 'primitive' societies, if the Aztecs for instance can be considered primitive. The written records on this subject fall into three categories: historical accounts written by hostile observers, myths and anecdotes told by natives to anthropologists about enemies and strangers, and ritual practices forming part of a complex cosmological system, recorded also by anthropologists. V Arens in her book *The Man-eating Myth* (1979 Oxford University Press, New York) rejects entirely all historical records of such practices and makes a strong case I think against accepting accounts in the first two categories. It is undeniable that accounts by missionaries and colonial administrators contain an in-built bias since the former always and the latter until quite recently have been strongly motivated to denigrate the social customs of native peoples for their own professional purposes. Indeed they do not need to tell lies or even be at all disingenuous about recording in good faith 'facts' about anthropophagy given them by native informants, for a reason which is made clear by Fitzjohn Porter Poole writing about the Bimin-Kikusmin of New Guinea (*Cannibals, Tricksters and Witches; Anthropophagic Images among Bimin-Kikusmin* 1983 (EC) pp 6–32). These tribes divide up the human race into four categories: (i) themselves; (ii) certain neighbours with whom they have regular cultural interchange ('human men'); (iii) groups with whom any interaction is indirect ('human creatures'); (iv) 'animal men', fearsome semi-mythical groups, known only from stories and hearsay, trolls to frighten naughty children. They attribute cannibalism to these in increasing degree—themselves who practise it under strict ritual conditions, their neighbours who they claim will eat Bimin-Kikusmin killed in war and raids, when they can get them, but at random only if they are witches. The 'human creatures' who consider man-flesh as 'ordinary food' are outside the ritual and kin system and hence practise incest, and

† Most of the recent references to anthropophagy in the anthropological literature, including those cited in the text under EC, are included in a Special Publication of the Society for Psychological Anthropology, *The Ethnology of Cannibalism*, edited by Paula Brown and Donald Tuzin, published by the Society for Psychological Anthropology, Washington DC 20009, 1983.

'animal men' who hunt man-meat avidly and prey on the last group. If this kind of attitude towards one's neighbours, near and remote, is representative (and there is no reason to think it is not, especially as the B-K admit their own cannibalistic practices), it would only need a little uncritical listening by a potential exploiter or slave-trader with a *parti pris* or indeed a perfectly honest missionary from an alien culture, to record the most horrific accounts which justify him in his efforts to *écraser l'infame*. There is moreover a kind of shameful dream of anthropophagy, a sort of fascination and a special frisson, which affects, I believe, all humankind for reasons which we shall come to in a moment. It is similar to but stronger than the guilty pleasure associated with the breaking of any other tabu, as in blasphemy and sexual swearing. If a tabu can be broken under socially acceptable conditions then the excitement associated with it is magnified, especially if those conditions are rather restrictive. At any rate it is agreeable if we can believe that some people do shocking things, even if we dare not do so ourselves. It is interesting that informants from among the B-K themselves expressed distaste or even disgust (see F Porter Poole) when speaking of their own cannibalism (small-scale and highly controlled as it was), even though it was essential in order to sustain and augment their own maleness or femaleness, which was its rationale. But the ambivalence was probably part of the excitement.

I make no claim to be a professional anthropologist, merely a philosophic observer, but perhaps with that proviso I may be allowed a little off-the-cuff analysis going somewhat beyond my specific sources. Firstly it seems to me that the sources make it unlikely that cannibalism was ever formally practised purely for nutritional purposes. Apart from availability there is absolutely no nutritional advantage to humans of human meat over pig meat and the tribes who practise ritual cannibalism are precisely those who do not have any great difficulty in getting adequate amounts of animal meat. There is also the considerable disadvantage that eating of fresh uncooked human flesh carries an appreciable chance of transmitting infections. I will consider the special case of Kuru in a moment but, although the normal stomach is pretty efficient at killing off most infective agents, some viral infections (poliomyelitis, AIDS, hepatitis, infectious diarrhoea) and many bacterial and parasitic ones can certainly be transmitted from foodstuffs taken by mouth; moreover any agents derived from man will be often well or indeed uniquely able to infect men. Many of these agents will be largely eliminated by efficient cooking through, but primitive cooking is evidently seldom efficient, and quite often the ritual of anthropophagy demands uncooked meat anyway. It surprises me that cannibalism has not been eliminated in social evolution for these reasons, but men whether primitive or not always suffer from an over-supply of imagination and generally prefer a fanciful explanation which fits in with their ideological obsessions to a rational one. Cats know better.

Secondly it seems that there are at least two explicit reasons for anthropophagy, depending on whether one is ritually eating one's enemies or one's relations. In the first case, although aimed at adding strength and reproductive force to the eater, it is done almost scornfully, since the prey was defeated anyway, which says little for its potency. In the second case, in Polynesia but apparently not in New Guinea, the ruler was equated with a god and an offering to him was entirely equated with a sacrifice to a god. In the third case which is especially characteristic of female cannibalism it is done altruistically, in order to rejuvenate the spirit of the dead progenitor, hero or neighbour and bring it back into the reproductive cycle.

The case of Kuru is an interesting though not a particularly unique one, except that it has been used to confound sceptics who did not believe in the existence of cannibalism at all. The practice of eating the brains of dead neighbours was established in the relevant New Guinea tribes (Gimi, Fore) as a rite of the third type, confined, like many others to females and pre-adolescents; this practice was thought to strengthen females but actually to be weakening to adult males. Though there is no documentation it is likely that the ritual persisted harmlessly perhaps for centuries until the advent of a quite new, highly stable and intensely virulent slow virus, present in quantity in the brain of sufferers, possibly brought from Europe and possibly derived from or at least related to the virus of Kreutzfeld-Jacob disease, a European virus infection causing, after a long incubation period, senile dementia with rather similar symptoms to Kuru. The sex and time incidence of the disease, confined to women or to men who could as boys have shared their mothers' meal, makes the association with female cannibalism almost certain, though historical evidence is rather sparse

154

(J Farquah and D C Gadjusek 1981 *Kuru* (New York: Raven)) and presumably as a result of indoctrination, both moralistic and hygienic, about the ritual, the disease is now disappearing.

Apart from noting the fact that human meat, whose anatomical source and in particular whether cooked or raw is generally strictly specified by any ritual that we know, I am not competent, as a non-professional, to make any analysis, though such would be I feel highly relevant to the theme of this book. Lévi-Strauss's classic *Le Cru et le Cuit* is the authority in this field, though not the easiest reading in the world, I confess, for the non-expert.

I would conclude by cautiously referring to traces of anthropophagy in Western cultures. I do not mean the anecdotes of 'demon butchers' and so on occurring in long seiges of European towns and in post-war famines, these only show that greed and hunger are at times enough to break any tabu. But after all our ancestors a hundred generations ago were as 'primitive' as any Fijian; we can easily imagine hearing stories that would embarrass us from the lips of a mere hundredth grandfather. It would be surprising if some traces of such practices had not persisted in the 'racial unconscious'. Indeed the story of the Sacrifice of Isaac, which is deeply embedded in the imaginations of my generation at least (though I expect that nowadays most Sunday-school children don't hear the words of Genesis but are given only a sanitized homiletic version), carries the explicit moral that the ritual, though aborted in this case—as it had to be since the whole future of the Chosen People depended upon the survival of the victim—was thought of as perfectly acceptable to Jehovah. Preparations were made for setting a fire under the victim and everything we know of sacrificial rites leads to the expectation of subsequent ritual cannibalism. There are even examples from New Guinea where animal flesh is substituted at some stage for human. Jephthah's daughter is another Biblical example and I do not believe that there is any evidence in the text that what Jephthah really expected his victorious army to meet was just a stray dog, as I was assured by the pious lady who read it to me when I was already too old to be quite easy in my mind about the matter.

Another quite essential reference to anthropophagy in our culture is the Christian Eucharist, though it is bad form to refer to it in this connection. The words of Christ on this are perfectly explicit and carry a charge of great beauty. Christian missionaries have had to face up to this dilemma. Marshall Sahlins (who discusses (*Raw Women and Cooked Man, and other 'Great Things' of the Fiji Islands* 1983 (EC) pp 33–50) the whole question of the relation of sacrifice to anthropophagy with acuteness and authority), says 'it would be difficult to agree with the Christian missionary who, on partaking of the Lord's Supper with a small group of Marquesan converts, thought he was witness to a remarkable religious change, since only a few years before these inveterate cannibals had been eating the flesh of their fellow men: "All had eaten human flesh and drunk the blood of their enemies. They were now sitting at the feet of Jesus, and in their right minds, eating and drinking the emblems of that body which was broken, and that blood which was shed for man" (Coan 1882 : 173) The problem, of course, Sahlins adds, is that cannibalism is always 'symbolic' even when it is 'real' (M Sahlins p 861).

Let me finish with a return to my title, The Feast of Atreus. Atreus of course served up the sons of his brother Thyestes to their father in a pie, as a revenge for some very raw dealing by Thyestes (hence the misfortunes of the House of Atreus all the way down to The Family Reunion). My title was not put in just to give a nice Classical gloss to a bald scientific discussion; but along with the Biblical stories I have referred to, of parents who threaten to kill and eat their children, it may carry much deeper implications. The Ur-tale is that of Chronos (Saturn) who ate his children way back near the beginning of things; many may remember the appalling image by Goya of this myth in, I think, the Prado. When a young mother calls her baby, or a young lover his inamorata, '...... so scrumptious I could eat you!' a love-hunger of possibly dubious origins is being expressed. The art critic who referred to a Boucher nude as 'positively edible' is an unconscious Saturnian.

(G Devereux 1980 The Cannibalistic Impulses in Parents in *Basic Problems of Ethnopsychiatry* (University of Chicago) pp 122–37; see also D Tuzin). G Devereux has convincingly developed the theory that these stories and innumerable others in myth and legend indicate the existence of a neurotic complex, a kind of mirror image of the Oedipus, whereby progeny go in terror of being eaten by their parents, and parents are felt to suppress the impulse to eat their young. The zoological correlates of this have been noted above; male parents consume their young out of rivalry, and female parents out of protectiveness—the nursling is felt to be still insufficiently separated from the maternal substance to be a separable being. From the psychic influence of this complex we may find the strength of the anthropophagy tabu and the guilty fascination of contemplating it. Cooking and eating human flesh is considered a specialty, like incest, of our neighbours next-door but one.

R M Laws

A PERSPECTIVE ON ANTARCTIC COOKERY

When I first went to the Antarctic in 1947 with the Falkland Islands Dependencies Survey (FIDS), now British Antarctic Survey (BAS), it was to spend 25 months on small Signy Island in the South Orkneys. There were only three of us in the first year and four in the second; we took it in turns to be cook for a week at a time. Facilities in general were primitive since, with an open-plan floor area of 12 ft × 24 ft, the kitchen area was naturally very small, though with a solid-fuel Esse cooker. Water was obtained for most of the year by melting snow. The food provided was greatly lacking in variety: tinned stew, tinned meat and vegetables, tinned pilchards, dried, diced vegetables, dried or tinned fruit, rice, flour, spices, pickles and bottled sauces. The only alcohol was an excess of full-strength Navy rum, but we made cider from dried apple rings and baker's yeast.

Because we lacked refrigeration, fresh material soon went off, although we acquired mutton carcasses, some fresh vegetables and fruit when ships visited us, no more than twice a year, we were, however, able to introduce variety by eating off the land, or rather ice!

Delicacies included young crabeater seals, especially filet or liver, leopard seal brains on toast, seal chitterlings (the small intestine of one species is several hundred feet long), fish and shag. The eggs of several sea-birds were appreciated though the whites of penguin eggs are an off-putting translucent bluish-grey and are better in cakes and omelettes than fried or boiled. Particularly to be avoided were giant petrels (flesh or eggs) and elephant seals which, although the subject of my PhD thesis, are repulsive, however cooked.

The following recipes are typical of those employed to make the most of local products. They were taken from Recipes of an Antarctic Cook by Gerald T Cutland (*Polar Record* 9, No 63, pp 562–9). Introducing the article the Editor of *Polar Record* wrote: 'The following recipes have been summarised from notes prepared at the Falkland Islands Dependencies Survey Station at the Argentine Islands, where the writer was a cook in 1956–57. His skill and initiative deserve acclaim among a wider circle. We therefore publish a number of his recipes based on local raw materials.'

TOURNEDOS OF SEAL PORTUGAISE

Seal meat
Garnish: tinned tomatoes, about
  2 per person, tinned peas,
  slices of fried bread

Sauce: 2 oz butter,
  1 tablespoon flour,
  butter and seasoning,
  tomato sauce, milk, salt,
  pepper

Cut meat into round pieces about 1 in thick, season and fry quickly in butter. To prepare garnish: heat tomatoes and peas in butter for a few minutes. To prepare sauce: melt butter in small saucepan and bring to the boil; add flour and cook for a few minutes, stirring continuously; add milk slowly with saucepan away from heat stirring continuously until sauce reaches required thickness; season, and flavour with tomato sauce; return to stove and reheat, but do not boil.

Place each piece of meat on a slice of fried bread and garnish with tomatoes and peas. Top each tournedos with tomato sauce, and pour remainder of sauce round the tournedos.

BRAISED SEAL HEART

Seal hearts   *1/4 cup reconstituted carrot*
6 tomatoes   *1 tablespoon each 'Bovril', flour,*
4 oz beef suet   *salt, pepper*
Water or stock
1/2 cup each reconstituted onion, turnip, peas

Ensure that all blood is washed from hearts and soak them in salt water for 2 or 3 hours. Fry vegetables until brown. Remove vegetables from pan. Cook flour in remaining fat until brown; add water, stock, 'Bovril', salt and pepper, stirring continuously to prevent lumps forming until gravy reaches required thickness. Return vegetables to stewpan and place hearts on top almost covering with gravy. Cover and simmer for 2 or 3 hours. Slice hearts for serving.

SAVOURY SEAL BRAINS ON TOAST

1 brain   *1 dsp tomato sauce*
3 reconstituted eggs   *3 oz butter*
Grated cheese, toast   *Salt, pepper, grated nutmeg*

The brains should be a milkish white colour, apart from the veins visible on the surface. Wash thoroughly in salt water removing loose skin and blood, then soak in fresh water for an hour, changing the water two or three times. Place in lined saucepan and cover with water, adding enough salt and vinegar to flavour the water, bring to the boil, and boil slowly for 15 minutes. Dry the brain on a cloth ready for cooking.

Chop brains into small pieces and mix with eggs, tomato sauce and nutmeg. Melt butter in pan and add mixture, cook for a minute or two, stirring continuously. Serve on hot buttered toast sprinkled with grated cheese.

ESCALOPES OF PENGUIN

Penguin breasts	*Batter*
Reconstituted onion	*Flour*
Salt and pepper	*Beef suet*
Milk	*1 tin mushroom soup*

Cut breasts in slices and soak in milk for about 2 hours. Dry, season and flour on both sides. Mix onion in batter. Roll meat in batter and fry in deep fat. Pour the mushroom soup over meat as sauce.

The diet now provided at the BAS Antarctic stations is very similar to what is eaten at home in Britain. Variety is somewhat less because all food has to be brought in infrequently by ship (in the case of the most remote station only once a year); fresh fruit and vegetables are therefore of very limited availability and meat is frozen, dried or tinned.

Professional full-time cooks produce a wide range of dishes representing a variety of national cuisines, from French to Indian. The kinds of food provided have changed. Walk-in deep freezes (even installed at Halley Station which is 60 ft down within the shelf ice) mean that a wide variety of frozen foods can be kept year round. To some extent the diet reflects changing tastes in the UK, and increasing interest in foreign foods such as pasta and rice in place of potatoes and a wider range of herbs and spices. The personnel on our stations probably feed better than their contemporaries in Cambridge colleges.

While they are working mainly inside the station building only about 3000 calories a day are needed; travelling with a dog sledge might call for up to 5000 calories a day; while skidoo[†] travel which is now the rule requires only about 3800 calories. Captain Scott's party man-hauling to the pole in 1912 were on a daily ration of 257 g protein, 210 g fat, 417 g carbohydrate providing 4600 calories. (Skidoo travellers today have 105 g, 190 g and 420 g respectively.)

The early explorers managed mainly on salted or dried meat and biscuits. Captain Scott's sledging rations in 1912 consisted only of pemmican, biscuits, butter, sugar, cocoa and tea. Pemmican was

† Skidoo is a 'motorized toboggan' with handlebars and tracks instead of wheels. It is the polar equivalent of a motorbike, but can pull heavy loads over the ice/snow—say 1000 lbs.

originally developed from a North American Indian recipe based on dried caribou meat, fat and wild berries, pounded together to make a bar. As used later by Polar travellers it was made from dried beef and beef fat and added vitamins. We were still using it in the 1950s. For present-day sledge travel rations are light, compact, easy and quick to prepare (to save fuel). The food is well-packed in standard BAS sledging ration boxes to last for twenty man-days. There are three kinds of freeze-dried meat, several varieties of dried soup, dried vegetables, rice, tea, coffee, drinking chocolate, orange drink, biscuits, chocolate, butter, sugar, dried milk and multivitamin tablets supplemented by a few extra 'goodies' to personal taste. Water is from melting snow and paraffin primus stoves are still the most dependable and compact system. These special sledging rations are expensive and it costs almost twice as much to feed a person at a field camp as it does at a research station.

Miriam Rothschild

WHALE'S MILK FOR BREAKFAST

At a certain period of my life I became profoundly interested in milk and my notebook was filled with strange pieces of information.

1. Life of a milk bottle. Average 34.58 trips (largely to replace broken ones $12,500,000 worth were purchased by dealers in the USA in 1937).
2. Elephant's milk is the sweetest—human milk next. Milk contains 90 times as much sugar as blood.
3. 3 lb of blood passes through the udders of a cow every 52 seconds so 200 lbs per hour.
4. Annual consumption of milk in Iceland 666 pints per capita. UK about half that.

At breakfast we tried out different sorts of milk. Thus we compared the taste of Jersey Cow and Short Horn milk, Freisian Cow and Kerry Cow milk, ass's milk and goat's milk. We even tried 'pigeon's milk' which in appearance and consistency resembles cottage cheese, but has a disagreeable sour taste of fermenting cereals—it completely lacks sugar. 'Pigeon's milk' is produced in the crops of both male and female birds and curiously enough is controlled by the same hormone as human milk, namely prolactin.

Great was the excitement when it was announced that the Lanes were about to become the first family in the UK to drink whale's milk for breakfast.

Derek Frazer and Professor Huggett had been to the Faroe Isles to conduct some scientific investigations on the female animals brought ashore by the local inhabitants. Derek Frazer had secured the milk and had preserved it in a thermos flask which was despatched to Elsfield from St Mary's Hospital. We all knew that whale's milk was as solid as blue cheese and had to be eaten not drunk. It was 49% fat and was squeezed into the baby's mouth from the mother's teat, like toothpaste out of a plastic tube. This is a practical solution of the difficulties involved in suckling under water. It avoids a loss of milk flowing into the sea, or conversely the

baby whale imbibing gulps of salt water rather than its mother's milk. Furthermore, all mammals, such as seals, which live in cold waters, have a very high concentration of fat in their milk, which is consequently solid rather than fluid.

The moment I handled the hospital thermos I knew something was wrong. There was a sloshing-around sound in the body of the flask suggesting water rather than thick cream or cheese. I gingerly unscrewed the top and looked in. The children craned their necks and held out their plates. Inside the thermos was a transparent yellow fluid, the colour of sweet Rhine wine. There had been a mix-up of bottles at St Mary's and we were about to serve whale's urine instead of milk! Eventually the right container was located and despatched to us. Whale's milk, as anticipated, was solid as Stilton cheese. It could no longer be described as fresh, and perhaps it was not a fair trial for taste and flavour. Small chunks were eaten very thoughtfully and voted revolting, and compared with rancid soap.

In the afternoon there was a party at All Souls College and I passed round the jar, offering a prize to anyone who could identify the contents correctly. There was not a single guess which came within even reasonable distance of the correct answer. So much for the great brains of Oxford. Next day the Royal Entomological Society did better. The jar was again handed round. It stopped in the grasp of the President, the late Norman Riley. 'This', he announced confidently, 'is cheese. But it's not one I have ever smelled before.' He won the prize, a bottle of Claret, Lafite 1947.

John Krebs

BIRDS AS FOOD

My gastronomic experience of the class Aves, like that of many of my readers, is restricted to a very small proportion of the 8800 living species. We have all eaten domesticated species such as chicken, turkey, duck, goose and quail, and some of us have sampled various species of wild duck, pigeon, and game birds such as grouse, pheasant, partridge, woodcock or snipe. But even the most experienced gourmet is unlikely to have eaten more than a dozen species and will almost certainly not have tasted our commonest native birds. Such culinary conservatism is of relatively recent origin in Britain. In the last century wheatears were served by dozens at inns in Sussex (W Yarrell 1839 *A History of British Birds* (London)), while in an earlier time (1519–1605) white storks and herons were served to the Lords of the Star Chamber and Sir Thomas Browne was said to be partial to young bittern (H B Cott 1946 The edibility of birds: illustrated by five years' experiments and observations (1941–1946) on the food preferences of hornet, cat and man; and considered with special reference to the theories of adaptive colouration *Proc. Zool. Soc. Lond.* **116** 371–524). The house sparrow used not only to be consumed with gusto, but was considered to be a powerful aphrodisiac: 'The sparrow is a full hot bird and lecherous, and the flesh of them oft taken in meat exciteth to carnal lust' (Seager 1896, cited in J D Summers Smith 1963 *The Houesparrow* (London: Collins)). Why have British eating habits with respect to birds become so narrow minded? In other parts of Western Europe, most notoriously Italy, millions of small birds belonging to perhaps more than a 100 different species are still slaughtered annually for culinary purposes. Although today the major lobby against harvesting wild birds comes from conservationists, this, being a rather recent development, cannot have been the original cause of the decline in bird-eating. More probably it was associated, as was the parallel decline in the variety of fish species eaten in Britain, with the general movement of the population away from the countryside into large cities and the consequent dependence of most people on mass-produced, easily transportable food.

I am as keen on conservation as the next man and I do not want to advocate adoption in Britain of bird-hunting on the Italian scale, but let me just consider for a moment what kind of harvest could be achieved from our common wild birds without detriment to their populations.

Numerically the most abundant birds in Britain are several species of songbirds. At least 10 of our native species have winter populations in excess of 10 million birds, including an estimated 30 million chaffinches, 37 million starlings, 25 million skylarks, 15 million house sparrows, 20 million hedge sparrows and 14 million blackbirds (P Lack 1986 *The Atlas of Wintering Birds in Britain and Ireland* (Calton: T and A D Poyser)). Harvesting at the right level does not have an adverse effect on natural populations because it simply replaces other, natural, causes of death such as starvation, predation or disease, which are more severe at high than low population sizes. In a typical small bird such as the robin, about half the adults and four fifths of the youngsters die each year and, because this mortality is proportional to population density if some of the birds were harvested, the survival rate of the remainder would increase. Taking the 80 gram starling as an example, a conservative estimate would be that an annual yield of 100,000 kg (1.25 million birds) could be taken without affecting the size of the British population. Since the starling is an agricultural pest and is slaughtered in considerable numbers in many parts of Europe for this reason, one might even wish to advocate a heavier cropping regime. While this kind of quantity is not going to provide a staple diet for the population, it does represent a fairly substantial crop for the gourmet market, similar in size to the annual harvest of red grouse. The herring gull at 900 grams, is one of our commonest large birds. It has a breeding population of about 300,000, but has been increasing at an alarming 15% per annum. Culling the breeding adults to keep a steady population would yield 40,000 kg per annum and probably twice this could safely be harvested by taking young birds before other kinds of mortality have acted.

This shows that there is some potential for harvesting wild birds that are not currently taken, but are starlings and herring gulls gourmet food? In general, which birds are likely to taste good and which are not? Opinions on the answer to the first question differ. According to some authorities, starlings taste bitter (H A Macpherson 1897 *A History of Fowling* (Edinburgh)) while others find them good if they are decapitated immediately (see Cott 1946) or if they have recently been feeding on fruit (Macpherson 1897). Herring gulls are reported to be excellent if eaten young (Cott 1946). The second question, the palatibility of birds in general, was analysed in some detail by the Cambridge zoologist Hugh Cott during the Second World War (Cott 1946). Finding himself in North Africa and the Middle East, Cott used his spare time testing the edibility of bird carcasses of some forty species to two kinds of predator: hornets and cats. Remarkably, he found not only that cats and hornets tended to agree in their preference when presented with a pair of carcasses, but also that the relative palatability of the various species to humans was broadly correlated with the hornet—cat ranking. Top of the gourmet league were skylarks, wrynecks (a small brown woodpecker—rather rare in Britain), house sparrows and greenfinches, while propping up the bottom of the table (no pun intended) were hoopoes, kingfishers, golden orioles and several black and white desert chats (relatives of the wheatear).

Cott's conclusion was that among small vulnerable species, conspicuous birds are less palatable than inconspicuous species. If, however, one moves to large species such as storks, geese and gulls the relationship between conspicuousness and nastiness breaks down. The interpretation of this suggested by Cott is that small palatable species have evolved crypsis as a means of escaping predators, while potentially vulnerable but inedible birds have evolved bright warning colours to deter predators, analogous to the black and yellow warning stripes of a wasp. Large species such as storks and gulls are not at risk anyway, so do not have to conceal their edibility behind a cryptic costume. This general picture is undoubtedly a simplification: age, diet and a host of other factors complicate the story, but as a first approximation, if you are stuck on a desert island wondering which birds to try to capture and eat, avoid the kingfishers and go for the species referred to by professional bird-watchers as 'LBJs' (Little Brown Jobs).

I do not expect my essay to persuade supermarkets and chainstores to stock sparrow, gull and skylark in the immediate future, but I am sure they will continue to sell that dullest (and therefore most challenging) of meats: frozen, battery chicken. Here is a simple version of tarragon chicken that uses chicken as a vehicle for other tastes and textures and provides a good entertainment while your guests try to work out what is in the stuffing.

Ingredients: 6 half chicken breasts, 3 courgettes, 3 teaspoons of dried tarragon (you can use fresh, but tarragon is one of the herbs that doesn't lose its flavour when dried), 50 g butter, 150 ml whipping cream, 200 ml chicken stock, 150 ml white wine.

Method: Skin the chicken breasts and slit part way down one side to make a pouch. Grate the courgette with a coarse grater, mix with the tarragon and fry for 1 min in the butter stirring continually. Season with salt and pepper. Stuff each chicken breast with about 1 dessertspoonful of courgette—tarragon stuffing and use a wooden cocktail stick to stitch the pouch closed. Arrange the chicken pieces in a dish and pour over the stock and wine to almost cover. Cover with foil and cook in a medium-hot oven for 40 minutes, by which time the chicken should be done and the stuffing will not have gone soggy. Decant the liquid, reduce by half and thicken with cream. Pour over the chicken and serve.

Richard Keynes

THE CHEQUERED HISTORY OF THE TYPE SPECIMEN OF RHEA DARWINII

From a letter from the artist Conrad Martens to his brother, Henry, written on board HMS *Beagle*, March 19, 1834: 'While here, as there was but little to be done in the way of sketching, I used generally to take my gun and was fortunate enough one day to bring home an ostrich, the only one indeed which as yet we had been able to kill, although great numbers had been seen. It was a young one and excellent eating.'

Charles Darwin, writing in Volume II of the *Zoology of the Voyage of HMS Beagle*, p 124: 'When at Port Desire in Patagonia (Lat 48°), Mr. Martens shot an ostrich; I looked at it, and from most unfortunately forgetting at the moment the whole subject of the Petises, thought it was a two-third grown one of the common sort. The bird was skinned and cooked before my memory returned. But the head, neck, legs, wings, many of the larger feathers, and a large part of the skin, had been preserved. From these a very nearly perfect specimen has been put together, and is now exhibited in the museum of the Zoological Society.'

From *The Beagle Record* by R D Keynes

J F Dewey

THE LENTIL

The lentil, a dried legume seed, is used, principally in Asia, to generate an immense variety of delicious and elegant dishes. Its

167

particular appeal is in its inherent simplicity upon which a subtle variety of cooking and flavouring techniques are imprinted. Generally, the dried pulses, beans, peas and lentils, should be picked over, washed and rehydrated before cooking although soaking is less important for lentils. At an early stage in the cooking, most pulses must be boiled vigorously for about ten minutes to break down their toxic lectins; this can be reduced to a very brief boiling for lentils which are low in lectins. The ingredients that I prefer and use in many combinations are: green, yellow or red lentils, finely chopped onion, macerated garlic, crushed root ginger, green chillies, tomatoes, tomato purée, black pepper, paprika, cayenne, turmeric, chilli powder, coriander, cumin, cardamom (these last three both in powder and/or seed form), fresh lemon juice and a good quality light cooking oil. I do not use salt because it reduces the subtle flavours of the spices. No recipes *per se* or quantities are given because these can be varied enormously to give a wide variety of textures and flavours.

The basic technique is, sequentially: fry the onions and garlic until transparent, but not browned, in a modest amount of oil, then add and gently cook the green chilli and ginger if used, add the spice combination of the day and cook gently to a thick paste that begins to stick to the pan, adding tomato paste and tomatoes, if used, at a late stage. Now deglaze the pan with boiling water and/or a little white wine and progressively add water until you have a vigorously boiling low-viscosity aromatic fluid. Now add the washed and rehydrated lentils and bring to the boil for a few minutes, then simmer until cooked, up to a maximum of thirty minutes. During early boiling, a frothy scum will rise to the surface; this may be removed to prevent a slightly 'gritty' final texture. Lentils may be cooked without the initial onion, garlic and spice frying; simply boil, then simmer all ingredients together for up to thirty minutes. Lentils soften and cook more quickly than other pulses and, if integral lentils are required, should not be overcooked. However, they may be cooked and/or mashed to a puree or soup in the Indian fashion. The cooked lentil dish may be finished with lemon juice and garnished with a vinaigrette dressing, finely chopped eggs, parsley, fresh coriander or chives. Lentil dishes may be puréed later as wonderful cold dips and as an accompaniment to other foods, particularly if refreshed with lemon juice and chopped parsley. They may be used also as 'body' for meatloaf dishes or can be baked or recooked as croquettes or pancakes. Above all, lentils are the most flexible and delicious of foodstuffs to which I have been addicted for many years. This article is an attempt to spread that addiction.

David Walker

IN PRAISE OF FRESH HERBS

A plant physiologist ought, you might suppose, to be able to take advantage of his craft when it comes to salads. (A plant physiologist, by the way, is one who pretends to be a biochemist when he is talking to botanists and a botanist when he is talking to biochemists, whereas, in reality, he is neither one thing nor the other.) Perhaps the application of his knowledge to salads may seem so slight and superficial that it is hardly worth noting but strangely enough even these trivia can make a remarkable difference.

I assume that our readers will agree that the dressing is probably more important than the salad itself and that garlic is an essential element of most dressings. If so, they will have none of this nonsense of rubbing the bowl with a piece of garlic and who wishes to go to the trouble of cleaning a garlic press? Instead you should slice a clove of garlic (this in itself facilitates peeling) and crush it, with a fork, in a teaspoonful of salt and half a teaspoonful of sugar against the side of the bowl. Leave this for twenty minutes (if you can) and osmosis and autolysis will combine to reduce the garlic to a fine white pulp which, in the presence of oil and vinegar (about 3.5 to 1), will yield a fairly stable emulsion. The vinegar, of course, has to be tarragon and tarragon, as every botanist will tell you, is as variable as the legendary durian. For many years I visited Robert Hill (a fellow Fellow of great eminence) every June for the pleasure of his company and the fact that he maintained three varieties of tarragon of such subtle flavour that when a sprig of each was left to mature in white vinegar for a few months even the aroma when the bottle was opened would have been almost enough to revive a dead fish (this is its next best use).

You should also grow basil, one of the few herbs that will do well in a pot on the kitchen window-sill during the winter, because you need this to go with the tomato which you will slice into the bowl. Personally, I often get carried away and throw in finely chopped parsley and celery and a touch of fresh coriander but then I never use precisely the same ingredients or the same proportions because a good salad should be as infinitely variable as a good wine. But, unlike wines, dressings do not improve with age (at least not after the first hour) and yesterday's crushed garlic is almost as much of an abomination as dried mint. That, of course, is all to do with post-harvest physiology—a subject too complex even to contemplate.

Finally, there is the lettuce. No one should waste a good dressing on monstrosities like 'Webbs Wonder' or 'Iceberg'. If you can, grow something exceptional like 'Tom Thumb'. If you have to rely on limp lettuce from a shop let osmosis come to your rescue again. Roughly torn leaves immersed in water will regain full turgor in 20 to 30 minutes. If they are then bundled into a tea towel and whirled violently about the head they will emerge as though they had been freshly picked on a May morning.

N W Pirie

POPULARISING UNCONVENTIONAL FOODS

Foods which are traditional in some communities may be unknown, ignored, called novel, or even abhorred, in others. Factors such as these, which restrict and retard widespread acceptance, change at curiously varied rates. Change may even be cyclical with alternating praise and denigration (Pirie 1984). Evidence from communities which have not yet been much affected by 'development' suggests that people initially chose an extensive range of food sources. They may use 50 to 100 plant species and most of the birds, fish, insects, mammals, molluscs and reptiles available locally. With urbanisation, and an unfortunate tendency to copy the food habits of foreign rulers or advisors, the number of plant species shrinks to a dozen or less and the number of animals to 3 or 4. Those communities lucky enough to become prosperous then increase the range of choice and approach the dietary variety made possible by modern supermarkets. Such variety is itself novel—as anyone who remembers shopping 50 or 60 years ago will agree. The important point is that, in spite of reiterated statements to the contrary, food habits are flexible. What agents bend them?

The intrinsic merits of a foodstuff are obviously relevant although they are seldom given prime importance. Maize and manioc spread so rapidly through Africa, on their merits, that they were often assumed to be indigenous. On the other hand, several years elapsed before as broadminded an observer as Arthur Young was convinced that potatoes were edible: it is said that tomatoes languished in unpopularity until the rumour started that they were aphrodisiac. Public opinion about the merits of foods is notoriously unsound. Nevertheless, it is a pity that these opinions have so little effect on what is eaten. For example: majority opinion holds that wholemeal bread is nutritionally preferable to white bread, but more white bread is eaten. Sober publicity for the real merits of a novel food is therefore unlikely to have much effect. It would be overpowered by the flamboyance of commercially motivated advertising. Furthermore, advertisers repeat their case daily: a scientist doing that would meet general disapproval.

Several countries are now moving, but with no obvious sign of haste, towards having scientifically based nutrition policies. Norway has probably moved furthest along this commendable route; nevertheless, fifty times as much is spent on advertising by food firms there as by the government on advice. It may be argued that advertisers and advisors have different objectives. One is trying to push a novelty into an already saturated market, whereas the other, in ideal cases at any rate, being aware of local malnutrition, would be calling attention to an underused resource. Scientists could learn something from advertisers but, because of their connections with government, they should not copy advertisers' techniques too closely or they will be accused of being dictatorial. Scientists have the advantage that they can more easily influence what is served in canteens, school meals etc. Novelties have often been accepted into the standard diet after being offered discreetly at first as an optional extra. Failures are inevitable. In spite of their wealth and experience, food firms succeed with only a tenth of their innovations. Failures happen with a specific product, presented in a specific manner, to one group in one place at one time. The outcome could have been different had any factor been different.

171

Only those novel foods which could make a practical contribution to nutrition in countries where there is now malnutrition are worthy of serious attention. Seeds are the dominant food throughout the world. Those which are most widely used become edible after minimal preparation and cooking, there are traditional methods for fermenting others to make them edible. Some, e.g. khesari (*Lathyrus sativus*) which contains a crippling neurotoxin, can be made edible if cooked in the manner suggested by Sir Hugh Platt (1596) '... boile your beanes, pease, beechmast, & c. in faire water ... and the second or third boyling, you shall finde a strange alteration in taste, for the water hath sucked out and imbibed the greatest part of their rankness ...'. The method is traditional in Brazil where the jack bean (*Canavalia ensiformis*) is called the 'seven water bean'. Processing such seeds in expensive and elaborate equipment is irrelevant though often profitable. The rich do not need the products: the poor could not afford them. What is being supplied when they are made is convenience rather than nutrition.

Projects which conflict with the basic principles of physics are equally irrelevant. Thus algae should be exploited if they grow locally. Bernal Diaz, who accompanied Cortez in the conquest of Mexico, described the use of *Spirulina* there (Pirie 1962). Although Lotka (1925) had an admirably quantitiative approach to most subjects, he led many scientists astray by suggesting the artificial cultivation of algae as a preferable alternative to growing conventional plants. The idea has been taken up, and abandoned, in most of the warmer parts of the world. It should have been obvious from the start that conventional plants, with ample leaf surface to catch light and CO_2, would outyield a monolayer of algae given comparable levels of cosseting. The cultivation of micro-organisms on petroleum is similarly absurd for physical reasons. About half the heat that would have been produced had the petroleum been burnt, has to be disposed of without allowing the temperature of the vat to exceed the tolerance of the micro-organisms. They, especially those which make mycelia, have a place among unconventional foods, but they will have to be grown on substrates such as the sugars or methanol which are already partly oxidised.

The most useful unconventional foods would be made from something which is already available but unused or underused. It is a pity that more groundnuts are consumed (mainly as peanut

172

butter) per head in USA than in India, although India is a major producer. Cotton seed was little used as human food until Incaparina was devised (Shaw 1970). In spite of the modest and self-denying honesty of publicity for the product, it is extensively sold in Central America. The idea of using cotton seed, except as animal feed, seems not to have caught on elsewhere. Ideally, preparative methods should be simple enough for use by poor and relatively unskilled people.

It is now thought unconventional to use dark green leaves as more than a colourful adjunct to a meal; the usual reason given for advocating more extensive use is that they supply vitamins and minerals. The presence in them of 20 to 30% protein (calculated on the dry matter), and similar amounts of starch, is overlooked. This neglect is new. Some figures for the amounts eaten by communities not yet afflicted by consenting culinary colonialism are collected elsewhere (Pirie 1981). A Transvaal proverb (Waldmann 1975) 'Meat is a visitor, but *morogo* (the local name for a 'spinach') is daily food' states the earlier situation succinctly. The main reason for advocating the rehabilitation of leafy vegetables is that they can give a greater annual yield of edible material than any other method of using land.

Plants are not the only source of underused foods which could be popularised. A few fish are poisonous; always or intermittently. These should be shunned except by experts. Otherwise, the vertebrates raise no real problems. Prejudices for and against some species are widespread but wholly irrational and unworthy of further discussion. Popularisation of invertebrates will not become an important issue until methods for ensuring a more abundant supply have been worked out. Their potential is enormous. Marine molluscs, e.g. mussels, depend largely on the 1.5×10^{12} tonnes of organic detritus suspended in the oceans. That renewable resource could be more fully exploited if mussels were given more attachment sites by erecting fences, or suspending ropes, in suitable coastal waters. This is already being done on a small scale, it gets less attention than the more glamourous activity of fish farming. It will be more difficult to harvest the deep water cephalopods on a large scale. E J Denton (1974) assembles evidence that sperm whales eat more than 150 megatonnes of cephalopods annually, and that the total population must weigh much more although this group of animals seems to be rare.

173

My personal experience is confined to the popularisation of protein extracted from leaves (LP). This is not proposed as a substitute for leafy vegetables, prepared in the normal manner, but as a supplement to them. It is now generally agreed that many people in industrialised countries eat too little fibre for the proper functioning of their guts. Nevertheless, there are limits. Structural fibre in leaves restricts consumption to an amount which would supply only 2 to 4 g of protein daily. That is not insignificant, it is as much as fish supply in the UK. LP contains little fibre, about 60% protein, and a useful amount of carotene (Pirie 1987); 10 to 20 g is the usual amount eaten. In many parts of the world, the carotene (provitamin A) is as important as the protein: vitamin A deficiency blinds 0.5 million people (mainly infants) annually. The technique of extraction is simple enough to be a village, or even family, process (Joshi *et al* 1984, Fellows *et al* 1986, Pirie 1987).

Artificial and real problems arise with novel foods. Before work can start in a region, the interest of officials must be aroused. They tend to assume that, as J A Lovern (1969) phrased it '... to be acceptable to the poverty-stricken, protein-starved peoples of the world a food must also be acceptable to the sophisticated palates (and even to the aesthetic concepts) of the well-fed.' That is the artificial problem: the real problems involve a study of local dietary habits to see where and how an unconventional food can be fitted in neatly, and with which conventional components it will be complementary. For example: LP, like several legume seed proteins, is somewhat deficient in sulphur amino acids, whereas maize and wheat grains are relatively rich in them. Experiments on rats confirm that LP and wheat are complementary.

Tasting panels can judge no more than the extent to which the qualities of a well-known existing food have been mimicked by one containing a novel component. Shah *et al* (1981), in Pakistan, were very successful in introducing LP in a manner which satisfied a tasting panel. We (Morrison and Pirie 1960, Byers *et al* 1965) approached the artificial problem by making things which looked interesting, could be eaten in one or two bites, and were portable so that they could be demonstrated away from the laboratory. LP is very dark green, it can be decolourised but the carotene would then be lost. A dark colour causes less comment when pieces are small. My technique of presentation is simple and effective. Instead of politely offering what we had made to visitors first, I, while still

174

explaining the merits of LP, started eating. After a few seconds one of the visitors invariably said 'Could I have some too?'; all the rest then joined in. If personal initiative is not encouraged in that manner, there is more initial hesitation and suspicious nibbling of minute pieces instead of straightforward eating.

In Papua New Guinea I met some resistance to LP from charming, able, and conventionally minded Australian nurses, but none from local children. At a school where English was taught, I handed out samples. When they were eaten I said 'Who would like another one?'. Every hand went up. In a village, I wandered round munching. Children followed expectantly and ate all I had with me. No problems arose with feeding trials in India (Doraiswamy *et al* 1969, Devadas *et al* 1978). The subjects in these trials were in institutions: valid measurements of growth etc. can be made in no other way. The charity 'Find Your Feet' (FYF) has organised and/or supported LP production, and use by people coming voluntarily for it, in Bolivia, Ghana, India, Mexico and Sri Lanka; projects elsewhere are being planned. As before, there were no problems when familiar foods, fortified with LP, were intelligently presented[†].

Successful popularisation depends to some extent on the enthusiasm of those who started work on LP and of Carol Martin, the chairman of FYF. It depends still more on the presence of a local enthusiast and a suitable local climate. The two do not always coincide. LP can be made from many different species but, in a semi-arid environment, none give lush growth. Without it, protein extraction, though possible, is not easy. The acceptability and nutritive value of LP are now thoroughly established. Nevertheless, we cannot claim that popularisation has been successful until, in suitable climatic regions where there is protein shortage, production units run throughout the growing season with no more outside subvention than is enjoyed by other aspects of agriculture.

† A 45 minute video showing some of this work is available from 'Find Your Feet', 13–15 Frognal, London NW3.

References

Blythe C 1978 Norwegian nutrition and food policy *Food Policy* **3** 163
Byers M, Green S H and Pirie N W 1965 The presentation of leaf protein on the table. II *Nutrition* **19** 63

Denton E J 1974 On buoyancy and the lives of modern and fossil cephalopods *Proc. R. Soc.* B **185** 273

Devadas R P, Kupputhai A and Sebastian S 1978 Effect of leaf protein on nitrogen retention in pre-school children *Ind. J. Nutr. Dietet.* **15** 107

Doraiswamy T R, Singh N and Daniel V A 1969 Effects of supplementing ragi (*Eleusine coracana*) diets with lysine or leaf protein on the growth and nitrogen metabolism of children *Br. J. Nutr.* **23** 737

Fellows P J, Davys M N G and Bray W 1986 The use of leaf protein as human food In *Recent Advances in Leaf Protein Research* ed I Tasaki (Nagoya: Iroha)

Joshi R N, Savangikar V A and Patunkar B W 1984 The Bidkin green crop fractionation process *Ind. Bot. Reporter* **3** 136

Lotka A J 1925 *Elements of Physical Biology* (Baltimore: Williams and Wilkins)

Lovern J A 1969 Problems in the development of fish protein concentrates *Proc. Nutr. Soc.* **28** 81

Morrison J E and Pirie N W 1960 The presentation of leaf protein on the table *Nutrition* **14** 7

Pirie N W 1962 Indigenous foods *Adv. Sci.* **18** 467

——1981 The need for more information about vegetables In *Vegetable Productivity* ed C R W Spedding (London: Macmillan)

——1984 Fluctuating food fashions *Interdisciplinary Sci. Rev.* **9** 149

——1987 *Leaf Protein and its By-products in Human and Animal Nutrition* (London: Cambridge University Press)

Platt H 1596 *Sundrie New and Artificial Remedies Against Famine*

Shah F H, Sheikh A S, Farrukh N and Rasool A 1981 A comparison of leaf protein fortified dishes and milk as supplements for children with nutritionally inadequate diets *Plant Foods Hum. Nutr.* **30** 245

Shaw R L 1970 The acceptability of Incaparina *Prot. Adv. Grp. Bull.* **9** 16

Waldmann E 1975 The ecology of the nutrition of the Bapedi, Sekhukuniland *Ecol. Food Nutr.* **4** 139

Sector VII Meals—Memorable or Otherwise

TWO VIEWS OF THE AMERICAN BREAKFAST

Geoffrey Dawes

Many years ago, when first I visited the United States, I soon discovered that the most delicious thing to eat there was breakfast. Ordering a 'gourmet' meal in a restaurant might prove a sad disappointment, thirty years ago. Of course, steak was almost universally good, and the amount, by our post-war European standards, impossibly lavish. However, I found, for instance, that the menu's 'tender little green peas, plucked at dawn and served with herbs for your pleasure', would prove to have been frozen, ready-minted, that sauces were not attempted, and that dessert meant ice-cream. The instinct for survival led to the discovery that in the modest little hotel in Manhattan where I stayed there was always a meal to be had of eggs, over or sunnyside up, bacon, tomato and links, with 'English' muffins and marmalade, all on the same plate and all first-rate.

Perhaps it is the formative nature of my earliest travels that have led me to become a breakfast cook. I have added mushrooms and—*horribile dictu*—fried bread to the Harbour Bar menu, and I allow a separate plate for home-made bread rolls and ginger marmalade, but I have tried to keep my breakfasts as sizzling hot as

177

theirs, so far, of course, as the arrival of the family at breakfast permits. Despite Calverley, I often feel that 'Fate cannot touch me, I have breakfasted today.'

Benjamin Franklin (1706–1790)

VINDEX PATRIAE, a writer in your paper, comforts himself, and the India Company, with the fancy, that the Americans, should they resolve to drink no more tea, can by no means keep that Resolution, their Indian corn not affording "an agreeable, or easy digestible breakfast." Pray let me, an American, inform the gentleman, who seems ignorant of the matter, that Indian corn, take it for all in all, is one of the most agreeable and wholesome grains in the world; that its green leaves roasted are a delicacy beyond expression; that samp, hominy, succatash, and nokehock, made of it, are so many pleasing varieties; and that johnny or hoecake, hot from the fire, is better than a Yorkshire muffin—But if Indian corn were as disagreeable and indigestible as the Stamp Act, does he imagine we can get nothing else for breakfast?—Did he never hear that we have oatmeal in plenty, for water gruel or burgoo; as good wheat, rye and barley as the world affords, to make frumenty; or toast and ale; that there is every where plenty of milk, butter and cheese; that rice is one of our staple commodities; that for tea, we have sage and bawm in our gardens, the young leaves of the sweet white hickery or walnut, and, above all, the buds of our pine, infinitely prefer-able to any tea from the Indies; while the islands yield us plenty of coffee and chocolate?—Let the gentleman do us the honour of a visit in America, and I will engage to breakfast him every day in the month with a fresh variety, without offering him either tea or Indian corn.

From a letter to the *London Gazetteer* of 2 January 1766.

R M Laws

A BARBECUE ON A LARGE SCALE

This is a true story which draws on my experiences in North America and East Africa. I was in Texas, staying with my old friend Professor Sayed el Sayed (an oceanographer well away from the ocean) at College Station. One evening we went out for a steak dinner at a plain and basic restaurant—board floor, checked gingham tablecloths and excellent barbecued T-bone steaks.

During the meal the proprietor suggested that we might like to see his kitchen facilities around at the back. There was a splendid stainless steel marinading cabinet and other equipment, but his pride was clearly the barbecue pit—a new term to me—of which he was inordinately proud. It was, he said, 'The biggest barbecue pit in Texas'. Although it was indeed splendid I couldn't resist the temptation to compare it with my facilities in Uganda when I was engaged on my research on elephants. I told him that we had had a much larger set-up altogether. First, I said, we dug a pit in the ground 15 yards by 5 and several feet deep. Next we brought in a large number of trees for fuel and made a fire. We then shot ten elephants and barbecued them in the pit—which took a long time of course. The meat was distributed to a large number of local people and was received with delight; we did this most nights. He was at a loss for words, but looked at me rather strangely and I returned to my meal. My host Sayed followed in a little while and said 'You've really upset him. He says "I don't know whether that Limey is pulling my leg or not"'. Sayed assured him I wasn't—but every time he goes back to that steak bar the proprietor raises it again—'That godamned Limey was pulling my leg wasn't he?'

The irony is that it was all true. In the course of my work we culled large numbers of elephants for management and research purposes. The elephant population was destroying the habitat it depended on—so there were thousands upon thousands of dead Terminalia trees for fuel. To help pay for the operation we sold the carcasses to a local butcher who cut them up and smoked great quantities of meat in these large pits for sale to the local population. I'm sure that Texan is still uncertain though!

179

William Mitchell

'THEY ORDER THIS MATTER BETTER IN FRANCE'†

Although I knew that, of course, chance plays an overwhelming part in life, I did not anticipate that a decision in 1972 to develop a new line of research would lead to one of the greatest gastronomic experiences of my life. The common thread in my earlier research had been the way that *disorder* in a predominantly ordered system determines its physical properties. During three years spent in Bristol doing this work I was exposed to the pervading influence of Nevill Mott and got to know Jacques Friedel. In the 1970s, stimulated and helped by new techniques (neutron scattering, laser light scattering, computer simulation) I embarked on a new line of research in Reading and later in Oxford, on the study of small amounts of *order* in a disordered system rather than the opposite.

One of the two groups which were already looking at this problem was that of Madame Dupuy in Lyon and therefore one was not totally surprised to receive a request from Madame Dupuy to become a member of the jury for the *Doctorat d'Etat* thesis of her colleague, Derrien. I jumped at the opportunity because there were some differences in our work which had not been fully reconciled and the chance of discussing Derrien's thesis in detail, both formally and informally, was too good to be missed.

I had already taken part in two *soutenances de thèse* in Paris and my infelicity with spoken French had, amongst our closer French acquaintances, given rise to an amicable tolerance of the traditional English eccentric linguistic incompetence. My wife is a Professor of French who ranks amongst the home grown French scholars in the study of French poetry. The combination is part of the eccentricity to which our friends responded—how together could I be so bad and Margaret so brilliant? Nevertheless, off we went to Lyon.

The jury duly assembled at 10.00 AM, led by Jacques Friedel who since those Bristol days followed a brilliant career in theoretical studies of defects and disorder in materials and who had married Nevill Mott's sister-in-law. Of course the French 'order this matter better'—the presentation by the candidate in front of the jury and,

† Laurence Sterne *A Sentimental Journey.*

180

behind, the rows of family, friends and colleagues; the speeches and questions from the jury; the replies from the candidate; the withdrawal of the jury; the agreement to award 'très honourable'; the announcement and shaking of hands; and the lively champagne party previously arranged in another room. All absolutely delightful—what marvellous occasions these French *soutenances* are!

But...! As we left the party, heading as we anticipated for the Faculty Cafeteria—still preferable to the tea and biscuits which traditionally follow an English D.Phil. viva—the Head of Department guided us—the jury, the candidate—to waiting colleagues who explained that, if we didn't mind, lunch was at a little restaurant in the environs of Lyon. Incredibly 15 minutes later we turned into the restaurant 'Paul Bocuse'. It was as if Callas and Gobbi were materializing before us for a divine performance. Four hours later we were to emerge. With no disrespect to Dr Derrien, my immediate recall of the occasion of his *soutenance* was what happened in those four hours, not, I regret, the preceding three.

It was not the anticipatory aperitif, chilled and sparkling though it was, but the subsequent splendours which are etched in my memory. *Les trois terrines*, as carefully ordered in their *assortissement* as any crystal: a foie gras spiked with the friendly truffle, an indefinable mousse curled into the lightest of brioches, and then the quintessential terrine, fruit of much marinading and moulding and modelling of texture, the wine—a humble Pouilly-Fuissé, but deliciously appropriate.

The arrival of the *Loup de mer en croute* was as sensational as that of Don Giovanni's last supper in one of the more lavish productions. Scales, fins, unwinking eyes, they were all most lovingly sculpted in that golden *croute* which opened up like a Russian doll to reveal the fish itself, inside which was hidden the ineffable *mousse de homard*. The rosy sauce Choron was served *a part*. This classic dish on a scale quite transcending the miniature effects of the *nouvelle cuisine* which was barely known in those days, was to my mind the apogee of the meal, the real triumph of the chef's and the pastry-cook's art, not to be approached by even the most ambitious of amateur cooks.

Aiguillettes de canard, that particular way of serving duck breasts in a pink, succulent fan, has now become widespread but then was unknown outside certain restaurants in France. Again they order this matter better, in a country where ducks are neither

Reproduced by permission of Paul Bocuse.

bred to be cushioned in fat or drained of their blood, that essential part of the sauce. But it was the sauce which was the real triumph, distilled and refined from the amalgam of duck and turnip. Devonian though I am and staunch supporter of the pasty, I had never thought this homely old faithful could be thus trans-mogrified.

We may have been far down in the wine stakes from Giscard's Margaux 1926, but there seemed to us nothing further to be desired than the Corton Clos du Roi, 1966.

The rest was, if not silence, to say the least a blur. Cheeses of the region, an iced cassis soufflé, digestifs; time, hours of it, passed and Jacques Friedel, pale, ascetic-looking, was the only one who remained unflushed. The drive back along the great river through a hazy Lyon was a hectic rush, the luxury of the Mistral—the now-defunct Marseilles–Paris express—a refuge from such an *embarras de richesses*.

It has been a hard act to follow.

Roy Pike

A ONE-DIMENSIONAL RESTAURANT

One of my favourite corners of the world is the Ligurian Riviera. A scientific collaboration with the Physics Department of the University of Genoa over a number of years has facilitated exploration of the architectural, geographical and gastronomic delights of this unique region. I will give an example of the last category in a moment but, for those who don't know the University, I might mention that the new Department of Physics is constructed along the lines of the Beaubourg in Paris and is well worth a look around as an architectural specimen.

To the west of Genoa, as far as Ventimiglia, lies the Riviera di Ponente and although, under the same felicitous collaboration, I have travelled this many times on my way to Nice and the French Riviera, passing through such romantic sounding places as Albenga, Alassio (shades of Elgar), Imperia and San Remo, it is at

Chiavari on the Levante side where the restaurant of my title is to be found.

The Riviera di Levante stretches from Nervi in the suburbs of Genoa down to La Spezia and, like the whole length of this Riviera coastline on the blue Mediterranean sea, is backed by the Ligurian Appenines. On the Levante side these mountains seem to fall right into the water with the happy consequence that restricted access to many of the tiny fishing ports and villages limits the influx of tourists to spoil their natural beauty.

Chiavari lies some 20 km south of Genoa on the ancient Roman Via Aurelia between the Portofino peninsula and the Cinque Terre. Readers who might decide to dine one day in Chiavari may work up a healthy appetite exploring either of these areas beforehand.

Portofino is an exquisite miniature pastel fishing port but now, like St Tropez, has been invaded by artists and tourists and cannot be recommended in high season. A four or five hour walk from Portofino will take one to the little port of San Fruttuoso and back or, better in the summer perhaps, one may explore the pine and olive groves of the peninsula from the pretty port of Camogli (houses of the wives); fishing widows were apparently well known before golfing ones! For a luncheon snack try a portion of *focaccia*, a savoury heavy flat bread which is a speciality here.

The Cinque Terre—Monterosso, Vernazza, Corniglia, Manarola and Riomaggiore—are almost inaccessible by road and can be walked from end to end by a rather wild mountain mule path which gives spectacular views over the sea. In the right season one may pluck the odd ripe fig from the tree or even the odd grape since the slopes yield a sweetish white wine called *sciacchetra* (chatterbox). For less athletic visitors I have to say that a railway line with many tunnels can be used to short circuit the mule track if necessary.

Let us descend to Chiavari with suitable appetite and find our way to the Via Bighetti in the old part of the town. This narrow street has a covered pavement of ancient stone arches along one side and, depending upon the time of evening, a line of tables will be set up under these, stretching in one-dimensional array as far as is necessary to accommodate available diners. In this way *Da Luchin* is always full but yet can serve whoever arrives by adding another table to the line. There is no facility for booking in advance.

The waiters have a special attire, namely, aprons, short trousers and boots. On one occasion I asked my friend Ara, wife of a professor of General Physics at Genoa, who is a talented artist as you may see, surreptitiously to sketch the scene.

An important ingredient in any Italian meal, of course, is the acoustic content. Apart from the normal Italian high-speed, high-volume parallel conversational practice, as distinct from the more usual British discreet serial type (only in Italy can one be complemented after dinner on the fluency of one's conversational Italian without having said a word!), specialities here are the intermittent clanging of local church bells and the incessant screeching of flocks of swallows which soar and dive constantly over the town.

Officially Da Luchin is a 'farinotto' (specialist at 'farinata') rather than a restaurant and for 'primo piatto' (first course) one should, without question, sample this speciality. Also of low dimension like the place itself, farinata is essentially a two-dimensional cooked mixture of 'farina di ceci' (flour of the chick-pea), water, olive oil and salt. The stirred ingredients are

Drawn by Ara Pontissia

poured into circular trays of about a metre in diameter to a depth of only a couple of millimetres. These are slid into special large wood-fired ovens and a tricky scientific business of levelling then takes place. This is done by dextrous positioning of long thin wedges under the edge of the tray to ensure uniform thickness of the fluid layer before it starts to cook. It is eaten ungarnished, simply as it comes from the oven, in flat slices on the plate, and very distinctive and delicious it is too.

As is customary for 'cucina casalinga' (home cooking) there is no written menu. A list of possibilities is issued verbally by the waiter in response to 'che cosa c'e?' (what is there?). I shall recommend the 'ripieni' (filled vegetables). For these one needs 'melanzane' (aubergines), 'cipolle' (onions), 'zucchine' and 'peperoni' (red or yellow peppers). The first three are boiled gently for five or six minutes but must not go too soft. They are then fashioned into small hemisperical shells like cups and laid out with the peppers tailored similarly. A filling or 'ripieno' is now prepared with the pulp only of the 'melanzane', chopped up beef (as for a hamburger), just a little 'mortadella di Bologna' or salami, or garlic and marjoram beaten up with raw egg to bind the mixture together. Salt and pepper may be added to taste. The 'cups' are filled with the mixture, topped with grated parmesan and breadcrumbs, especially the 'melanzane' and 'zucchine' but also a little on the 'cipolle' and 'peperoni', and placed carefully on an oiled baking tray in a moderate oven to brown.

The protein content of the meal so far may be low for some appetites and so a dish of 'frittura' (mixed small fried fish) or 'polpi' (octopusses) might follow. To drink, a wine specially bottled 'per il farinotto Luchin' is 'Bianco Pittorino, frizzante a fermentazione naturale', a light, slightly sparkling white wine which should serve the occasion very well. It is drunk, of course, *ad libitum*.

My counsel at this point would be to ask for 'il conto', which should not be more than 15–20000 Lira per person, and to repair around the corner to the pasticceria 'Defilla' in the Piazza Giacomo Matteotti under the gaze of the statue of Garibaldi. Here one takes coffee and the very special Defilla 'sorrisi' (smiles) of Chiavari. These are individually wrapped liqueur chocolates of 'maraschino fortissimo'. The covering is of Turinese 'Cioccolato Gianduja', named after the classic mask of that city. As a digestive I am partial myself to a glass of Sambuca, preferably with the canonical coffee bean in the bottom of the glass, but others may prefer the more conventional Grappa of one sort or another.

The town boasts a nice park and a long beach and since one's own dimensions might possibly have increased a little a gentle stroll might be advisable to conclude the evening.

George Temple

MONASTIC MEALS

As a Benedictine monk I turned first to Caput XL of *Sancti Benedicti Regulo Monachorum*. Under the inviting title 'De Mensura Potus' I read: 'Credimus Heminem vini per singolos sufficere per diem'. Commentators have reached no agreement as to the meaning of 'hemine'. Estimates vary from half a pint to a pint.

But I can speak from experience of two dishes served at Quarr Abbey.

On abstinence days a very savoury dish is served consisting of gobbets of tunny fish cooked in an egg custard.

After the lengthy office at midnight at Christmas a highly spiced pâté of rabbit is served in the Refectory. This is known by the appropriate name of 'Réveillons'.

This brings me naturally to the subject of breakfast.

Thirty years ago a very good breakfast was served on the 8.00 AM train from Liverpool Street to Cambridge.

That was as nothing compared to a breakfast served one fine Sunday morning by Priestley, the Dean (?) of PhD students at Cambridge. I arrived at his house as bidden at 9.00 AM, having taken the precaution of hearing Mass in the Chaplaincy at 8.00 AM. The door was open but no one had arrived. Hearing my entry the host hurried downstairs in a dressing gown and assured me that the other guests and food would soon arrive.

At 9.30 a train of college servants appeared carrying relays of grapefruit, omelettes, fried bacon and eggs, lamb cutlets, boiled eggs, cereals, stewed fruit, cream, toast, butter, marmalade and excellent coffee. I staggered to my lodgings at noon and I needed no lunch.

To crown my observations on breakfast I must mention that a certain Benedictine abbey found a place in the *Good Food Guide*—as renowned for its breakfasts—but, alas, that was some years ago.

To conclude I will quote from the excellent novel *Gryll Grange* by Thomas Love Peacock. Dining with his friend, Squire Gryll, the Reverend Doctor Opinien proclaimed that:

> There is much to be said for the bream. In the first place, there is the authority of the monastic brotherhoods, who are universally admitted to have been connoisseurs in fish, and in the mode of preparing it; and you will find bream pie set down as a prominent item of luxurious living in the indictments prepared against them at the dissolution of the monasteries. The work of destruction was rather too rapid, and I fear the recipe is lost.

I must add a reference to the classical work of Anthelme Brillat-Savarin. entitled *Physiologie du Goût ou Méditations de gastronomie transcendante* from which I cull the following story.

The young Anthelme was a choirboy at S. Clothilde in Paris, and, one fine day, he and his fellows were taken by coach to a Cistercian monastery to sing at the Mass of S. Bernard and thereafter to be entertained to dinner by the monks. Passing quickly over the Mass Brillat-Savarin describes the meal in loving detail, noting especially, in a corner of the refectory, an array of about 100 bottles of wine on which a fountain of cold water continually played. The meal concluded with coffee, served in bowls of Sèvres china from which, he says, the reverend Fathers drank with a noise of spouting whales. (I quote from memory.)

Section VIII
Travel, biographical, historical

Brian Flowers
with the (not inconsiderable) help of Mary Flowers

PLAGIARISM IN THE POT

'I have no special gifts,' Einstein is reputed to have said in answer to some pestilential pressman who was endeavouring to interview him on the subject of his genius, 'just an insatiable curiosity.'

An oversimplification no doubt, but cannot this dictum be applied to the casserole as well as to physics?

When I was first married my wife heard me praise a colleague's mathematics. 'That chap has real elegance,' I sighed admiringly. Mary, who knew next to nothing about maths, and still isn't interested in what used to be, in part, the source of our livelihood, but was even then an adventurous cook, expostulated. Flinging down her copy of *Vogue* magazine she snapped, 'You're crazy. How can that jumble of numbers, symbols, squiggles and dots be *elegant*? Now look at this beautiful Dior skirt, it must cost a bomb. I wonder if I could copy it. They might have it in Harrod's. I could try it on, sneak a look at how it is put together and then pretend I don't want it after all. It would take some working out, but it is elegant. Or maybe I could invent something along the same lines.'

She had no idea how close in meaning both our statements had been.

The good cook needs elegance, whether in copying, adapting or inventing from scratch. He or she requires imagination as well as curiosity, a sharp eye for what may be adapted, the ability to analyse, to synthesise and to copy shamelessly, and then the imagination to introduce an original touch. That's really just like doing science.

Of course, standard techniques are necessary in cooking as in physics. You have to know that you can't make a soufflé in a tepid oven, or a Vitello Tonnato in five minutes. You need to be very exact in your freezing and microwave techniques. But so much of that can be found in the boring little handbooks that accompany each new kitchen appliance, and can easily be worked out by virtue of our training.

The pedestrian sort of cook follows his recipe books slavishly. The good cook reads them on the bus or in bed for the sake of inspiration rather than instruction. Isn't this more like advanced studies, post-graduate work if you like, that leads you beyond the confines of merely getting it right?

How many of us can invent new dishes, find out what lies beyond carefully guarded secret recipes, and improve on the original? 'Is this something out of Mummy's head?' asked one of our sons when in his early 'teens (he didn't mean Cervelli con Funghi), 'or did you pinch it from someone else?'

For example, if you find yourself saying, 'I seem to have this disgusting orangeade left over from a children's party,' you can throw it out, drown it in gin or use some of it to make an unusually delicious iced soup of carrots with good curry paste.

Then comes the art of copying. Take the case of the Chinese seaweed. That crisp, seductive vegetable, enjoyed from Peking to Putney but almost impossible to find in a recipe book. I knew all about it. I suffered from my wife's total obsession with the nature and preparation of this delicacy. We asked countless Chinese, from respected colleagues to to knowledgeable-looking waiters. They were, without exception, inscrutable. We once ate it in the house of a French friend who whispered in answer to my wife's urgent pleading, 'I have to confess, I ordered it from a Chinese restaurant, an excellent one, I give you the telephone number.' We were back to square one as far as this piece of research was concerned. A few

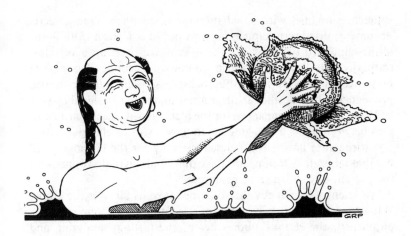

weeks later we were enjoying a particularly good Cantonese lunch in Chelsea. Suddenly my wife looked as if she were going to give birth. 'The Trade Description Act', she gasped, and almost threw the menu at the astonished waiter. She remained unusually silent until every last scrap of her 'seaweed' had been consumed, after which she fled from the Lotus Flower Garden as if she were being chased by one of the improbably ferocious dragons which adorned the walls. Just what had sparked off this particular outburst, I wondered. 'Could I have a look at the menu again?', I asked the waiter. 'Seaweed', I read clearly. No mistake there. But, then in tiny print underneath, too small to see without extra-strong spectacles, the minute, qualifying word, 'Greens'. It still didn't quite make sense so I returned to the relative peace and quiet of my office.

That evening I came home to find my wife looking the way I feel after completing a lengthy piece of algebraic manipulation. 'Sorry to give you the same vegetable you had at lunch, but there is grilled halibut instead of chicken and almonds.' Pause. 'I had to strike while the iron was hot,' she added casually as if nothing really mattered now. Then I tasted it. Greens? Nothing could be further from that overcooked early cabbage of our youth that was reputed to be good for the bowels. It was in fact a culinary replica of what we had enjoyed earlier in the day except that it was slightly less greasy. (Nowadays there exists a 'low fat' version.) She had cracked the code: just a handful of spring greens or large-leaf spinach, shredded with a Sabatier far more finely than a secret document; dried scrupulously, spread out over a clean cloth in the airing-cupboard (we now use the microwave oven on a very low setting), and deep fried for a couple of seconds. No marine mysteries or rarities from the rocks: just plain kitchen-garden provender. She has since spent hours rummaging in the alleyways of Hong Kong and Singapore for the ideal utensil for preparing this dish between bouts of nagging me to have a sort of chip pan with a fine wire gauze basket constructed specially for the purpose. I tell her that laboratory technicians have quite enough to do coping with the present-day shortage of resources.

We scientists are lucky that our jobs take us all over the globe. When our day's work is done, our lectures given, our meetings adjourned, the serious studies begin: the tasting, analysing and remembering the local delicacy put before us. It may be a sliver of fish taken from a fragrant marinade by an exquisite, kimono-clad creature in an ethnic hostelry on the slopes of Mount Fuji and seared on a beautiful stone so hot that it could have shot straight up from the earth's core, or it may be a vegetarian Tali prepared by a Brahmin cook in a simple Bangalore home and eaten with the fingers of your right hand only. (It matters not if you're left handed. Sinister agility is reserved for a very different purpose!) All the spices have been freshly ground and will require careful identification. Small samples must be retained to show to Mr Patel who keeps a useful shop just off the Euston Road. Nearer home there is that sublime feast of fish with saffron, olive oil, garlic and white wine, which may or may not be called 'Bouillabaisse', depending upon one's school of thought. Indeed, we once inadvertently started a verbal fight in a small Vieux Port restaurant in Marseilles (*mérite un détour*), because *M le Patron* answered our questions in a manner his clients did not approve.

I have sometimes almost lost my companion and cook of many years, fearing that I should have to return from some distant land without her. It has required enormous courage on my part to negotiate the labyrinths of subterranean kitchens from Mexico to Madras in order to remind her that our flight is due to leave shortly and she has yet to arrange the spoils of these expeditions in a way that will not arouse dangerous suspicions in the nostrils of some over-zealous customs officer.

Then, even before taking care of such incidentals as the letters that have accumulated on the doormat, my dirty socks and our jet lag, the synthesis begins. It lasts some days until the flavours and fragrances of the last port of call have crystallized, and the dishes and those that develop from them become part of the repertoire.

'Those Buddhist monks didn't cook the capsicums quite so long. If there were more fresh coriander leaves it would be even better. Do you think we dare introduce some of those dwarf turnips? The tofu from the health shop is extremely dull, I must go to Gerard Street.' So it goes on. It is every bit as much of a compulsion as that which urges us on in our own fields of research. By the time we've finished with it the work of those good monks has been plagiarized and varied out of all recognition, and a new dish has seen the light of dawn.

George Bernard Shaw said 'The reasonable man adapts himself to the world, whereas the unreasonable man tries to adapt the world to himself. Therefore all progress depends upon the unreasonable man.' (He never thought of an unreasonable woman, of course.) So if you are not interested in being unreasonable in your demands for super food, really good, exciting cooking is not for you. One day I shall get it all on to a hard disc. How curious that we should call up 'menus' on our computers.

Alan Cook

MEALS AND DRINKS IN MANY PLACES

My reflections on cooking and cuisine do not arise from any application of the principles or techniques of physics to the preparation of food; the connection I make between physics and cooking is that, thanks to my pursuit of physics, geophysics and astronomy having taken me to many countries, I have had the chance to sample good (and bad) cooking in varied places. My recollections are moreover coloured by other circumstances. When I was still a graduate student about 1951 I made some measurements of gravity at Bad Harzburg in Germany. No regular hotels were open then, and I stayed in a British Army Officers' Mess. It was summer time, and I remember breakfast, both for what we ate, but also for the pleasure of having breakfast out of doors on a terrace with a view of wooded hills, after the privations of wartime. Ever since, I have taken great pleasure in breakfasting out of doors. Another breakfast I recall is the one that it used to be possible to have on a train that left Edinburgh for Aberdeen at 8.00 AM. After the sleeper from King's Cross, it was indeed the start of a new day to be served morning rolls, kippers, Dundee marmalade and excellent coffee, alas no longer possible.

I have acquired rather definite views on how I like things cooked. The essential thing is that the cooking, however it is done, should be brought to just the right stage for the best flavour and texture, when very little sauce should be needed. Pretentious descriptions on menus tell you that some dish is 'masked' with an elaborate sauce, too often only too correct a word. I have found that Italian cooking in Italy frequently satisfies my criterion (as in roast veal with a thin rich juice, or *bollito misto con salsa verde*, provided it is done in Bologna, or *pasta carbonara*, or with just butter and garlic, or a *sole alla mugnaia*) while Italian restaurants in England or the USA seem to follow presumed local taste with thick alcoholic creamy sauces that suppress the flavour of the meat or fish. Many American restaurants do follow elaborate practices but I recall some simple dishes cooked in a refined way—sucking pig in a restaurant in the mountains above Boulder in Colorado, chowder at the seaside, kidneys Turbigo in Los Angeles. Another delight of American cuisine hardly involves cooking—the ubiquitous crisp salads with various vegetables and fruits.

Trieste has some good restaurants with simple but careful cooking—fish at the seaside, meat on the Carso, with spicy salads and various fresh fruits from the hills, like wild strawberries or blackberries, in season, for dessert. I was first introduced to good Italian restaurants by a friend who was a train enthusiast and spent his holidays in France selecting his train journeys so that he had *correspondences* at stations with *buffets gastronomiques*. From him I learnt of Sabatini in Florence, where I had orange sherbet in the skin of the orange. A pleasure of being head of a house in Cambridge is that you can persuade the kitchen manager to do what you want and I had oranges with their own sherbet served at dinner just recently.

It is always a challenge to try to reproduce a dish experienced or read about. From the Récamier restaurant in the Rue Récamier in Paris, I brought back the idea of *Quenelles de Brochet, sauce*

Nantua—time consuming to make, and dependent on the chance availability of a pike. *A la Recherche du Temps Perdu* introduced me to *Pouding Nesselrode*, served to M. Norpois by Marcel's family and we have had success with that, but I have not yet ventured to attempt the great macaroni pie described in *The Leopard*.

I have experienced the three great cuisines of the world from time to time. As well as in Trieste, Venice and Florence I have had, of course, notable meals in Bologna and in Rome. I have had Peking Duck at the Peking Duck Restaurant in Beijing and been of a party that clapped spontaneously at the sight of a display of dishes at a Chinese banquet. And as for France, what can I add to all that has been written on the French table? Just two things, I think. One delight of France is that you may almost always find a good meal wherever you stop in howsoever unpretentious a restaurant. The other is that I have lunched in the Auberge de l'Ill at Illhaeusern, near Colmar in Alsace, graced with three stars in the Michelin and offering the most exquisite care in cooking. The menu bears record: *Boudin fumé de foie gras, Mousse de saumon, Canard Sauvage roti, Fromage, Fraises,* accompanied by *Tokay d'Alsace.*

Good food must have good wine. Physics and geophysics, I am happy to say, have taken me above all to California, to the Napa Valley, and to sites of other great vineyards, sources of some of the world's greatest wines. It is a great pleasure to make the acquaintance of notable wineries and their products, especially the splendid Chardonnays and Cabernet Sauvignons, as well as some surprises. Zinfandel is not so well thought of perhaps, but well made and matured it can be magnificent. Wine makes friends; it was Frank Turner, of the Earth Sciences Department at Berkeley, who gave me a bottle of a very old Zinfandel that was a revelation. He did not have his own vineyard, but making wine is an important occupation of some Berkeley physicists, I am happy to say. Of course, the University of California at Davis has a leading biotechnology department, set up long before biotechnology was a fashionable word, almost as 'in' as information technology. But winemaking is biotechnology if it is anything, and Davis has a department.

Truly I can say that my pursuit of the sciences has been sustained by some very agreeable nourishment.

Maurice Bartlett

OVER HALF A CENTURY OF INTERNATIONAL 'HICCUPS'

One very worthwhile 'perk' for research workers and scholars, especially perhaps on the scientific side, is the opportunity, through international conferences or other exchange invitations, to visit many countries throughout the world. This on occasions creates minor problems, some, though not of course all, of which are associated with food and drink. I do not suppose that my own reminiscences of a few of those that were are all that extraordinary, but I have ventured to set them down, if only as a reminder to younger travellers of what they might sometimes have to beware of.

My first experience of European travel occurred while I was a Cambridge undergraduate, taking advantage in about 1930 of a vacation scheme to visit Germany. I was anxious to improve my German, and crossed by cargo boat from Grimsby to Hamburg, where I was domiciled with a professor and his wife. Unfortunately for my intentions, a Harrow schoolboy was there as well; and, while we had some exciting adventures together paddling along the waterways in a canoe, we naturally conversed in English. The meals we were served were plain but palatable, reflecting a careful rather than austere household cuisine. On Sunday evening it was usual to have a cold collation; and, after my English companion had left some salami on his plate, I was secretly amused to see it appear again on his plate the next day.

My first visit beyond Europe was many years later, to the United States in the autumn of 1946, when the UK was still on food rationing, and bookings on trans-Atlantic liners made by special permission. I travelled on the *Queen Mary*, which docked first at Halifax, Nova Scotia, before proceeding to New York, being extensively occupied by British war-brides of Canadian servicemen. In spite of a crowded ship, the catering staff produced an excellent menu at each meal, the only problem, about which all the passengers were warned, being that our meagre war-time diet had not conditioned us to such repasts—in particular, the succulent white bread rolls had to be viewed with the utmost caution.

On my arrival in the USA I had to travel down to North Carolina, where I had been invited as an 'exchange visitor' at a new Department of Mathematical Statistics at Chapel Hill. The British are reputed not to know how to make coffee, but I certainly soon realized that the Americans did not know how to make tea. A recollection in a station buffet in Washington DC of a glass of warm water already mixed with milk into which a tea-bag had been inserted still makes me shudder. I found further, after arrival in Chapel Hill, that the English 'tea-break' did not exist on the university campus; but my well-being was fortunately resuscitated by the discovery of a Viennese tea-room not far from the campus, where the tea (with cakes) was all that it should be. The predilection of Americans for strong cocktails as against milder aperitifs I also found rather off-putting; when I was first offered sherry as an alternative, I am afraid that my instinctive question 'Is it *real* sherry?' was, even if pertinent, not all that well received.

After North Carolina, I think Sweden was my next invitation abroad, with lecturing commitments in Uppsala, Stockholm and Lund. I had arrived by ship at Göteborg in the morning, and was travelling on to Stockholm around mid-day by train. One of the first problems I encountered was the Swede's apparent facility of eating meals at any convenient time. Having neglected to reserve a booking for lunch on the train, I was lucky to secure a seat at the last sitting at 2 PM. Before leaving the restaurant car, as there was some time still to go before the train was due in Stockholm, and I was scheduled to go on immediately to Uppsala, I thought perhaps I should make sure of a further meal on the train. However, when I was told that seats for dinner were then only available for the first sitting, and was told further that this sitting was due to start at 3 PM directly we had finished lunch, I gave up.

During my stay in Uppsala I enjoyed a very pleasant family invitation with my professional host there, Herman Wold. I was introduced to the Swedish custom of guests raising their glasses to each other during the meal, although it was explained to me that (for obvious reasons if there are many guests) it was not etiquette to raise one's glass to the hostess. The main course was regarded as rather special and included reindeer meat-balls; the association from my childhood of meat-balls or rissoles with 'left-overs' did not, I trust, linger for long in my mind.

The Swedish propensity for eating meals at all hours was evident

199

also in their restaurants, where meals could linger on, partly because a bill was never presented until asked for. On my last afternoon in Stockholm I was due to catch a fast train for Lund, where I was to give an evening lecture. Herman Wold had thoughtfully arranged for us to have a farewell dinner near the railway station at 4 PM. The attractive Swedish smorgasbord, often made a complete meal, is equally often a glorified hors d'oeuvres. There were so many dishes set out, even at our private table for two, that it was impossible to sample much of their contents (what happens to the half-empty dishes and tins when they are taken away?) It must have been well after 5 when this course was finally concluded, and the main course brought on. At 5.30 I began to get anxious, and persuaded Herman to skip dessert and coffee in order for me to catch my train. On arrival at Lund I was at once whisked away to have dinner before my lecture; I did not have the effrontery to refuse, and finally rose to give my lecture in a replate and somewhat bemused state.

Moscow was one of my next international destinations; I was invited there in 1956 as one of the British delegates to a mathematical conference. In fact, for obscure reasons, the passengers in our plane from Helsinki all landed up first in Leningrad. After a long delay we were taken to an imposing hotel and although by this time it must have been 11 PM we were invited to order anything we liked to eat. One passenger decided to test out this invitation, and ordered caviar and champagne for 'starters'; but he was politely informed that 'anything' meant 'anything available'. After dinner we felt more comfortable, but retired rather disconsolately to bed, because our luggage (including pyjamas, shaving gear etc.) was still on the plane. I had the uncharitable thought that perhaps our luggage was being deliberately withheld, so that the next day all the visitors from bourgeois Britain would appear a very scruffy lot. (This was no doubt unjustified, at least my wife and I had a similar experience in February 1987, when our British Airways flight from Los Angeles to London had to turn back because of engine-trouble; we were put up for the night at a sumptuous hotel, but again without our luggage.)

When we finally arrived at Moscow airport the next day, I was welcomed as though the 24 hour delay had never existed, giving me the impression that the passing of time seems of no consequence to the Russians. This impression was accentuated when an exhausting morning visit to the Kremlin did not allow us to get back to our hotel for lunch until 3 PM; but all the restaurant staff were waiting for us as though this was our regular lunch hour. The final conference banquet I had regretfully to miss, having succumbed to what seems often to be referred to as the 'Mexican bug' (though on my one visit to Mexico nothing untoward happened to me, susceptible as I am on foreign travels to this kind of upset). The next day I was due to return to England, and I was presented with some caviar to take as a cure. I am glad to say with some success. I have no wish to labour over what might be regarded as an indelicate topic, especially in a book concerned with food and drink; but I might add that I have often carried a flask of cognac for such an emergency (tablets from the chemist are nowadays an efficient alternative).

My flask, for example, stood me in good stead on a visit to Rome for an international conference. By chance I had arrived at the reception desk of the same hotel where Professor Sir Ronald Fisher FRS, an illustrious but notoriously irascible colleague was also hoping to stay. We had both, as we thought, taken care to reserve rooms 'with bath'. The desk clerk was adamant that we had not, no doubt bearing in mind that the American contingent would be insisting on such facilities. He was a little shaken when we both produced documentary evidence of our reservations, but after further vehement discussion could only be persuaded to 'discover' one such room, the other being 'without bath'. Fisher being not only more distinguished, but also older, than me, I felt impelled to relinquish my own claim; but I lived to regret it after having to make a series of nocturnal journeys down a very long hotel corridor. As on various other occasions, my flask came in handy at that time.

Another international tour took me to Calcutta, where I visited the Indian Institute of which Professor C R Rao, FRS was then Director. I was accommodated at a guest-house close to the Institute, and was intrigued before retiring to notice the night-porter's recumbent position across and just inside the doorway. In the morning at breakfast the housekeeper triumphantly produced a boiled egg for me as a special favour, so that I was embarrassed to find that the egg was hardly warm and probably not properly boiled. Mentally I assessed the risk of some dire infection, but politeness triumphed over my anxiety, fortunately with no ill effects. At that time J B S Haldane and his wife had emigrated to India and were living nearby. They took me to an Indian restaurant for a curry which I was assured was their mildest, leaving me wondering what the hottest curry would have been like.

This tour then took me on to Japan, where, apart from the discomfort at times of no sensible chairs to sit on when eating, nothing of a culinary nature occurs to me now as worth mentioning, interesting as some of their food was. Indeed, a more memorable encounter with Japanese colleagues occurred in England, when a Japanese professor came to Oxford, where I then was, to work in my Department. Shortly after he had arrived with his wife, my wife and I took them both by car to a pleasant traditional English tearoom in Chipping Campden, in the Cotswolds. The Japanese seemed delighted with this occasion, possibly comparing it with their own 'tea-ceremonies'. The inevitable camera was produced, which the Japanese professor insisted must take our photograph, himself included, while we were having tea. We all positioned ourselves expectantly, waiting for the time-release shutter and accompanying flash, but nothing happened. The professor fiddled a bit with his apparatus, and tried again, but still nothing happened. With a broad grin, he exclaimed: 'Made in Japan'.

Some time later during his stay he invited my wife and myself to dinner in their apartment. The food, as far as I can recollect, was good, but if I have difficulty in recollecting what it was, this was because my Japanese host plied me with cognac throughout the meal (my wife not being offered a drop). I never discovered whether this was a Japanese custom or whether our Japanese visitor thought that it was an English one.

Round about the close of my full-time academic appointments, I visited Australia a number of times. My wife and I enjoyed these visits, including their food and wine, the latter especially being both of high quality and moderate price. The only embarrassing incident I recall occurred when we were guests at an Australian Academy of Science dinner when formal dress was required. I was, or so I thought, well equipped for such an occasion. However, we were flying back from Adelaide to Canberra just in time for the dinner, and my one pair of black shoes, unlike the rest of my evening wear which had been left in our apartment in Canberra, had been taken with me to Adelaide for semi-formal gatherings. When we arrived back in Canberra, I discovered that my suitcase had been mislaid. I was obliged to appear correctly clad apart from the conspicuously brown pair of shoes I had travelled in—I was of course sure when we arrived for the dinner that everyone was staring at them.

One problem with recalling these trivial incidents is that one tends to remember more and more of them; and, after all, they *are* somewhat trivial. So, even although there are several countries I have not mentioned, I think I should stop. I see, however, that I have not referred to France. It will perhaps help to discount any suspicion that I have not dwelt on the more positive aspects of food and drink if I say that I have a great admiration for French food and wine, not only in France, but in French restaurants elsewhere.

To date my last professional commitment has been in May 1987 when my wife and I visited that delightful Swiss lakeside city of Lausanne. We experienced again there that disconcerting custom in Swiss restaurants, unconductive to maintaining a slim figure, of producing a second helping of the main course (on a clean plate) as large, if not larger, than the first helping. However, our visit also brought back memories to us of some happy hours together with a friend and colleague of mine, Dr Hilary Seal, whom I first met at Yale (where he combined a flourishing actuarial practice with a university lectureship). He had retired with his wife and family to a house not far from Lausanne, where he still used to lecture until his sudden death a few years ago. Before then he loved to drive the four of us over the Swiss border into France, where he would seek out a restaurant extracted from the Michelin guide, so that we could sample, and appraise, their menu, and store it in our memory for future reference.

Rudolf Peierls

FIRST ENCOUNTER WITH ENGLISH FOOD

My first visit to England was a summer holiday in 1928, and I came again in 1933—as it turned out, to stay. The first experience of food was mainly in boarding-houses and rather average restaurants. The magnificent breakfast in these places fully justified its fame on the Continent, and the afternoon tea (known on the Continent as

'five-o'clock-tea', although I have never met a place where it was served that late) was equally attractive. But the rest of the meals seemed strange. It took some time before I understood the system.

In a thoroughly democratic country it would not do for the cook to impose his or her taste on the guests, so everything was boiled until only a neutral matrix remained. Then at the table the guests could add salt, pepper, mustard, ketchup, Worcester sauce, etc., to generate any desired flavour. My theory seemed confirmed by the observation that many people would add salt, pepper and other condiments to their food before tasting it.

This custom led an English couple into trouble when at dinner in a famous restaurant in Paris they asked the waiter for salt and pepper. The patron appeared and threw them out. They had insulted his food by suggesting it was not perfectly seasoned.

I also had disappointing experiences caused by similarities with familiar foods: when first offered brown bread I expected rye, and was taken aback by Hovis. When I first met junket, I took it to be yoghurt until I tasted it (or rather failed to detect any taste). Minted peas were unfamiliar and made my wife suspect that the cook had by mistake used tooth powder instead of salt.

In the thirties coffee was, in the places we could afford, an overrated pastime, but this was not unfamiliar, because we were used to Germany. There in comparable places the coffee was similar, particularly in Saxony where the local coffee is often called *Blümchenkaffee* (flower coffee) because you could see through it the little flower painted at the bottom of the cup.

It took us some to discover the best of English food, then served mainly in private homes. Now, some fifty years later, excellent English food is much easier to come by, though the old style of cooking, conforming to my theory, can still be found occasionally.

One custom which seems to me strange is still met quite often. That is treating potatoes as a vegetable, to be served with a main dish which is itself based on potato (cottage pie) or on pasta or rice. Sometimes two different forms of potato (boiled and roast). Such a surfeit of carbohydrates seems peculiarly English.

Other puzzles did not relate to the nature of the food, but to terminology. Why did butchers' shop windows distinguish between English and Canterbury lamb? Was not the cathedral city in England? (For that matter was 'Botany Wool' some kind of cotton?)

One commodity which is even today not too widespread is fruit ice cream. Too often it is replaced by a concoction containing neither real fruit nor real cream. I might therefore end with an easy recipe, learned from our daughter, Mrs Joanna Hookway. Liquidise 8 oz of fruit (e.g. strawberries or raspberries, if necessary defrosted; dried apricots, soaked, are excellent). Whip half a pint of cream, not too stiff, and add to the fruit, with the juice of half a lemon and sugar to taste. Put in the freezer and forget it. (The usual procedure of stirring the mixture during freezing to avoid crystallisation is not necessary here, because crystallisation is prevented by the air bubbles in the whipped cream, and the lemon juice stabilises the whipped cream.)

David Tabor

A TRAVELLER'S REFLECTIONS ON THE EGG

Travellers to conferences and other worthy destinations often have problems with eggs. By eggs I do not mean the base for something else or as a carrier of all sorts of garnishes; I mean eggs as eggs or, as the philosophers would say, 'das Ding an sich'.

For the average hotelier the least troublesome way of preparing an egg is by boiling it but for the client there are two basic difficulties: until you break into the egg you do not know how hard or soft it is, nor can you tell how fresh it is. Furthermore you would have to eat most of it before you discover whether there is a speck of blood in it or not. In some countries it is customary to shell the whole boiled egg for the client and place it in a glass container with a whiff of salt and a pat of butter. The theory, according to my wife, is that boiled eggs taste better when eaten out of glass just as tea tastes better when drunk out of fine china. Does a crystal-cut-glass container, I wonder, improve the flavour even further? The fact remains that the boiled egg is inherently an unknown quantity until it is cracked and tasted.

All other forms of egg preparation involve breaking the shell and dealing with the contents. The form with the most artistic appeal is the fried egg particularly if it is fried only on one side. The brilliant yoke gleams like the golden iris of a Cyclops in a luminous white sclera of albumen. Sometimes the yolk is too hard, sometimes too soft. Often the egg retains too much browned butter which may dominate the delicate flavour of the egg itself. This is even more marked if the egg is fried on both sides: it is also in danger of becoming too rich.

Scrambled eggs, shirred eggs and omelettes all fall into a single class—the white and yolk are thoroughly mixed. Most commonly the bottom is too brown and the top too raw. To avoid the rawness the egg is often overdone and as a result many restaurants serve a product that is tough and rubbery in texture and tasteless. There is a hint here for the chemical engineer who might be looking for a substitute for leather.

Apart from baked eggs which have no particular appeal to me the most eggy egg is the poached egg. The egg is slid onto the surface of simmering water and left there until it is done. Often a minute drop of vinegar is added to the water since this coagulates the protein in the albumen and prevents the white from spreading. A more controlled way is to use a poacher where individual metal cups, spread with a soupçon of butter, are heated by boiling water. The trick is to make the white of the egg firm, and the yolk firm but runny. The egg should be slid onto a thin slice of brown bread or lightly toasted bread, spread sparingly with unsalted butter. The egg may be lightly seasoned with salt but not with pepper.

It is very difficult to obtain poached eggs that are well and consistently prepared. Maybe there is not enough demand or too much care is involved. From Towcester to Tokyo, from Sydney to San Francisco I have nearly always found that the restaurant poached egg is little different from a fairly-hard boiled egg. I wonder if some whizz-kid will invent a computer programme which will define the poaching time in terms of the size of the egg (grades 1 to 4), the relative size of the yolk (an arbitrary grade from 1 to 3), the age of the egg (uncertain) and the altitude of the kitchen since this determines the boiling temperature of the water. 'Poached by computer' on the menu could be a new gastronomic inducement.

The poached egg is ideal for those with a delicate palate. It is an excellent form of protein and energy and if not eaten to excess is good for you. It is cheap. It is also delicious.

Elsie Widdowson

RESEARCH ON COOKING

Over sixty years ago a graduate of Cambridge University who had just completed 3 year's postgraduate work under Professor F G Hopkins obtained a small grant from King's College Hospital to help him obtain his medical qualifications. He was loosely attached to the biochemical department and, under the influence of Dr R D Lawrence, himself a diabetic, he became interested in diabetes. At that time the diet of diabetics was carefully rationed, especially as regards carbohydrate. Very few analyses of the carbohydrate content of cooked foods were available compared with the large number of those carried out on raw materials. As the carbohydrate of many foods is altered by cooking, and as most foods are eaten cooked, the difficulty of making use of the existing analyses for diabetic diets was at once apparent. Accordingly the medical student, R A McCance, set out to analyse cooked as well as raw fruits and vegetables for available carbohydrate, separating as far as he could the readily soluble sugars and starch from the relatively unavailable pentosans, hemicelluloses, cellulose and lignin, now often termed 'dietary fibre'. He dealt with 109 different plant materials, about half of them cooked by ordinary domestic methods, and each was analysed on six separate occasions. He did all this work single-handed, along with his medical studies, and the results were published in 1929 in the *Special Reports Series* of the *Medical Research Council* No. 135, under the title 'The carbohydrate content of foods'.

Before this report was published the manuscript was submitted to E P Cathcart, Professor of Physiology at Glasgow. Professor Cathcart was concerned with the nutrition of the poor and well-to-do and he said that from the point of view of the general public protein and fat were more important than carbohydrate. He thought that these constituents should be determined. The Medical Research Council provided R A McCance with an assistant, and a much larger study began on meat and fish. Fifty kinds of meat, besides poultry and offal, were analysed after cooking by standard methods, and over 60 varieties of cooked fish were similarly studied. In every case the method of cooking was described and the material was analysed for inorganic constituents as well as water, nitrogen, fat, and carbohydrate when present.

Detailed investigations of losses of nutrients from meat when roasted, steamed or boiled were made, and the 'pellicle' theory, originally propounded by Liebig, and still believed in by many cooks today, was shown to be completely without foundation. The theory states that all cooking of meat should commence at a high temperature. This coagulates the proteins on the outside of the meat and an impermeable skin is formed which retains the salts and soluble nitrogenous compounds which Liebig regarded as the 'goodness' of the meat. McCance found that the losses of nutrients from meat when roasted, steamed or boiled in water were due to 'shrink' of the muscle fibres, and these losses were the same whether meat for roasting was put into a cold or hot oven, and whether a joint of beef for boiling was put into cold or hot water. The results of the study were published in 1933 in a second *Medical Research Council Special Report* No. 187 with the title 'The chemistry of flesh foods and their losses on cooking'.

R A McCance did all the cooking for these studies himself, and he did it in the main kitchen at King's College Hospital. At about this time I had just finished my PhD at Imperial College, and I was desperately looking for a job involving research. Such jobs were hard to come by in the early thirties, so I was advised to train as a dietitian. I was all set to take the first Postgraduate Diploma Course in Dietetics at King's College of Household and Social Science under Professor Mottram, and before the course started I was sent to King's College Hospital for training in large-scale cooking in a general hospital kitchen. While I was there I often saw a white-overalled gentleman bringing joints of meat into the kitchen and cooking them in the oven or steamer. I asked the cook who he was and she told me that he was Dr McCance and that he was doing 'Research on Cooking'. I was naturally interested and one day I plucked up courage and spoke to him. He invited me to visit his tiny laboratory, where he told me about the work he was doing on meat and fish, and his previous study on the available carbohydrate of fruit and vegetables. The outcome of this was that he invited me to join him, got a grant for me from the Medical Research Council and we started another study on plant foods. We re-analysed cooked and raw fruit and vegetables for nitrogen and inorganic constituents as well as for the separate carbohydrates, glucose, fructose, sucrose and starch. We also studied losses from vegetables on cooking; in some ways these may be more important nutritionally than those from meat because material lost from meat is generally consumed while water in which vegetables have been boiled is thrown away. Vegetables do not 'shrink' when exposed to heat as meat does, but the cell walls collapse and soluble consti-tuents leach into the surrounding water. The extent of the loss varies with the time of cooking and the surface area of the pieces that are cooked. The skin of potatoes is remarkably impermeable, and potatoes boiled in their skins lose hardly any nutrients at all. These findings were published in 1936 in a third *Medical Research Council Special Report*, No. 213 entitled 'The nutritive value of fruits, vegetables and nuts'. Sadly the stocks of all three *Reports* were destroyed in a fire started by enemy action in World War II, and they have been out of print ever since.

I completed the dietetics course in my spare moments, and as part of it I spent 6 weeks in the diet kitchen at St Bartholomew's Hospital. Much of my time was occupied calculating diets for patients, using American food tables. All the foods in these tables had been analysed in the raw state which I knew gave figures quite unrepresentative of the cooked foods as served to the patients. I realised that with a little more analytical work we should have all the material needed for making comprehensive tables of the composition of British foods, both cooked and raw. The result was *The Chemical Composition of Foods* first published in 1940.

While we were preparing these tables the question arose of including figures for the composition of cooked dishes made from several ingredients. Since one of the main uses of the tables was likely to be the calculation of the chemical composition of diets of men, women and children, most of whom eat such cooked dishes, we decided to do our best to give some information about this. Most of the recipes were taken from standard cookery books. The dishes were cooked by a dietitian and 90 were included in the first edition of the tables. The second edition was prepared in wartime, and published in 1946. About 20 'economical' recipes were added, using for example dried egg, 'Household' milk and potato for pastry. As time went on some cookery experts became rather critical of our original recipes, so for the third edition of the tables the whole of this section was revised with the help of members of the cookery department of King's College of Household and Social Science. However, we kept in a few of our favourite recipes. When a fourth edition of the tables came up for discussion we felt the time had come for us to hand over the responsibility to younger people, and the planning was taken over by a joint Medical Research Council–Ministry of Agriculture, Fisheries and Food Committee. Composition of cooked dishes was still included, but completely revised yet again, using recipes recommended by other cookery experts. A few of our favourites were omitted, including three passed on to me by my mother, born 1877, died 1984. I offer them as a tailpiece and a tribute to her. (See section IX, page 241.)

Naomi Datta

DOMESTIC SCIENCE

The 'Clockwise' feeling of wanting to be in two places at once is familiar to everyone who has combined a job with bringing up children. I was 30, and well launched as a medical bacteriologist, when I had my first baby. I soon went back to work and tried to get home for her 6-o'clock feed. But I could not find any time at which to leave the Public Health Laboratory, at Colindale in North London, so as to reach home at 6.00. If I left at 5.00, say (I forget the exact times), I would be at home by about 5.30, but because of the traffic, if I stayed until after 5.00, I was regularly delayed until well after 6.00. I wish I had kept a record of the times taken on those journeys, so as to plot a graph showing 6.00 as an impossible arrival-time.

Later, by the time I had three children, I worked in the Department of Bacteriology of a teaching hospital, where I had time for research and where travelling to and fro was much easier. Bacteriology is, or was, a discipline related to cooking and gardening. The nutrient media were prepared in the Media Kitchen and inoculated, or sown, with bacteria. Most of the latter, unlike garden plants, grew up overnight in a $37°$ incubator. The apparatus of a laboratory was quite like that of a domestic kitchen. When my research, on antibiotic resistance, came to a critical point, I wanted to stay on and finish the experiment but I also wanted to get home to my family. I resolved this by taking work home with me—Petri dishes containing colonies of bacteria to be tested and plates containing antibiotics. After I had cooked supper, and it was eaten and cleared away, and the children unhurriedly put to bed, I came back to the kitchen. There I picked bacterial colonies, inoculated the antibiotic plates and then incubated them in the airing cupboard. At first I used my gas hob as a Bunsen burner to flame my wire loops, but later took to using pre-sterilised wooden tooth-picks, discarding them straight into a pan of boiling water. I did not take home dangerous pathogens and I knew that I was putting my family at no risk, though I suspect that under present-day regulations this sort of home-work may be illegal. The temperature of the airing cupboard was no more than $30°$ but I could usually detect growth next morning; if not, a few more hours in a $37°$ incubator gave the result. One of the pleasures of bacteriology is seeing the results of an experiment on the following morning. It is exciting to open the incubator and look at the cultures and if the experiment has failed, at least one is rested and fresh and less down-cast than when failure comes at the end of the day.

Another link between my kitchen and my laboratory was my Grant bath—a rectangular, thermostatically controlled water-bath, about 100 cm × 50 cm in area, 50 cm deep, with an electric stirrer and a lid. I used it constantly in the lab, at 56° for keeping agar media molten, ready for use, or at lower temperatures, 37° or 42°, for bacteria or bacteriophage held in tubes in metal racks. The thermostat could be turned up to 100°, when the water did not quite boil but reached simmering point. Our chief technician had made me a trolley to hold the bath at bench height, which was most convenient. At Christmas, I took my bath home. I had no pan big enough to boil a ham, but the Grant bath was just right and easily transported on its trolley. After the holiday, the smell of boiled bacon persisted, despite all attempts at cleaning.

When I retired, I thought I might miss my bacteria and the everyday work in the laboratory but, in fact, I do not. I still have my kitchen and also a garden for growing things.

E R H Jones

A CHEMIST LOOKS AT SOME FOOD PRODUCTS

Lea and Perrins Worcestershire Sauce

For more than a century this invaluable adjunct to the cuisine has been available worldwide. John Lea and William Perrins, chemists or druggists, entered into partnership in 1823, and they carried on a lively business in Worcester making and selling medicaments, toiletries and so on, and also providing a service as analytical chemists. Lord Sandys, lately Governor of Bengal, who had retired to live at Ombersley Court, near Worcester, asked them to make up a sauce from a recipe which he had brought back from India. His Lordship expressed himself as entirely satisfied with their product, but Messrs Lea and Perrins considered it to be 'an unpalatable, red-hot, fire water'. Next year, during the annual spring-cleaning and stocktaking, a quantity which they had left over was being disposed of, when its aroma attracted attention. On tasting it again, to their great surprise, they now found it to be piquant and appetising. Sales began in 1842 and by 1855 they were selling 30,000 bottles a year. Maturing, of a physical, chemical or biological

212

nature is a not unimportant part of food manufacture and a fortunate accident preserved this widely famed product for posterity.

From *Imperial Tobacco Group Review* 1970 **1** 14 and *The Road to Aston Cross* by Louise Wright, 1975.

McDougalls Self-raising Flour

When his father died of cholera in 1832 Alexander McDougall, then 23, supported the family first as a shoemaker and then as a teacher in Carlisle. After moving to Manchester he became headmaster of the Day School attached to the Mechanics Institute which, in his time there, gained a good reputation for science teaching. His interest in science and his entrepreneurial instincts were fostered in the lively Manchester atmosphere and especially in the famous Literary and Philosophical Society where he made contact with Angus Smith, fairly called the first public health chemist. Although by 1837 he had his own school at Chorlton-on-Medlock, he decided to go into the manufacture of useful chemical products. Success came with 'McDougalls Disinfecting Powder' which, fulfilling an urgent need of the times, was widely used in the 1850s for sewage treatment. Its popularity did not long survive competition, but it made McDougall wealthy and, more importantly, its use of carbolic acid (phenol) led Joseph Lister in Edinburgh to the famous experiments which gave us antiseptic surgery.

McDougall's lasting fame came with the marketing of a 'phosphatic yeast substitute' for bread making. But bakers could not be converted to its use and so McDougall and his sons (five of them helped in the business) made and sold their own 'self-raising flour' and then had to go into the milling field themselves to obtain enough raw material of the right quality. The flour-milling venture is now part of the Rank, Hovis, McDougall group and the chemical activity was hived off as Cooper, McDougall and Robertson, well-known in the agricultural chemicals business.

From *Notes and Records of the Royal Society* 1974 **28** 257.

Magnesia, Soda Water and Three Scientific Generations of Henrys

After his apprenticeship as an apothecary Thomas Henry set up in his own business in Knutsford, Cheshire. He moved to the centre of the-then country town of Manchester in 1764 where, as was normal in those days, he established a good medical practice. Whilst working for a couple of years as an assistant in Oxford he had become interested in the production of 'magnesia alba', widely used in the relief of gastronomic ailments. With some understanding of the chemistry involved he was able to refine the process, 'Henry's Calcined Magnesia' became almost a household word (they ceased advertising about 1780) and was manufactured by T and W Henry in Manchester until the 1930s.

Almost complementarily, and initially with a medical purpose, they made soda water and there is reference to the establishment of a factory in Birmingham, with help with the pumping equipment from James Watt junior (Boulton and Watt), in order to counter the concern that Schweppe (*sic*) might get established there.

Thomas Henry's third son William became, of necessity, a partner in the business with the result that his educational opportunities were much reduced. However, he did manage to get some fragmentary scientific training at Manchester and at Edinburgh and this was sufficient for his astute mind to perceive the scientific principles behind the soda water process and so to elucidate what came to be known as Henry's law, governing the relationship between liquids and gases dissolved in them. This was described to the Royal Society in 1802 and six years later earned him the Society's highest honour, the Copley Medal.

With little scientific training, but strong entrepreneurial instincts, Thomas and William Henry made many and varied contributions to science and technology. Disappointingly, William's only son Charles, after a sound formal education (M.D. Edinburgh) and with superb opportunities of collaboration with some of the 'great ones' in an exciting period of scientific development (he became a Fellow of the Royal Society like his father and grandfather before him) gave up a promising scientific career for the comfortable life of a country gentleman in Herefordshire.

From W V Farrer, K R Farrer and E L Scott *RIC Reviews* 1971 **4** 35; *Ambix* 1973 **20** 183; 1974 **21**, 179, 208; 1975 **22** 186; 1976 **23** 27; 1977 **24** 1.

Nicholas Kurti

BIRD'S CUSTARD: THE TRUE STORY

It is widely believed that Bird's custard is one of the earliest examples of 'convenience foods' or of regrettable substitutes designed purely to reduce the cost and the time of preparation of a dish. Nothing could be further from the truth. Indeed, the invention of Bird's custard is a shining example of alleviating a deprivation caused by cruel nature.

Alfred Bird, whose father taught astronomy at Eton, was born in 1811 in Birmingham and in 1837 established himself as an analytical and retail pharmaceutical chemist there. When he married Elizabeth Lavinia Ragg he faced a challenge which was to influence his career. His young wife suffered from a digestive disorder which prevented her from eating anything prepared with eggs or with yeast. But Elizabeth Lavinia was apparently yearning for custard to go with her favourite fruit pies so Alfred Bird started experimenting in his shop. The result was the custard powder bearing his name and based on cornflour, which when mixed with milk produced, after heating, a sauce reminescent in appearance, taste and consistency of a genuine egg-and-milk custard sauce.

The young wife was overjoyed and this substitute custard became the normal accompaniment to puddings at the Birds' dinner table, though, when they entertained, genuine custard sauce was offered to their guests. Then came an occasion when, whether by accident or by design, 'Bird's custard' was served and Alfred must have been gratified to hear his guests declare that it was the best custard they had ever tasted!

This then was the beginning of the firm Alfred Bird and Sons Ltd of Birmingham which for 120 years remained a family business, first under the chairmanship of the founder, then of his son, Sir Alfred Bird Bt and then of his grandson Sir Robert Bird Bt. While the firm's main product remained custard powder Alfred Bird's other invention to circumvent his wife's digestive troubles, namely baking powder, was also manufactured and was used during the Crimean war so that British troops could be given fresh, palatable bread.

Alfred Bird was a Fellow of the Chemical Society and, a few months after his death on 2 December 1878, a brief obituary was published in the *Journal of the Chemical Society*, Vol. 35, p. 206, 1879. It described at some length Bird's interest in physics and meteorology, thus 'He constructed a beautiful set of harmonized glass bowls extending over 5 octaves which he used to play with much skill' and 'in 1859 he constructed a water barometer with which he was fond of observing and showing to others the minute oscillations of the atmospheric pressure' But of Bird's Custard Powder—not a word!

The help of the City of Birmingham Public Library is gratefully acknowledged.

Section IX Recipes

Anthony Bradshaw

LIBERATED BREAD

Does cooking display insidious relics of sexism in this country—the female sex presumed to be delighted to be bent over the stove for long hours? I hope not. But what other reason is there for so little interest in labour saving cookery? Why otherwise does every bag of flour I can find have printed on it recipes which are tedious and unnecessary? Everyone I know thinks home bread making is complex and time consuming, when it need not be. The only alternative I can think of is that these complex recipes are an insidious sell of shop bread by the multiple bakers.

The first three crucial savings of time and trouble that anyone can make in bread making are to (a) rise the dough only once (twice is unnecessary), (b) use the oven both to rise and bake it (saves carrying the bread from one place to another), (c) not bother to cover it during the rising process (the standard recommendation is to put the dough into an oiled plastic bag, but this is a tedious business). The next saving comes from remembering that bread making is a biological process in which the yeast is thermophilic working fastest when it is warm, $35°C$ and not $15°C$. The final saving comes from using the newly available small-grained dried yeast which can be mixed direct with the flour. Rising once is the greatest saving—a carefully conducted blind test on the family showed that nobody could tell once-risen from traditionally twice-risen bread—if anything the once-risen was preferred.

This recipe takes 15 minutes of work, after which the product is ready in one hour. It uses black treacle to provide a more interesting taste, but this is not essential. We use wholemeal or granary flour because we prefer it. The simplicity of the work involved is very relaxing; the biology always intriguing. The quality will beat what you buy in the shops.

Ingredients

1.5 kg (1 bag) bread flour (wholemeal or granary, or white if you must, but made from hard wheat—beware of special home grown wholemeal flours because they are usually made from wheat varieties which are poor in gluten and difficult to make into a strong dough).

1 dessertspoon salt

2 sachets (12 g) fine grain dried yeast (old fashioned large grain dried yeast must be mixed with water first)

1 heaped dessertspoon treacle or malt (optional)

$1\frac{3}{4}$ pint hot water (out of the tap or at least 60 °C (140 °F))

Method

Mix the flour, salt and yeast together in a large basin. Dissolve the treacle in the water and add to the flour. Mix the lot together with a large fork or spoon, and then continue with fingers. Knead until the mixture forms a coherent dough (about 1 minute). Lift out of the bowl and knead energetically on a clean table or working surface while you read the newspaper for 5 minutes (the dough will not stick now). Swiftly put rounded humps weighing about 1 lb each into suitable greased tins, and into an oven set to 70°C. Leave to rise for 25–30 minutes, until dough has doubled in height (may take longer if dough is not warm enough). Turn up temperature to 225°C (450°F) and cook for 30 mins. (Top should be light brown and dough begun to shrink from tin, but bread will be soft and moist.)

This makes about six loaves which are too much to eat in one go. Just put the spares into a freezer in plastic bags.

Stephen Mason

A HOT PORRIDGE BREAKFAST
MADE POSSIBLE BY THE ADVENT OF THE
MICROWAVE OVEN

Mix a teacup full of porridge oats, of the precooked 'quick' variety, with milk to a mobile slurry in the bowl intended for subsequent use at table. Add a small pinch of salt, and sugar to taste if so desired, and cook for three minutes at full power in the microwave oven. During the final minute, lower the power setting if the mixture boils. After extraction of the bowl from the oven, add cold milk to cool the now-cooked porridge for immediate consumption. The use of a pottery bowl is essential. Plastic bowls in the oven release unpleasant and doubtless harmful substances, and the bowls themselves tend to spontaneously distort and then disintegrate.

P Steptoe

FISH A LA PROVENÇALE (FISHPOT)

Place in a fireproof dish thick slices of onion and tomatoes, then slices of turbot, and cover with thick slices of onion and tomato, all mixed with herbs. If you have no olive oil, put small dabs of butter in between and on top. Bake in a moderate oven. Serve with thinly sliced potatoes baked in butter and grated cheese.

This is a basic recipe. If you do not like turbot then halibut is an excellent alternative. Herbs such as marjoram, basil, 'mixed', can be added as well as peppercorns, turmeric, a generous pinch of saffron, salt and pepper. A good spoonful (tea) of capers gives just a hint of sharpness which makes a difference. Most important is the addition of garlic.

It can be served with rice or jacket potatoes.

John Postgate

JOHN POSTGATE'S MEDIAEVAL LEEKS

Put some cooking oil in a casserole and place on a hotplate. Slice three average leeks longitudinally and cut into about 2 cm lengths. Add them to the warm oil such that some pieces get gently fried but the majority do not. Chop about $\frac{1}{2}$ lb of mushrooms into fair-sized pieces and add. Chop $\frac{1}{2}$ an apple into small pieces and add; feed remainder of apple to passing child or horse. Add a pinch of powdered ginger, a good shake of nutmeg, a shake of dried celery seed or celery salt, white pepper, knife-tip of commercial Marmite, a little salt—less than you might think because the Marmite is salty. Stir in a teaspoonful of self-raising flour and add a small wineglass of cider. Stir, transfer to an oven at $220°$C and cook for 30 minutes. Best if cooked earlier in the day and re-heated for dinner.

Steven Weinberg

ANHYDROUS ZUCCHINI

Those who take a morose view of the biological limitations of the human species should consider the zucchini. In countless British and American restaurants, this vegetable (courgettes to native FRSs) is boiled to the point of disintegration, and served in a watery stew of tomatoes and onions. It is natural to conclude that zucchini is an evolutionary dead end, kept under cultivation only by a government subsidy of ill-advised agriculture. Yet zucchini can be quite good to eat, and without excessive trouble. Here is my own recipe.

First, wash your zucchini. I don't know why, but zucchini come rather dirty from the greengrocer. Perhaps grocers can't believe anyone will actually eat zucchini.

Next, slice each zucchini unevenly, the slices averaging 5–10 mm thickness. The point of their being uneven is that then some slices will get cooked up more rapidly, and you can eat them while you're cooking the rest.

Then, put some olive oil in the bottom of a skillet, enough to wet the bottom everywhere, and heat it on a high flame for a minute or two. Put the zucchini slices in the oil, and turn them over nervously several times until they begin to brown.

At this point, you can begin to be inventive. Add salt or soy sauce, and also garlic or oregano if you like. As slices become golden brown, remove from the pan and dry on a paper towel. Try not to eat them all before you have a chance to bring them to the table.

Walter Welford

CHISWICK VEGETARIAN RISOTTO

Ingredients
Rice (Uncle Ben's long grain works well)
An onion
An aubergine
A red sweet pepper (green will do almost as well)
Italian red vermouth
Soya textured vegetable protein or TVP (unflavoured
    Protoveg chunks are best)
Cooking oil (soya oil or olive oil if you can afford it)
Knorr vegetable stock cubes

Method
The quantities suggested above will serve two or three people as a main course. Chop up a medium sized onion and cook it in about a tablespoonful of cooking oil in a large saucepan until it is slightly brown. Add a level coffee mug full of the rice and stir and cook until the grains look transparent (one or two minutes). Add three of the same mugs full of water just off the boil, cover and bring to boil gently. Add one or two chopped up vegetable stock cubes, pour out a large wineglass of the vermouth and drink some of it. At about the same time as you add the water put a small cupfull of the TVP in a pan with some boiling water, half cover and cook gently.

Wash and dice half the aubergine and wash and slice the pepper (taking out the seeds) and add them to the rice; this should be done about 5 minutes after adding the hot water to the rice. At this point also the TVP should have softened by absorbing water; strain away its water and add the TVP to the rice; stir, reheat to boil, cover and leave to cook gently until all the water has been absorbed by the rice.

The water should all have gone about 20–25 minutes after adding it to the rice and by then the risotto should be ready, but stir it and check by tasting; at this point also you should have drunk all the glass of vermouth.

Serve in a heated dish with grated cheese; with a salad and some wine this makes a good main course.

Notes

The only critical point is that the volume of water added to the rice should be three times the volume of the rice; other quantities can be varied according to taste within wide limits. Also any other preferred aperitif may be used instead of the vermouth.

The aubergine and the pepper should *not* be skinned and there is no need to leave the aubergine in salt to 'take away the bitterness'; modern aubergines don't seem to need this.

Hans Kornberg

OEUFS LYONNAISE: A RAPIDLY PREPARED FISHLESS DISH

The first thing to be explained about this recipe is the title. Some 40 years ago, after the end of the Second World War but not after the end of food rationing, I had the good fortune to be asked to spend part of my summer vacation, in the company of fellow undergraduates, in helping to run a small hotel on the Cornish coast, that made up in atmosphere what it lacked in staff. Meat rationing being what it was, most of the meals consisted mainly of local (and deliciously fresh) fish. However, even the most succulent fish can begin to pall if it is compulsory and the staple diet. In response to an incipient rebellion from some of the guests, I hastily put together the following dish (made possible by the fact that a local farmer let us have eggs in profusion, for exorbitant payment and never-ending free drinks in *The Fisherman's Arms*). To my (and everybody else's) surprise, this guaranteed fish-free dish is not only easy to prepare and very filling but is jolly good. Try it!

Ingredients (for 4 people)

4 large onions
6 eggs
Mustard (powder)
Wine vinegar
Sugar, salt
A reasonably strong Cheddar-type cheese
Milk (re-constituted powdered will do)
8 oz spaghetti or other pasta
Frozen peas

Method

(1)   Peel and slice onions. Melt butter sufficient to cover the bottom of a stout pan; add a (roughly equivalent amount of) corn oil. Cook the onions over low heat, with occasional stirring, until they are translucent and soft but not brown. At the same time,

(2)   Bring the 6 eggs to boil in initially cold water; simmer for 10 minutes. While all this is going on, you will have ample time to do two more things:

(3)   Put a large saucepan of water on to boil, for the spaghetti; put a small pan (containing only about 100 ml of water) on low heat, ready ultimately to receive the peas. This will give you time now to make the all-important mustard sauce.

(4)   Melt a good tablespoonful of butter (to hell with cholesterol for one evening!) and stir in enough plain flour just to absorb all the fat and to form a very sticky cake. Add milk slowly: it is best to warm the milk ahead of this step, as this gives a lump-free white sauce. Approx. three-quarters to one pint is plenty; if desired, water can be used for, say, the last quarter pint instead of milk. The amount of liquid to be added can be titrated against the viscosity: add only enough to make a thick sauce. Set aside. Now mix two good dessertspoons of mustard powder with approximately four times as much wine vinegar to form a thin yellow liquid; add two

good dessertspoonfuls (if that is the correct plural form) of caster sugar, a couple of teaspoons of salt and a couple of twists on the pepper grinder. Pour this mixture into the warm white sauce, simmer but not boil, and taste: it should be a little too 'sweet and sour' and a little too hot—if it causes you to wonder whether you have overdone the seasoning, it will be just right when it ultimately meets the buffer zone of spaghetti!

(5) Put the spaghetti into the briskly boiling water; set timer for 12 minutes.

(6) Put the onions as a thick layer into the bottom of an oven-proof dish.

(7) Cool the eggs under running water; peel and slice: dot the slices evenly over the layer of onion. Pour the mustard sauce evenly over this mixture: it should cover, but not drown, it.

(8) Grate 3–4 oz of cheese over the contents of the dish and place under the grill. Now

(9) Put the peas into the boiling water in the small pan; bring back to boil and let simmer for about 3 minutes. (Taste! Mushy peas are a splendid Northern dish, but not with this.). If all has gone to plan, everything will now be ready to serve simultaneously ... and it should all take less than half an hour to do.

George Series

SAVOURY PUDDING

A delicious old-fashioned accompaniment for lamb, pork or poultry. It is not in any standard cookery book: the weights given here are approximate. Whatever combination of ingredients is used the pudding is always appetizing.

100 g flour or flour mixed with breadcrumbs or porridge oats
200 g chopped onion
2 eggs
Mixed herbs
Salt and pepper
A little milk and water

Mix the flour (or flour mixture) with the chopped onion, herbs, salt and pepper. Beat in the eggs. Add enough milk to make a very stiff batter.

Baking is usually complicated by the presence in the oven of the joint of meat—but this is not obstacle to the resourceful cook. Put me in the baking tin with the joint (but you'll find me difficult to serve up). If you want me neat and tidy, put a medium-sized baking tin with a little lard or dripping on a high shelf in the oven, and wind me up to regulo 6 (200°C–400°F) as nearly as possible. Reduce the temperature gradually; allow about an hour to cook me. If I'm ready before the meat, take me out of the oven and eat me cool.

TANGERINE AND CHEESE SALAD

A tasty snack, quick and simple to prepare.

Mix small cubes of cheese with segments of tangerines. In summer, add a little chopped mint. At Christmastime, throw some tangerine skins on the log fire for a fragrant scent in the room.

R R Jamison

TURKEY STUFFING

Stuff a turkey with a combination of sliced whole oranges, apples, onions, sage and onion, thyme, chestnut stuffing, raisins and currants, sausage meat. Cover with bacon and foil and cook 4–5 hours at gas mark 3. The extra mass and water content produces an outstandingly tender and well flavoured bird.

Richard Southwood

LAPIN L'ELZIÈRE

Ingredients
  1 rabbit, jointed (sans tête)
  'Root' vegetables as available (e.g. potatoes, carrots, salsify, etc.)

'Fruit' vegetables as available (e.g. aubergines, tomatoes,
   mushrooms, courgettes, etc.)
Small whole onions and/or shallots
4 rashers bacon
Wild herbs (marjoram, thyme)
Parsley and bay leaves, garlic, salt, pepper
Vin de table (blanc)

Method

Fry rabbit briefly (if facilities available—not essential).

Rub inside of casserole with cut garlic clove.

Make bed of sliced root vegetables and place rabbit joints on top: pack between joints with small whole onions and/or shallots.

Cover with wine and water (50:50 mixture) and fresh herbs, add salt and pepper to taste.

Place in oven and cook briskly for 10 minutes.

Then add 'fruit' vegetables, sliced, and top with bacon, parsley and more herbs; add wine as necessary and simmer until rabbit is tender—about 3/4 hour.

Leave on warm stove for a short while—about 10 minutes—before serving.

This dish was concocted at L'Elzière—a small hamlet in the Cevennes—using local ingredients and minimal cooking facilities. (Minimal washing-up of cooking utensils too!)

H Gutfreund

CULINARY EXPERIMENTS

IN POST-WAR CAMBRIDGE

The early 1950s provided my first post-war opportunities for foreign travel. Several trips to Austria, Italy and France as well as a prolonged stay in the United States whetted my appetite for more exciting fare than was readily available in the Cambridge of that period. Raw materials gradually became more plentiful for adventurous cooking in England and I was encouraged to experiment

226

with pots and pans during my time off from the laboratory. I did not have adequate cooking facilities in my rooms in Jesus Lane so I borrowed kitchens in various friends' houses to try out recipes which I obtained from three sources: my mother, continental cook books and imitation of dishes which I had enjoyed in restaurants abroad.

At first I only attempted simple dishes like *Reiss Fleisch* and Goulash—on the latter I could improve on the *Concise Oxford Dictionary* definition of 'highly seasoned stew of steak and vegetables'; this sounds like English institutional cooking. Slowly I graduated to more sophisticated dishes such as *Gigot à la Clinique*, prepared in collaboration with Alice Orgel, and my favourite party piece which is described below and goes by different names. It was first known to me as *Rinds Rouladen* but was given the more elegant name of *Oiseaux sans Tête* by Christian de Duve when he dined with us in our own house some ten years after my Cambridge culinary exercises.

Cambridge in the 1950s was socially and intellectually a most exciting place. Everybody who was anybody in the new science of molecular biology or in biophysics passed through. Visitors were not only involved in stimulating discussions but also well entertained. Good food and wine were gradually appreciated by many who were too young to have known them before wartime and post-war shortages threw a curtain over culinary pleasures.

A place of special social delight was the 'Golden Helix' where Francis and Odile Crick provided a most hospitable environment. I was given the freedom of their kitchen on several occasions. Although it was difficult to compete with what Odile could provide, I was able to entertain mutual friends. Once I received a rather doubtful compliment from George Kistiakowsky, who was a hero to an aspiring kineticist. After a meal of *Oiseaux sans Tête* and a good Burgundy, he said to me 'Freddie you are wasting your time in science.' However, I doubt whether I should have had a more pleasant time than in my present career, had I followed that of a chef!

When I prepare a scientific paper I always enjoy writing the introduction and the conclusions. The description of the experimental detail is sometimes tedious. In the present case the experimental detail—the recipe and instructions—are much less quantitative than those essential for my biophysical papers. Much of the final preparation depends on taste and judgement; nothing needs to be done accurately!

The Recipe

Thin slices of best braising beef are required. In England one should ask for it to be cut as for beef olives. It is usually necessary to beat it thinner. On a recent occasion in Washington I was pleased to hear the butcher's assistant say 'Ah, you want to make *rouladen*', after hearing my description. She proceeded to cut the beef wafer thin, which was ideal. The slices are spread out and seasoned with salt, black pepper and paprika pepper.

A bed of finely cut onions, making a layer between $\frac{1}{2}$ and $\frac{3}{4}$ inch thick on the bottom of a saucepan in which some bacon bits had been fried, is cooked gently while the next operation is in progress.

Rice, lightly boiled and drained, is the basis for the filling. To this should be added all or some of the following finely cut ingredients: onions, crispy fried bacon, green peppers, mushrooms. The mixture is seasoned to taste with salt, black pepper and paprika pepper powder and bound together with a raw egg.

The *rouladen* are made by putting a heaped tablespoon of the filling on slices of meat about the size of a large postcard. The slices are rolled up and tucked in at the ends; if necessary secure with a toothpick or cotton. Pack the rolls tightly on top of the onions, close the pan and cook in an oven at 300 $^{\circ}$C for about two hours.

The final preparation requires the temporary removal of the *rouladen* from the saucepan. The remaining sauce is then put in a blender and returned to the pan. Under gentle heating add a little sour cream and red wine; add further seasoning to taste. This is where the real test for the artist comes; it involves further tasting and getting the amount of cream, wine and seasoning just right. When this is done, return the *rouladen* to gentle heat on top of the stove.

This dish is best served with pasta and salad.

Peter Richardson

MISH-MUSH

This dish has a curious name. The dish is quick and simple to prepare, and allows the cook much opportunity for subtle variety in flavour. The name tells nothing about the cooking or the taste, but somehow it has stuck in the family as the right name.

Begin by cooking 1 lb mince (hamburger) in a large frying pan. The meat should be in loose, small pieces, and cooked only to the point that the red colour is lost. A 10 or 12 inch pan is ideal. Liquid fat should be drained while retaining the meat in the pan. A tin of condensed soup of creamy texture (e.g. mushroom, celery) should be stirred in, and half its volume of water added. Spices, mixed in the bottom of a cup while the meat was cooking, are added and stirred in. A typical spice mix might include chilli, ginger, cardamom, black pepper, mustard, fennel seeds, salt; alternatively a more herbal mix might be used, including basil, rosemary, thyme, etc. with some salt and pepper. One and a half cups of quick or instant rice are added and stirred to prevent burning on the low to moderate heat used in this phase. It is advisable to taste the cooked mix at this point and add spices if needed to tune the mix to taste. The mix will serve 3–4 persons. Cooked mix can be kept in a refrigerator, and people may eat this rewarmed or even cold (then sometimes with a dash of ketchup). The overall cooking time, from cold pan to serving on plates, is about 20 minutes.

This savoury dish was designed to keep the cook fairly uniformly busy during preparation, while having the heating part of the cooking process running throughout. The spice and herb mixture is what makes the dish different each time. Thus people do not tire of it, and can explore their favourite flavours. A good starting point is to use $\frac{1}{4}$ to $\frac{1}{2}$ teaspoon of each of 6 to 8 spices, and explore different proportions and strengths. The choice of greens to go with the dish may be balanced against the intensity and style of spicing. Thus a strongly spiced version may go well with a white cabbage or green beans; a more herbal version may suit a salad. Other additives may be introduced to the basic dish, such as raisins, or chopped nuts, for added variety and inflections of flavour.

Michael Dewar

SOME CHINESE RECIPES

Here are three Chinese recipes, modified more or less extensively from ones acquired here and there. One of them (Outer Mongolian Lamb) is really an original contribution, though distantly based on Hunan lamb. All three dishes can be frozen with very little loss, provided they are reheated in a microwave oven. The only casualties are the peanuts in Kung Po chicken which get a bit soft. If possible, add these after reheating.

I think the instructions are fairly clear. The temperatures are Fahrenheit and measures American; i.e. 1 cup = 8 oz; 1 oz = 2 Tbsp (tablespoons) = 6 tsp (teaspoons). Marinade the meat or chicken for at least two hours.

I have also included a recipe for boiled rice which is not only simpler but also much better than any of the standard ones. The original version came from India, to accompany curry, but it is excellent with Chinese dishes if you like rice to be in separate grains and not glutinous, as we do.

KUNG PO CHICKEN

This was my first real success. I do think it is better than any I have had at any Chinese restaurant. But be warned; if you follow the recipe, it will be *very* hot, unless your red peppers are very anaemic. If you like *really* hot Indian curries, or red-hot Texas chilli, fine; otherwise try it first with a lot fewer peppers!

Ingredients
1 lb boneless chicken breasts, cut into bite-sized pieces
2/3 cup shelled and skinned peanuts
10 medium size dried hot red peppers, seeded
1 Tbsp chopped ginger root
Marinade
1 Tbsp cornstarch
2 Tbsp water
White of one large egg

Sauce

    1 Tbsp cornstarch in 2 Tbsp water
    2 Tbsp soy sauce
    2 Tbsp Hoisin sauce
    2 Tbsp rice wine
    1 tsp Chinkiang vinegar
    1 Tbsp sesame oil

Preparation

Heat one-and-a half cups oil in a wok to 375°; add the peanuts and stir till they are just beginning to turn golden (about 2 minutes), then strain. Since they go on cooking, it is important not to fry them too long.

Pour the oil back into the wok; heat to 400°; add the chicken and stir at maximum heat until it is all cooked (2–3 minutes). Strain (not in the same strainer as the peanuts; otherwise the nuts get soggy).

Wipe the wok out with paper, add 3 Tbsp oil, and heat to 375°. Add the red peppers and stir till they are almost black all over. Don't take fright; they really do need to be almost incinerated. The flavour comes largely from the semi-burnt peppers and it is delicious. However, this step does fill the place with extremely pungent fumes. If you can't carry it out under a hood, at least do it by an open window, preferably with a fan blowing the fumes outside. When the peppers are done, add the ginger and stir till just beginning to turn golden. Add the chicken, stir till hot, add the sauce, stir till it thickens, then serve.

OUTER MONGOLIAN LAMB

A contribution from 6808 Mesa Drive, named on the basis that if lamb in Outer Mongolia were as good as this, people would travel there to get it.

Ingredients

    1 lb lean lamb, shredded (leg is best; anything else is wasteful)
    1 large (or two small) red bell pepper(s) cut into small chunks
    1 small can water chestnuts, halved into slices
    5 dried hot red peppers, deseeded
    2 Tbsp chopped garlic
    1/2 cup chopped spring onion

Marinade
2 Tbsp light soy sauce
1 Tbsp rice wine
Sauce
2 tsp cornstarch in 2 Tbsp water
3 Tbsp rice wine
3 Tbsp light soy sauce
1 Tbsp sugar
1 Tbsp Hoisin sauce (or a bit more)

Preparation
Heat 2 cups of oil in a wok to 375°, add the water chestnuts, stir till they are crisp and the bubbling has subsided (about 1 minute), strain.

Return the oil to the wok and reheat to 375°, then add the red bell pepper and stir till it is well cooked and tender (about 2 minutes), then strain.

Return the oil to the wok and heat to 400°, add the lamb and stir till it is well cooked (about 3 minutes), then strain.

Heat 3 Tbsp fresh oil to 375°, add the hot red peppers and stir till they are black (see Kung Po Chicken), add the garlic and stir till the bubbling subsides and the garlic is just beginning to change colour, add the lamb and stir till it is hot, add the red peppers and water chestnuts and stir till they are hot, add the sauce and stir till it thickens, then add the spring onion, stir, and serve.

Notes
Water chestnuts. All the books assure one that canned water chestnuts are a disaster. This is not true if they are precooked as indicated above. They end up just as crunchy as fresh ones and taste almost as good.

Outer Mongolian Chicken or Beef. The same dish can be made with equal success using chicken or beef. With beef, just substitute it for lamb in the recipe above, either shredded or cut into small thin slices. With chicken, use 1 lb chicken breast, prepared, marinaded and cooked in the same way as for Kung Po Chicken.

SWEET AND SOUR PORK

This is a *very* good version of this classic dish. It is slightly modified from a recipe I found somewhere from a restaurant in Hong Kong.

The original version used green or red bell peppers. Red ones are much better and they also add to the appearance of the dish. The usual restaurant versions with half-cooked green peppers are calculated to sabotage the strongest digestion.

Ingredients
- *1 lb pork tenderloin, about 1/3" thick, cut into pieces about 3/4" square*
- *1 large (or two medium) red (or yellow) bell peppers, deseeded and cut into bite sized pieces*
- *1 small can sliced pineapple, cut into chunks*

Marinade
- *1 Tbsp cornstarch*
- *1 Tbsp water*
- *1 Tbsp soy sauce*
- *1 egg yolk*

Sauce
- *1 Tbsp cornstarch*
- *4 Tbsp water*
- *4 Tbsp rice vinegar*
- *4 Tbsp tomato ketchup (Heinz)*
- *4 Tbsp sugar*

Preparation
Coat each piece of the marinaded pork with cornstarch, drop into a lot of very hot (> 400°) oil, at least four cups if using a wok. A deep fry works well but is rather extravagant because it is very difficult to recover the oil. Fry till brown (about 2 minutes), then strain. Reheat the oil to 400°, add the pork, refry till crisp.

Heat 2 Tbsp oil in a wok to 400°, add the peppers, stir till tender (2 minutes), add the pineapple, stir till hot, add the sauce, stir till it thickens, add the pork and stir till everything is hot and well mixed, then serve.

Notes
(a) The pork must be cooked in a *lot* of *very* hot oil. It should be added right at the end to keep it crisp. So it is best to cook the other things in another wok, or in a frypan, while the pork is frying.

(b) Don't be surprised at the tomato ketchup! China has always absorbed good things from elsewhere and this is one of them.

Worcester sauce is another—though here the Chinese have developed their own version. Perhaps there is also a Chinese tomato ketchup too by now, but I haven't come across it.

BOILED RICE

Half fill a large saucepan with water, add 1–2 teaspoons of salt, heat till boiling vigorously, then add the rice (long grained is best), 1 cup being ample for two.

Boil for 15 minutes (exactly!), strain, spray with cold water, and drain well.

Spread the rice out to dry in a large dish with a lid, leaving the lid off, preferably for at least two hours.

About half an hour before the rice is needed, cover the dish with its lid and put it in an oven at 200° to warm up.

That's all there is to it! So much for the mystique about cooking rice! The original recipe, which I inherited from my mother, told one to boil the rice, tasting bits from time to time, till just cooked, i.e. until the individual grains are just no longer hard. I have found this rather harassing procedure quite unnecessary. Every brand of long grained rice I have tried has always needed 15 minutes. If yours happens to end up hard or too soft, you may need to alter the time. However, once you have calibrated your own brand, I'm sure you will find the time needed is always the same.

M J Whelan

JAPANESE DISHES

Here are a couple of Japanese dishes I have learnt about during my travels in the East.

SUKIYAKI

This is a winter dish which is the best known of the so-called 'nabemono' dishes (nabe = pan; mono = thing), a sort of casserole, which traditionally is cooked in a heated skillet on the table in front of the guests, enabling them at the same time to get some warmth from the cooking. However, with the traditional method guests are advised to wear bibs to protect themselves from splashes, so in the

West it is best to cook it in a large deep frying pan on the kitchen stove and bring it to the table. The following recipe serves 4 or 5 adults.

Ingredients

$1\frac{1}{2}$ lb beef (e.g. topside)
8 oz leeks
12 oz shirataki (also known as konnyaku, a sort of spaghetti-like material)
8 oz tofu (a bean curd cake)
2 oz beef suet
1 teacup soy sauce
1 teacup soup (e.g. beef consommé)
$\frac{1}{2}$ teacup sake (rice wine)
4 oz sugar
Bamboo shoots, cabbage, spinach, carrots, mushrooms, and anything else that you fancy

Some of these ingredients may be difficult to obtain, so try the following substitutes.

For shirataki — pre-cooked spaghetti.
For tofu — pre-cooked Yorkshire pudding cut into 1″ squares.
For bamboo shoots — parsnips.
For sake — a dry sherry.

Preparation

The beef must be sliced thinly, like bacon. It helps to partially freeze the beef before slicing with a machine. An English butcher often needs much persuasion to perform this task properly, usually because he cannot see the point of cutting beef so thinly. Clean and slice the vegetables and mushrooms, and cut the tofu into cubes.

Mix the soy sauce, sake, sugar and soup and heat. Melt the suet in the pan and cook the leeks until tender. Add the meat, the other ingredients and the sauce mixture and cook on a stove for 20 minutes, stirring occasionally.

Serving

In Japan *sukiyaki* is traditionally served by breaking a raw egg into a bowl, and using it as a sauce. The *sukiyaki* is transferred a little at a time to a guest's bowl and stirred into the raw egg. However, some Japanese now have reservations about eating raw egg. A spoonful or two of the sauce from from the pan serves to wet the bowl instead. Eat with chopsticks or with a fork and spoon.

SUKANA A LA SUKEDA

This is a summer dish, which I have christened after Mrs Sukedai, who showed me how to prepare it. It is a broiled fish fillet.

Ingredients

Fish fillet, e.g. cod or haddock
Carrots, onion, greenpepper, kidney beans,
   Chinese cabbage

Preparation

Construct a boat of aluminium foil slightly larger than the fillet and which can be folded over to completely enclose the fillet. In fact a double boat (boat within a boat) is useful, since it protects against leaks and also gives a space between the boats for disposing of fish bones.

Add salt and pepper to the fish and sprinkle with white wine.

Clean and slice the vegetables, and lightly pre-cook the beans and carrots in boiling water.

Thinly butter the bottom of the aluminium boat, cover with the vegetables and put in the fish. If required grate some cheese on the fish. A mixture of soy sauce and sugar can be used as a seasoning instead of wine.

Heat in an oven for 15 to 20 minutes at 200°C.

Serve with a slice of lemon if required.

Olga Kennard

KENNARD FAMILY TORTE

Ingredients

For the meringue
   250 g hazelnuts
   280 g vanilla sugar
   8 egg whites

236

For the cream
    8 egg yolks
    8 Tbsp vanilla sugar
    2 Tbsp chocolate
    300 g butter (creamed)
    A drop of rum

Method

For the meringue

Roast the hazelnuts in the oven until golden yellow.

Rub off the peel with a clean cloth.

Grind in a blender or similar appliance then mix with the sugar (preferably sugar in which a stick of vanilla has been kept).

Beat the egg whites until quite stiff and add the hazelnut/sugar mixture.

Spread out on a large buttered baking plate and bake in a moderate oven until nicely set. Allow to cool. (Oven 350°F first then reduce to 300–250°).

For the cream

Beat the egg yolks with the 8 Tbsp of vanilla sugar over steam until thick (10 minutes).

Melt the chocolate in water with a drop of rum then add to the beaten egg yolks.

Wait until the mass is cool then add to the creamed butter.

Cut the meringue into 3 long strips and sandwich these with the cream.

Michael Grace

RUM PIE

After a summer of physics at the Argonne National Laboratory, my wife and I returned home via the White Mountains of New England. We spent several days at a small inn renowned for its cuisine and in glorious surroundings with the Fall colours at their best. One of the dishes which drew people from great distances for Sunday lunch was Rum Pie.

Ingredients

1 envelope of gelatin
$\frac{1}{4}$ cup cold water
2 cups light cream
2 egg yolks
Pinch of salt
$\frac{1}{4}$ cup granulated sugar
2 Tbsp rum
2 egg whites
6 Tbsp castor sugar
Chocolate shavings
Baked 9" pie shell

Method

Sprinkle gelatin on cold water—let soften for 5 minutes. Scald cream in a double boiler. Beat egg yolks with a fork. Stir in salt and granulated sugar. Stir in scalded cream and return mixture to double boiler top. Cook over hot, not boiling water, stirring constantly until smooth and as thick as custard sauce—about 5 minutes. Remove from heat—add gelatin, stir until dissolved. Pour into bowl and chill until it mounds slightly when dropped from a spoon. Add 2 tablespoons of rum (or a little more). Beat egg whites quite stiff and slowly add 6 tablespoons of castor sugar beating until stiff. Combine with the rum custard. Poor into the baked pie shell and sprinkle with chocolate shavings. Keep refrigerated at all times.

David (Cecil) Smith

'LESLEY'S LEMON PUDDY'

This absurdly easy recipe produces a dessert which rivals syllabub in flavour, and exceeds it in popularity. There is a perennial demand for it at departmental and research unit parties, and it is also produced at small dinner parties—when the recipe is often quietly solicited afterwards (the speed and simplicity of preparation never fails to surprise the enquirer).

Ingredients (for 6 people)
  20 fl oz plain yoghurt
  10 fl oz double cream
  Finely grated rind ('zest') of 2 lemons
  Juice of 1 lemon
  6 dsp castor sugar

Directions
Mix together and beat up well. Chill in a refrigerator.

N.B. Any leftovers freeze well.

Martin Aitken

YOGHURT FOOL AU COINTREAU

Strain, through a cheesecloth overnight, one pint of natural yoghurt, preferably home made. To the resultant soft cheese add $\frac{1}{4}$ pint of lightly whipped cream. Mix into a chopped banana, orange, apple and a few seeded grapes which have been marinated in 3 tablespoonfuls of Cointreau. Chill and serve sprinkled with toasted flaked almonds.
Serves 4.

E Lester Smith

PLASMOLYSED BANANA

Some people find banana indigestible, or of rather unpleasant texture. Both faults can be obviated by plasmolysis.

Mash a ripe or nearly ripe banana roughly. Sprinkle with half a teaspoon of sugar (preferably castor or icing), then mash more thoroughly. The sugar increases the osmotic pressure inside the cells and plasmolyses them; this reduces the fruit to a palatable pourable cream. It can be improved for some palates by a dash of lemon juice or with cream.

Anthony Hewish

FOOLPROOF FUDGE

Occasions arise in the life of any physicist when no amount of expertise in his craft can compensate for the lack of elementary skills in the kitchen. I have in mind grey afternoons near Christmas, or damp August days in the West Country when mist and drizzle roll off the granite moors and outings from the holiday cottage are best forgotten. At such times very young people require diversions. To colleagues in this situation I suggest a simple activity—make some fudge! If the name recalls memories of an unpleasant, pale, crystalline and buttery substance unwisely purchased from a homemade sweetstall, I hasten to add that this is different. My instructions lead to the production of a delightful sweetmeat, deep golden brown and rich caramel in flavour. Never has it failed to elicit generous praise in any company. Only the simplest ingredients are required but a thermometer is recommended.

Take one tin of evaporated milk (410 g), one block of margarine (225 g), one bag (1 kg) of granulated sugar and two generous tablespoons of golden syrup.

Warm the margarine and evaporated milk, adding the sugar and golden syrup when the fat has melted. Stir over a low heat until the sugar has fully dissolved and then bring gently to the boil. The mixture will be frothy at first, before settling down to bubble smoothly, so use a saucepan which is only half-filled initially. Continue boiling until the temperature reaches 240 °F, stirring occasionally to check that no browning occurs at the base of the pan. The brew will darken as it nears the final temperature and should acquire a tempting smell. Finally cool the pan in cold water and beat vigorously with a wooden spoon until the fudge consistency is obtained. At this stage it should be poured, with slight encouragement, into a greased tin. After cooling for about one hour it may be cut into squares. There is a small chance that you will end with soft toffee instead of fudge. In this case return to the saucepan and boil again for two or three minutes before cooling and beating.

In the unlikely event that you wish to keep a sample for some future occasion, wrap in a plastic bag and place in the freezer. Do not be tempted to improve an excellent product by using real butter instead of margarine. I have always found that the cheapest fat produces the best flavour. Additions such as chopped raisins, rum or vanilla etc., may be introduced at the beating stage.

Seymour Rabinovitch

BOILED CAN: A DELECTABLE CARAMEL SAUCE

Take one can of sweetened condensed milk (the viscous material—not to be confused with the fluid evaporated milk-stuff), large or small according to one's needs. Place in a saucepan without opening, cover with water and a lid, and boil for a period of approximately 1 to $1\frac{3}{4}$ hours, according to the degree of caramelization that is sought (check water level from time to time, of course). The time of cooking may be altered at one's personal discretion upon suitable experimentation. Remove from saucepan, open can, empty into a bowl, stir the contents lightly to ensure homogenization. Spoon over ice cream, cake or other material of choice. Enjoy!

Elsie Widdowson

THREE RECIPES

These three recipes were passed on to me by my mother, born 1877, died 1984. I offer them as a tribute to her.

TOFFEE
A sure success on sweets stalls at village fêtes.

8 oz sugar
1 oz butter
1 tsp vinegar
5 oz golden syrup
1 Tbsp water

Place all the ingredients in a saucepan and heat gently till melted. Boil rapidly for 10 minutes or until a small portion, dropped into cold water, becomes brittle. Pour into a buttered tin and mark into squares while still warm.

LEMON CURD
This has won several people prizes at cookery competitions.

> *8 oz sugar*
> *2½ oz butter*
> *3 eggs*
> *Juice of 3 lemons*

Place the butter, sugar and lemon juice in a double pan, heat gently and stir till melted. Add the beaten eggs one by one and cook slowly, stirring all the time until the mixture coats the back of a wooden spoon.

CHEESE STRAWS
A great favourite as a donation to the 'eats' at coffee mornings.

> *4 oz flour*
> *4 oz butter*
> *6 oz cheese*
> *1 egg yolk*
> *½ oz water*
> *1 level tsp salt*

Rub the butter into the flour. Add the grated cheese and salt. Bind to a stiff paste with the egg yolk and water. Roll out thinly and cut into narrow strips, twisted if desired. Bake in a hot oven for about 10 minutes.

John Cornforth

SEVILLE ORANGE MARMALADE

Apparatus
Pressure cooker (1 gal; 4.5 litres), preserving pan (2 gal; 9 litres), orange squeezer, egg slicer, thermometer, small saucepan, strainer, large wooden spoon, cutting board and knives, muslin.

Non-metric measures are British, not US.

Ingredients
Seville oranges (4 lb; 1.8 kg)
Lemons (1 lb; 450 g)
Sugar (8.5 lb; 3.85 kg)
Water (3 pints; 1.7 litres)

Procedure
Scrub the fruit with water and a vegetable brush. Halve the fruit, remove pips near the cut surface, squeeze out juice, remove the remaining pips and halve the fruit again. Tie the pips in muslin and put them with the fruit (lemons first) and 2 pints (1.1 litres) of water into the pressure cooker. Bring to high pressure (15 lb/in^2; 1 kg/cm^2) over medium heat and cook for 13 minutes at pressure. Allow pressure to reduce before cooling in water. When cool enough, cut the fruit into strips with the egg slicer. Untie the muslin

and boil it briefly with the pips in half a pint (0.3 litres) of water. Strain off the liquid extract and repeat the process with another half-pint of water. Combine the fruit, juice, cooking water and extraction water in the preserving pan, add the sugar, bring to the boil and boil rapidly until the temperature reaches 104.4 °C (220 °F); this takes only 15–20 minutes. Stop heating, and after 10 minutes pour into clean hot jars and cover. The yield is about 14 lb (6.35 kg).

Naomi Datta

ORANGE MARMALADE

Here are two recipes for marmalade. Both make beautiful gels, suspending cut-up peel, neither too hard nor too soft, amber-coloured, with the variations from translucent yellow to brown of real amber. Their two flavours are not identical but both are good, sharp and orangey with a hint of ginger, though no ginger was added.

RECIPE A

> 4 lb Seville oranges
> 4 lemons
> 8 lb demerara sugar

Boil the fruit whole, in a covered pan, with just enough water to cover them, until soft, about 1½ hours. Keep the water. When cool, cut up the fruit, including peel, and remove the pips. Boil the pips in some of the water for 10 minutes, then discard the pips and put their water back. Put the cut-up fruit back in the water, bring to the boil and gradually add the sugar, stirring. Continue boiling, with stirring, till the marmalade sets when tested on a cold plate. It sets quite quickly. Bottle in jars.

RECIPE B

> 8–12 Seville oranges, according to size
> 3 sweet oranges

2 lemons

Sugar, $\frac{1}{2}$ demerara, $\frac{1}{2}$ granulated

Cut up the fruit, saving the pips, and measure in a pudding basin. Cover the pips with water, let them stand, then boil. To each basin of cut fruit, add $1\frac{1}{2}$ basins water. Simmer thoroughly till soft. Leave for several days or *at least* 24 hours. Measure in basins again. To each basin of fruit-and-water, add one of sugar. Add the fluid from the pips. Boil till it sets when tested on a cold plate. Bottle in jars.

With both recipes, colour and flavour can be varied by changing the sugar, more granulated for paler, part raw, unrefined for dark colour and molasses flavour.

In neither of these recipes are the ingredients accurately defined. Those of Recipe A nearly are but '4 lemons' may vary considerably in size and weight. (It used to be very easy to shop for the ingredients but now adjustments have to be made, since oranges are sold by the pound and sugar by the kilo.) Recipe A I had from my mother-in-law, Alexandrena (Rena) Datta. Recipe B is from my mother, Ellen Henrietta Goddard, usually called Billy or Bill. It is not an American recipe, though having the ingredients measured by volume makes it read like one. The proportion of sugar to fruit is clearly defined; what you have to buy is uncertain though an approximation is easy enough.

I like to think that the recipes are characteristic of the two very different women who supplied them. Both were born over 100 years ago. Rena was a Scot, a determined, single-minded person, not at all interested in cooking or domesticity. (The marmalade recipe is the only one I ever had from her.) She had a busy, interesting life, spent mostly in England, Switzerland and India, though she travelled and worked in many more countries. She was a teacher and an organiser. But she never forgot, or ceased to regret, that her formal education was incomplete; she had had, so as to earn a living, to give up her place as a mathematics undergraduate at Glasgow University. Her marmalade recipe is effective and time-saving.

Bill, my mother, had very little education, not for financial reasons but just that it was not considered necessary for a girl. Compared to Rena's, her experience was narrow, bounded by her home, family and local community. We had holidays abroad, but among English people. Bill enjoyed cooking. She was full of humour, sympathy and curiosity but she was not curious about science, about how things work, politics or ideas. She did not mind being teased about her ignorance of, say, her own insides. (Writing this, I wondered if she really minded at all, but concluded that no, she did not, and enjoyed laughing at herself.) Her marmalade recipe is far from time-saving. Cutting-up of raw oranges is obviously much harder than of cooked ones. Why use so much water? It only has to be boiled off. And why stand the cooked fruit for a day or more? No further softening or fermentation is likely (the season for Seville oranges is January). Bill would not have asked herself these questions and had time enough not to have to rush.

Alphabetical List of Contributors

(For.Mem.RSs are prefaced by *fm*, co-authors by *c*.)

249

Index

253